Table of Contents

32   Chapter 3 Vegetables and Sides

45   Chapter 4 Poultry Mains

60 Chapter 5 Seafood Mains

70 Chapter 6 Meat Mains

In our evaluation of the top slow cookers, the Ninja multi-cooker was by far the largest and heaviest appliance. This, however, hardly be a surprise given the might of this monstrous machine. In addition to being a slow cooker, it also functions as a pressure cooker, steamer, and air fryer, and can sear, sauté, and roast food. It's important to keep in mind that due to its size, it takes up a lot of room and is difficult to lift.

It's a pleasure to utilise as a slow cooker. Everything may be prepared in one spacious, non-stick metal pot thanks to the sear and sauté functions. We prepared a beef stew in the slow cooker to test the sear function. The meat and vegetables rapidly began to caramelize due to how quickly it heats up. The huge, vibrant digital display was simple to operate and had distinct sections for each function. The slow cooker includes a high and low setting, with 15-minute intervals for cooking. The Ninja automatically changes to warm when the food is ready, and the timer displays how long it has been at that temperature.

Except for the lid of the pressure cooker, every removable component is ceramic-coated, dishwasher-safe, and non-stick. This phase of the washing-up is a little challenging because the main unit and lids have weird crevices that are challenging to get into. The pressure cooker lid, which was a little challenging to attach, is necessary for the slow cooker. It seems fairly large and putting it on required several attempts. However, as we used it more, it became simpler.

Due to its size and scope, the Foodi MAX is different from conventional multi-cookers. It makes soups, stews, and curries, and because it has two tops, it can also be used as an air fryer to brown meat, veggies, steaks, and seafood. It performed admirably in our tests and was simple to use. But because it's so large, think carefully before investing whether you really need the features and capacity.

What is Ninja Foodi MAX Multi-Cooker ?

When you want home-cooked meals but are too lazy to make them yourself, the Ninja Foodi Max is an excellent purchase. It has nine culinary modes inside its user-friendly design that make it simple to roast, bake, grill, crisp dishes, and more while also saving you time and energy. It's among the top Instant Pot substitutes we've tried.

In fact, the Ninja Foodi MAX 7.5L Multi-Cooker OP500UK (to give it its full name) can air fry food with up to 75% less fat than conventional methods and pressure cook food up to 70% faster than conventional methods. Large families will find its enormous 7.5 litter capacity to be a terrific alternative, but you will need a countertop large enough for it or enough storage space.

The Ninja Foodi Max is a step up from the 4.7 and 6L versions and the company's largest multi-cooker to date. The Ninja may appear very large at first sight; at 42cm high, 38cm wide, and 11.3kg, it isn't the kind of appliance that will blend into the background, but rather one that is intended to be a focal point of your kitchen's "working triangle." Except if you have a separate pantry where you can store the bulky countertop appliances.

However, the curved body's black and stainless steel realization is fashionable. All the cooking settings are available on board in an easy-to-use digital display that may be operated with a single button click. With options like pressure cooking, steaming, grilling, air crisping without oil, baking, roasting, and dehydrating, your standard built-in oven may appear quite obsolete. In addition to a cook and crisp basket, there is a two-tier reversible rack for cooking main dishes and sides at the same time. This is useful for layering veggies with meats, poultry, or fish.

After use, we simply washed the cooking pots in warm soapy water and gave the rest of the appliance a wipe down with a moist cloth. The design's 7.5 litre cooking pot and 4.7 litre cook and crisp basket are easy to clean - it comes with ceramic-coated, non-stick, dishwasher-safe elements.

Ideal for large families: The Ninja Foodi Max is a step up from the 4.7 and 6L versions and the company's largest multi-cooker to date. The Ninja may appear very large at first sight; at 42cm high, 38cm wide, and 11.3kg, it isn't the kind of appliance that will blend into the background, but rather one that is intended to be a focal point of your kitchen's "working triangle." Except if you have a separate pantry where you can store the bulky countertop appliances.

Cooking features for a complete meal in one pot: There are nine cooking options on the multi-cooker. The primary lid, which has an integrated grill that heats from above, is required for the other options; some use the pressure cooker lid, while sauté and sear are used without a lid. More details on each cooking function are provided below, but I found that after using one with a pressure lid and one without, the rest was simple to understand and the settings were simple to adjust for my cooking style.

The Ninja beeps to let you know when cooking is finished and then switches to the keep warm mode to prevent your food from getting cold. If you discover that the food requires more time to cook, simply repeat the process by choosing the function, temperature, and time again.

Impressive crisping technology: It has TenderCrisp Technology, which crisps food after cooking for an actual oven-cooked flavour. Despite having an instruction booklet, we quickly figured out how to operate it after playing about with it. Instead of forcing you to consult the manual, a preset cooking option will suggest the most typical temperature you'd need and provide a time for that function. Nevertheless, the outcomes from the Cook & Crisp basket were superb, nearly on par with those from any air fryer. There were only a few chips that were a little pale, and the majority of the chips had nice browning without being burnt at the edges.

Dishwasher-safe: Although the bigger containers are simpler to wash by hand because otherwise, they would virtually take up the entire dishwasher, it is nice that the majority of the Ninja Foodi MAX's components are dishwasher-safe. The biggest hassle is having to constantly remove and wash the silicone ring from the pressure cooker lid. Despite this, the ring keeps absorbing odor, which is typical of pressure cookers; Ninja offers replacements because of this. It's beneficial to have separate rings for savory and sweet foods.

Cooking 70% quicker: While the healthier Air Crisp option enables you to cook chicken strips, fish fingers, and French fries with little to no oil, pressure cooking allows you to cook succulent steaks, pork, and curries up to 70% faster than traditional cooking methods. You may also prepare entire meals in one pot, equipped with a 2-tier reversible rack. You can even cook from frozen using this cooker.

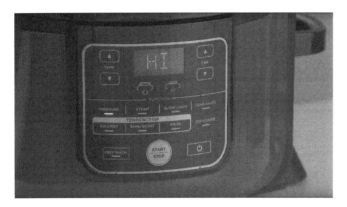

COOKING FUNCTIONS

PRESSURE: Use pressure to swiftly cook food while preserving softness. When cooking delicate items at a high temperature, use steam.

SLOW COOK: Cook your meal for a longer amount of time at a lower temperature.

YOGURT: To make creamy homemade yogurt, pasteurize and ferment the milk.

SEAR/SAUTÉ: Utilising the device as a cooktop for various cooking tasks, such as browning meat, sautéing veggies, and simmering sauces.

AIR CRISP: With little to no oil, air crisp adds crunch and crispness to cuisine.

BAKE/ROAST: Use the appliance as an oven for a variety of baked goods, tender meats, and more.

GRILL: To caramelize and brown your food, use a high temperature.

DEHYDRATE: Dehydrate fruits, vegetables, and meats for wholesome snacking.

After steaming, slow cooking, or pressure cooking, the appliance will automatically transition to the Keep Warm mode and begin counting down. If you choose to hit KEEP WARM to turn it off, Keep Warm will turn itself off after 12 hours. The goal of the Keep Warm mode is to maintain food at a temperature that is safe for consumption rather than warming it from a chilly state.

OPERATING BUTTONS

FUNCTION: Press FUNCTION, then select a cooking function using the START/STOP dial.

TEMP: Pressing TEMP will allow you to change the pressure and/or temperature of the cooking process.

TIME: Select TIME, then change the cook time using the START/STOP dial.

START/STOP dial/button: Use the dial to select a cooking function, cook temperature, and cook duration. START/STOP dial/button: Click the button to start the stove. The current cooking function will be stopped if the button is pressed while the appliance is still cooking.

POWER: Pressing the Power button turns off the appliance and halts all cooking modes.

Air Crisp

The Ninja Foodi performed an excellent job air frying the chicken. The meat was delicious and the skin was crunchy. The Ninja Foodi did poorly when it came to air-crisp chips, though. We manually configured the Foodi to cook our homemade chips in our fan oven at the same temperature and for the same amount of time, so we were dismayed when they turned out overcooked. There was not much potato inside, and the exterior was overly crispy and nearly rock-hard. Since then, we've tested these settings, and while the outcomes are improved, they still fall short of how the Ninja Foodi air fryer and most of its competitors cooked the chicken and made the chips.

1. Either the Cook & Crisp Basket or the reversible rack should be placed in the pot. A diffuser ought to be fastened to the basket.
2. Fill the Cook & Crisp Basket or reversible rack with ingredients. Put the lid on.
3. To select AIR CRISP, turn the START/STOP dial after pressing FUNCTION.
4. It will show the current temperature setting. Press TEMP to select a temperature between 150°C and 200°C, then spin the dial.
5. Cooking changes the cooking time in minute increments up to an hour, press TIME, and then turn the START/STOP dial. Simply add an additional 5 cookies to the cook time to preheat your appliance. To start or stop cooking, press START/STOP.
6. If necessary, you can lift out the basket and open the lid while the food is cooking to shake or toss the ingredients for more equal browning. Close the lid after lowering the basket back into the pot. Once the lid is shut, cooking will automatically begin again.
7. The appliance will beep and show DONE when the cooking time is finished.

Grill

The grilling function of the Ninja Foodi falls short of several of the other functions, which compete favorably with your standard oven. It's a useful addition, but using it is far less adaptable and efficient than using a regular grill. First off, you'll have a hard time fitting more than two chicken breasts on the rack comfortably due to the size of the Foodi. Another restriction is the rack's height. The grilled food cannot be placed closer to or further away from the grill element.

1. Either use the instructions in the recipe or place the reversible rack in the pot in the upper grill position.
2. Arrange the ingredients on the rack, then cover.
3. Select GRILL by rotating the START/STOP dial after pressing FUNCTION.
4. To change the cooking time in minute increments up to 30 minutes, press TIME and then turn the dial.
5. To start/stop cooking, press START/STOP.
6. The appliance will beep and show DONE when the cooking time is finished.

Baking/Roasting

We used the Bake/Roast option to twice roast potatoes throughout our tests. Using store-bought roasties from frozen the first time, and fresh potatoes the second time. Both batches of potatoes were wonderful, unlike the underwhelming results when air-fried chips. Given that the skins of the smaller batch of frozen potatoes were already cooked, they bordered on being extremely crispy, but overall, the potatoes had fluffy interiors and crunchy exteriors. The fresh potatoes, meantime, had the greatest homemade roast potatoes we've ever made, with the ideal balance of flavour and texture. We don't say that casually. We used the Ninja Foodi to bake fudge cake in its cooking pot after baking chocolate muffins on the grilling rack using the same Bake/Roast mode. Both of the dishes came from packets and tasted exactly how we expected them to when prepared in a conventional oven.

1. Fill the pot with the necessary ingredients and equipment. Put the lid on.
2. Select BAKE/ROAST by turning the START/STOP dial after pressing FUNCTION.
3. It will show the current temperature setting. In order to choose a temperature between 120°C and 200°C, press TEMP and then spin the dial.
4. To change the cooking time, press TIME, then crank the START/STOP dial in minute increments up to 1 hour, and then in 5-minute increments from 1 hour to 4 hours. To start or stop cooking, press START/STOP.
5. The appliance will beep and show DONE when the cooking time is finished.

Dehydrate

We cut up bananas and put them in the pot since we were interested in seeing how well the dehydration setting worked on fresh ingredients. Although the results were as delicious as banana chips from the shop, making them took up to six hours on the recommended 60 degrees as the machine gradually sucked the life out of the bananas before crisping them.

1. Lower the two-tier reversible rack into the pot, then arrange a layer of ingredients on top of the rack.
2. Place the top layer over the reversible rack as shown below, holding it in place with its handles. After that, add a further layer of ingredients to the top tier and secure the lid.
3. Select DEHYDRATE by turning the START/STOP dial after pressing FUNCTION.
4. It will show the current temperature setting. To select a temperature between 40°C and 90°C, press TEMP and then turn the dial.
5. Press TIME, then spin the dial to change the cook time up to 12 hours in 15-minute intervals.
6. To start the dehydration process, close the lid and press START/STOP.
7. The appliance will beep and show DONE when the cook time is finished.

Sear/Sauté

We used Sear/Sauté option on to slow cooking and searing. Many recipes call for frying items before adding them to a slow cooker, such as onions for curries or beef pieces for stews. The Ninja Foodi, not so. At the stroke of a button, you may switch from searing or sautéing food to slow cooking. Simply add the remaining ingredients, choose "Slow Cook," and then choose the cooking period. Although you may technically "fried" things in standard slow cookers, they never reach a high enough temperature to get the desired caramelized color. If you're a fan of slow cookers, this particular Ninja Foodi feature is a game-changer.

1. Fill the pot with ingredients.
2. Select SEAR/SAUTÉ by turning the dial

after pressing FUNCTION. It will show the current temperature setting. Press TEMP, then choose LO, LO:MD, MD, MD:HI, or HI by rotating the dial.

3. To start/stop cooking, press START/STOP.

4. To switch off the SEAR/SAUTÉ feature, press START/STOP. Press FUNCTION, then rotate the START/STOP dial to the appropriate cooking function to change the cooking function.

Slow Cook

1. Ingredients should be added to the pot. The pot should not be filled past the MAX line.

2. Place the pressure lid in place and move the pressure release valve to the VENT setting.

3. Select SLOW COOK by turning the START/STOP dial after pressing FUNCTION. It will show the current temperature setting. To choose HI or LO, turn the dial after pressing TEMP.

4. Press TIME, then turn the dial to change the cooking time by 15-minute intervals up to a maximum of 12 hours.

5. To start/stop cooking, press START/STOP.
.

Yogurt

1. Fill the saucepan with the necessary amount of milk.

2. Place the pressure lid in place and move the pressure release valve to the VENT setting.

3. Select YOGURT by turning the START/STOP dial after pressing FUNCTION. It will show the current temperature setting.

4. Press TEMP, then choose YGRT or FMNT using the dial.

5. Press TIME, then spin the dial to change the incubation time between 8 and 12 hours in 30-minute increments.

6. To start pasteurization, press START/STOP. While pasteurizing, the unit will display BOIL.

7. The device will beep and indicate COOL when the pasteurisation temperature has been reached.

8. After the milk has cooled, the device will show the incubation time, followed by ADD and STIR.

9. Take off the pressure lid, then skim the milk's surface.

10. Combine milk and yogurt cultures by stirring. To start the incubation process, install the pressure lid and click START/STOP.

11. The countdown will start after FMNT appears on the display. The device will beep and display DONE when the incubation period is finished. Until it is turned off, the device will beep once per minute for up to four hours.

12. Up to 12 hours before serving, chill yogurt.

Pressure Cook

1. Fill the pot with the ingredients, at least 250 ml of liquid, and any other necessary equipment. Past the PRESSURE MAX line, DO NOT continue to fill the pot.

2. Place the pressure lid in place, and then switch the pressure release valve to the SEAL setting.

3. Select PRESSURE by rotating the START/

STOP dial after pressing FUNCTION. The standard pressure level will be shown. To choose HI or LO, turn the dial after pressing TEMP.

4. Turn the dial after pressing TIME to change the cooking time in minute increments up to an hour, and then in 5-minute increments from an hour to four hours.

5. To start or stop cooking, press START/ STOP. As pressure builds inside the device, PRE will be visible on the display. When it has reached its maximum pressure, the device will start counting down.

6. The appliance will beep, go into Keep Warm mode, and start counting up once the cooking time is up.

7. Allow the appliance to depressurize naturally, or, if the recipe specifies it, quickly release the steam by turning the pressure release valve to the VENT position.

Tips for Using Accessories

The Ninja Website offers a huge selection of Ninja Foodi Max 9-in-1 Multi-Cooker accessories (opens in a new tab). The Ninja Foodi Max 7-in-1, which is likewise 7.5L, shares a lot of parts. Costs range from £4.99 for spare parts to £24.99 for a new cover or cooking pot. If your pot is used frequently, it would be worthwhile to invest in one of these so you have a backup while the others are being washed.

However, it's not just about the spare components. To make cooking easier, Ninja offers some reasonably priced tins and racks. You can get a roasting sling to help you quickly move meat into and out of the pot, a Ninja skewer stands to cook up to 15 kebabs at once, and a crisping rack to hold items like taco shells and bacon, for instance. Since I enjoy baking, I chose a silicone muffin tin and a tube pan, which functions similarly to a bundt shape for round cakes.

Both are of excellent quality and are dishwasher-safe, based on my experience using them. Instead of a muffin with a flat bottom because of the shape of the muffin mold, you get a little off-center half-egg, as seen in the picture below. Although it doesn't influence the taste, it may not be the muffin that some home bakers are accustomed to. But I believe that this mold is fantastic for things like muffins made with eggs or omelets.

It is simple to remove baked goods from the tube pan thanks to its detachable base. I used this to bake cakes, bread to share, and bread to rip, and I was pleased with the outcome. I would prefer Ninja to have a typical loaf or cake tin, appropriate for more conventional baked goods.

Cleaning and Caring for Ninja Foodi MAX Multi-Cooker

After each usage, the appliance needs to be completely cleaned.

1. Before cleaning, unplug the device from the wall socket.

2. Use a moist towel to clean the control panel

and the base of the stove.

3. Dishwasher-safe items include the pressure lid, cooking pot, silicone ring, reversible rack, Cook & Crisp Basket, and detachable diffuser.

4. The anti-clog cap and pressure release valve can be cleaned with water and dish soap.

5. After the heat shield has cooled, clean the crisping lid by wiping it down with a moist cloth or paper towel.

6. Fill the cooking pot with water and let it soak before cleaning if food residue adheres to the cooking pot, reversible rack, or Cook & Crisp Basket. AVOID using scouring pads. If scrubbing is required, use a nylon pad or brush with a liquid dish soap or non-abrasive cleaner.

7. After each use, let all pieces air dry.

Removing & Reinstalling the Silicone Ring

Pull the silicone ring section by section outward from the silicone ring rack to remove it. Either side of the ring can be mounted facing upward. Section by section, press it into the rack to reinstall.

Remove any food particles from the silicone ring and anti-clog cap after use.

To prevent odour, keep the silicone ring clean. The smell can be eliminated by washing it in the dishwasher or warm, soapy water. It is however typical for it to take in the aroma of some acidic foods. It is advised to keep several silicone rings on hand.

Additional silicone rings are available for purchase at ninjakitchen.co.uk.

NEVER take the silicone ring out too forcefully as this could damage the rack and the pressure-sealing ability. Replace any silicone ring that has cracks, cuts, or other damage right away.

Why does it take my unit so long to reach pressure? When does pressure start to increase?

• Depending on the chosen temperature, the cooking pot's current temperature, and the temperature or quantity of the contents, cooking times may vary.

• Verify that your silicone ring is flush with the lid and fully seated. If placed properly, you should be able to rotate the ring by giving it a small tug.

• When pressure cooking, make sure the pressure lid is completely closed and the pressure release valve is in the SEAL position.

Why does the clock go so slowly?

Instead of setting minutes, you might have done such. When setting the time, the display will read HH:MM and the time will advance or backward by minutes.

How can I detect if the appliance is under pressure?

To show that the unit is developing pressure, whirling lights will appear on the screen.

When I use the Steam function on my device, a lot of steam comes out of it.

Steam evaporating through the pressure release valve is typical while cooking. For steam, slow cooking, and sear/sauté, keep the pressure release valve in the VENT position.

Why am I unable to remove the pressure lid?

The pressure lid won't unlock as a safety measure until the appliance is totally depressurized. To quickly discharge the pressurised steam, turn the pressure release valve to the VENT position. Steam will suddenly erupt from the pressure release valve. The appliance will be prepared to open once all of the steam has been discharged. To avoid spatter, rotate the pressure lid counter clockwise before lifting it at an angle. Avoid lifting the lid up straight.

Is a loose pressure release valve normal?

Yes. The loose fit of the pressure release valve is deliberate; it makes it simple to switch from SEAL to VENT and helps regulate pressure by releasing a tiny quantity of steam while cooking to produce excellent results. For pressure cooking, please make sure it is turned as far as possible toward the SEAL position, and for quick releasing, please make sure it is turned as far as possible toward the VENT position.

How much time does it take the unit to depressurize?

Quick release lasts no more than two minutes. Depending on the type of food, amount of liquid, and/or combination of food and liquid in the pot, natural release can take up to 20 minutes or longer.

The Ninja Foodi MAX 7.5L Multi-Cooker OP500UK has what cooking modes?

Pressure cook, steam, slow cook/yoghurt, sear, air crisp, grill, bake/roast, and dehydrate are some of its modes.

4-Week Meal Plan

Week 1

Day 1:
Breakfast: Denver Egg Muffins
Lunch: Butter Carrots
Snack: Chimichurri Beef Strips
Dinner: Pecan-Coated Salmon
Dessert: Arborio Rice Pudding

Day 2:
Breakfast: Cheddar Bacon Egg Muffins
Lunch: Red Cabbage with Apples
Snack: Rice Beef Meatballs
Dinner: Courgette Chicken
Dessert: Flavourful Chai Latte

Day 3:
Breakfast: Ham Egg Burritos
Lunch: Corn on the Cob
Snack: Beef Short Ribs
Dinner: Spiced Prawns Scampi
Dessert: Chocolate Hot Cocoa

Day 4:
Breakfast: Veggie Burritos
Lunch: Cheese Asparagus
Snack: Tasty Prawns with Parsley
Dinner: Thai Beef Chuck
Dessert: Mochaccino Cheesecakes

Day 5:
Breakfast: Hash Brown Casserole
Lunch: Orange-Flavour Beetroot
Snack: Firecracker Chicken Meatballs
Dinner: Lobster Tails with Lemon-Butter Sauce
Dessert: Blackberry Crisp with Almond Topping

Day 6:
Breakfast: Sausage Sandwiches
Lunch: Green Beans with Almonds
Snack: Vegan Pizza
Dinner: Bourbon Chicken
Dessert: Friendly Steel-Cut Oatcake

Day 7:
Breakfast: Homemade Yogurt
Lunch: Basic Butter Polenta
Snack: Turkey Meatballs
Dinner: Tiger Prawns with Sausage Slices
Dessert: Red Wine-Poached Pears

Week 2

Day 1:
Breakfast: Granola with Cranberries
Lunch: BBQ Tofu Cubes
Snack: Baby Bella Mushrooms
Dinner: Homemade Boeuf Bourguignon
Dessert: Pineapple Tapioca Pudding

Day 2:
Breakfast: Chocolate Granola Bars
Lunch: Green Cabbage in Chicken Stock
Snack: Cherry Salad
Dinner: Mexican Flank Steak in Beef Stock
Dessert: Chocolate Chickpea Pudding

Day 3:
Breakfast: Hard-Boiled Eggs
Lunch: Simple Cinnamon Applesauce
Snack: Chicken Lettuce Wraps
Dinner: Rubbed Pork Ribs
Dessert: Crème Brûlée

Day 4:
Breakfast: Steel-Cut Oats with Chopped Apple
Lunch: Chickpeas Hummus
Snack: Sticky Chicken Wings
Dinner: Simple Beef and Broccoli
Dessert: Fruit Cheesecake with Chocolate Crust

Day 5:
Breakfast: Simple Porridge
Lunch: Pinto Beans
Snack: Sausage Seafood Gumbo
Dinner: Mushroom Tuna Casserole
Dessert: Easy Dulce de Leche

Day 6:
Breakfast: Whole Milk Yogurt
Lunch: Lightened-Up Mashed Potatoes
Snack: Pork Meatballs
Dinner: Turkey Loaf with Mashed Potatoes
Dessert: Mexican Cinnamon Hot Chocolate

Day 7:
Breakfast: Vanilla Banana Bread
Lunch: Mashed Sweet Potatoes
Snack: Beef Barbecue
Dinner: Maple-Soy Chicken Thighs
Dessert: Mulled Orange Wine

Week 3

Day 1:
Breakfast: Cream Berries Cake
Lunch: Vegetable Medley
Snack: Cheese Chili Mac
Dinner: Homemade Boeuf Bourguignon
Dessert: Chocolate Cake

Day 2:
Breakfast: Cheeses Egg Bites
Lunch: Tasty Bulgur Pilaf
Snack: Lemon Chicken Thighs
Dinner: Harissa Chicken Breasts
Dessert: Oat Strawberry Crisp

Day 3:
Breakfast: Egg Ham Burritos
Lunch: Cooked Beans
Snack: Spiced Prawns Scampi
Dinner: Smoke Whole Chicken
Dessert: Digestive Biscuit Cheesecake

Day 4:
Breakfast: Toast Casserole
Lunch: Apple Squash Porridge
Snack: Cheese Chicken Fajitas
Dinner: Fish in Orange Sauce
Dessert: Vanilla Crème Brûlée

Day 5:
Breakfast: Baby Spinach Frittata
Lunch: Butternut Apple Smooth
Snack: Mushroom Ham Scramble Mug
Dinner: Bacon & Beef Flank Steak
Dessert: Vanilla Caramel Popcorn

Day 6:
Breakfast: Banana Toast Casserole
Lunch: Turnips with Alfredo Sauce
Snack: Cabbage with Bacon Slices
Dinner: Pork Chunks with Pickled Red Onions
Dessert: White Rice Pudding

Day 7:
Breakfast: Poblano Frittatas
Lunch: Onion Turnips Mash
Snack: Savory Bok Choy
Dinner: Poached Salmon with Skin
Dessert: Lemon Apples

Week 4

Day 1:
Breakfast: Coffee Egg Bites
Lunch: Carrots Turnips Mix
Snack: Chickpeas Hummus
Dinner: Lemon Chicken Breast Halves
Dessert: Hazelnut Soufflé

Day 2:
Breakfast: Chocolate Cherry Porridge
Lunch: Honey Carrot Puree
Snack: Quick Cauliflower "Rice"
Dinner: Sweet Onion Beef Carnitas
Dessert: Lemon Graham Cheesecake

Day 3:
Breakfast: Cinnamon Banana Porridge
Lunch: Sweet Potato & Carrot Medley
Snack: Rice Mix Stuffed Peppers
Dinner: Glazed Baby Back Ribs
Dessert: Apple Rice Pudding

Day 4:
Breakfast: Southwest Breakfast Casserole
Lunch: Glazed Carrots
Snack: Courgettes and Tomatoes Mix
Dinner: Rosemary Lamb Chops
Dessert: Frozen Berry Crisp

Day 5:
Breakfast: Giant Pancake with Berry Compote
Lunch: Honey Glazed Baby Carrots
Snack: Mango Fish Tacos
Dinner: Saucy Chicken Thighs
Dessert: Simple Chocolate Pudding

Day 6:
Breakfast: Homemade Huevos Rancheros
Lunch: Garlic Aubergine Dish
Snack: Curry Prawns
Dinner: Salmon with Broccoli & Potatoes
Dessert: Greek Yogurt Bundt Cake

Day 7:
Breakfast: Blueberry French Toast
Lunch: Savoy Cabbage
Snack: Beef & Pork Meatballs
Dinner: Onion Prawns Risotto
Dessert: Vanilla Tapioca Pudding

Chapter 1 Breakfast

Denver Egg Muffins

Prep time: 10 minutes | Cook time: 5 minutes | Serves: 4

4 large eggs
2 tablespoons whole milk
¼ teaspoon salt
⅛ teaspoon black pepper

4 tablespoons diced ham
2 tablespoons diced onion
2 tablespoons diced green pepper
2 tablespoons sharp Cheddar cheese

360ml water

1. Spray four silicone muffin cups with cooking spray and set aside. 2. In a small bowl, whisk together eggs, milk, salt, and pepper. Evenly distribute egg mixture into four muffin cups. 3. Evenly divide up ham, onion, and pepper and drop equal amounts into each filled muffin cup. 4. Top each with ½ tablespoon cheese. 5. Add the water to the cooking pot, place the reversible rack in the pot in the lower position and drop the lower rack through the reversible rack handles. 6. Arrange the muffin cups onto the rack. Top them with a paper towel and a piece of foil crimped around the edges. 7. Install the pressure lid and turn the pressure release valve to the SEAL position. 8. Select PRESSURE COOK, set the cooking temperature to HI and adjust the cooking time to 5 minutes. 9. When cooked, let the unit naturally release pressure. 10. Remove foil from the top of muffin cups and then carefully remove egg muffins. Enjoy immediately and refrigerate any leftovers.
Per Serving: Calories 148; Fat 10.18g; Sodium 402mg; Carbs 5.36g; Fibre 0.4g; Sugar 3.27g; Protein 8.97g

Steel-Cut Oats with Chopped Apple

Prep time: 15 minutes | Cook time: 10 minutes | Serves: 4

80g steel-cut oats
125g unsweetened applesauce
1 teaspoon ground cinnamon

½ teaspoon ground nutmeg
¼ teaspoon fine sea salt
720ml water

1 apple, peeled, cored, and chopped
Milk, as needed

1. Combine the oats, applesauce, cinnamon, nutmeg, salt, and water in the cooking pot. Stir the ingredients. 2. Install the pressure lid and turn the pressure release valve to the SEAL position. 3. Select PRESSURE COOK, set the cooking temperature to HI and adjust the cooking time to 10 minutes. 4. When cooked, let the unit naturally release pressure. 5. Stir the oats, and then add the apple. Add milk until you reach your desired consistency. Enjoy with your favorite toppings.
Per Serving: Calories 113; Fat 2.47g; Sodium 165mg; Carbs 27.41g; Fibre 5.4g; Sugar 9.5g; Protein 5.28g

Cheddar Bacon Egg Muffins

Prep time: 10 minutes | Cook time: 5 minutes | Serves: 4

4 large eggs
2 tablespoons whole milk
¼ teaspoon salt

⅛ teaspoon black pepper
2 slices cooked bacon, crumbled
2 tablespoons diced chives

2 tablespoons sharp Cheddar cheese
360ml water

1. Spray four silicone muffin cups with cooking spray and set aside. 2. In a small bowl, whisk together eggs, milk, salt, and pepper. Evenly distribute egg mixture into muffin cups. 3. Evenly divide up bacon and chives and drop equal amounts onto each egg muffin. Top each with ½ tablespoon cheese. 4. Add the water to the cooking pot, place the reversible rack in the pot in the lower position and drop the lower rack through the reversible rack handles. 5. Arrange the muffin cups onto the rack. Top them with a paper towel and a piece of foil crimped around the edges. 6. Install the pressure lid and turn the pressure release valve to the SEAL position. 7. Select PRESSURE COOK, set the cooking temperature to HI and adjust the cooking time to 5 minutes. 8. When cooked, let the unit naturally release pressure. 9. Remove foil from the top of muffin cups and then carefully remove egg muffins. Enjoy immediately and refrigerate any leftovers.
Per Serving: Calories 204; Fat 15.66g; Sodium 385mg; Carbs 2.61g; Fibre 0.1g; Sugar 2.16g; Protein 12.54g

Ham Egg Burritos

Prep time: 5 minutes | Cook time: 5 minutes | Serves: 4

4 large eggs	⅛ teaspoon black pepper	4 (25cm) flour tortillas
30ml whole milk	65g diced ham	4 tablespoons salsa
¼ teaspoon salt	1 tablespoon butter	25g grated Mexican-blend cheese

1. In a small bowl, whisk together eggs, milk, salt, and pepper. Mix in ham. 2. Add the butter to the cooking pot; press FUNCTION and turn the dial to select SEAR/SAUTÉ. 3. Press TEMP and turn the dial to select HI, and press START/STOP to begin cooking. 4. Melt the butter, and then pour in egg mixture and ham; stir them with for 3 minutes until no longer runny. 5. Divide egg scramble evenly among four tortillas. 6. Spread salsa on eggs and top with cheese. 7. Roll into burritos and enjoy immediately or freeze.
Per Serving: Calories 283; Fat 14.59g; Sodium 794mg; Carbs 27.28g; Fibre 1.5g; Sugar 3.48g; Protein 10.33g

Veggie Burritos

Prep time: 5 minutes | Cook time: 6 minutes | Serves: 4

4 large eggs	1 tablespoon butter	4 (25cm) flour tortillas
30ml whole milk	2 tablespoons diced onion	4 tablespoons salsa
¼ teaspoon salt	2 tablespoons diced red pepper	25g grated Mexican-blend cheese
⅛ teaspoon black pepper	15g chopped mushrooms	

1. In a small bowl, whisk together eggs, milk, salt, and pepper. 2. Add butter to the cooking pot; press FUNCTION and turn the dial to select SEAR/SAUTÉ. 3. Press TEMP and turn the dial to select HI, and press START/STOP to begin cooking. 4. Melt the butter, and then pour in onion, pepper, and mushrooms; cook them for 1 minute until onions are soft. 5. Pour in egg mixture and continue to cook 3 more minutes until eggs are no longer runny. 6. Divide egg scramble evenly among four tortillas. 7. Spread salsa on eggs and top with cheese. Roll into burritos and enjoy immediately or freeze.
Per Serving: Calories 276; Fat 12.7g; Sodium 727mg; Carbs 27.69g; Fibre 1.7g; Sugar 4.04g; Protein 12.41g

Homemade Yogurt

Prep time: 5 minutes | Cook time: 8 hours | Serves: 8

1.9L ultra-pasteurized or ultra-filtered milk	2 tablespoons plain yogurt with live active
175g sweetened condensed milk	cultures

1. Start with a very clean the cooking pot cooking pot. 2. In a medium bowl, whisk together milk, condensed milk, and plain yogurt. Add the mixture to the cooking pot. 3. Press TEMP and select FMNT, and press TIME and turn the dial to adjust the cooking time to 8 hours. 4. Install the pressure lid and press START/STOP to begin incubation process. 5. When done, remove lid and refrigerate yogurt for a minimum of 8 hours. 6. Use within ten to fourteen days.
Per Serving: Calories 138; Fat 5.71g; Sodium 126mg; Carbs 12.93g; Fibre 0g; Sugar 13.62g; Protein 8.87g

Hash Brown Casserole

Prep time: 10 minutes | Cook time: 20 minutes | Serves: 4

200g frozen hash browns	60ml whole milk	⅛ teaspoon black pepper
6 precooked breakfast sausage patties	½ teaspoon hot sauce	50g shredded sharp Cheddar cheese
6 large eggs	¼ teaspoon salt	360ml water

1. Arrange frozen hash browns on the bottom of the Cook & Crisp Basket. 2. Place sausage patties in a single layer on top of hash browns with one in the centre and five around edges. 3. In a small bowl, whisk together eggs, milk, hot sauce, salt, and pepper. 4. Pour egg mixture over hash browns and sausage. Sprinkle cheese over top of hash brown casserole. 5. Place a paper towel on top of the basket and tightly cover with foil. 6. Add the water to the cooking pot, place the Cook & Crisp Basket on top of diffuser and press down firmly. 7. Install the pressure lid and turn the pressure release valve to the SEAL position. 8. Select PRESSURE COOK, set the cooking temperature to HI and adjust the cooking time to 20 minutes. 9. When cooked, let the unit naturally release pressure. 10. Remove the foil and paper towel from the top of the pan. Serve immediately.
Per Serving: Calories 419; Fat 30.43g; Sodium 626mg; Carbs 19.92g; Fibre 1.8g; Sugar 2.75g; Protein 17.48g

Sausage Sandwiches

Prep time: 10 minutes | Cook time: 9 minutes | Serves: 4

4 large eggs
2 tablespoons whole milk
¼ teaspoon salt

⅛ teaspoon black pepper
360ml water
4 English muffins

2 teaspoons butter
4 breakfast sausage patties
4 slices Cheddar cheese

1. Spray four ramekins with cooking spray and set aside. 2. In a small bowl, whisk together eggs, milk, salt, and pepper. 3. Pour the mixture evenly into four ramekins; wrap ramekins tightly in foil. 4. Pour 360ml water into the cooking pot, place the reversible rack in the pot in the lower position and drop the lower rack through the reversible rack handles. 5. Arrange the ramekins onto the rack. 6. Install the pressure lid and turn the pressure release valve to the SEAL position. 7. Select PRESSURE COOK, set the cooking temperature to HI and adjust the cooking time to 8 minutes. 8. When cooked, let the unit naturally release pressure. 9. Heat the sausage patties in the clean cooking pot at HI for 1 minute on SEAR/SAUTÉ mode. 10. Remove each egg from its ramekin and place on one half of English muffin. Top each egg with a sausage patty and a slice of cheese. 11. Place other half of the English muffin on top to create a sandwich.
Per Serving: Calories 413; Fat 24.83g; Sodium 778mg; Carbs 28.75g; Fibre 2.6g; Sugar 3.14g; Protein 19.83g

Cream Berries Cake

Prep time: 10 minutes | Cook time: 35 minutes | Serves: 8

230g unsalted butter, at room temperature, plus extra for greasing the pan
250g plain flour, plus extra for preparing the pan

2½ teaspoons baking powder
1 teaspoon fine sea salt
150g granulated sugar
1 large egg

180ml milk
300g fresh berries
240ml water, for steaming
1 (400g) container cream cheese frosting

1. Butter and flour the bottom of the Cook & Crisp Basket. 2. Combine the flour, baking powder, and salt in a medium mixing bowl. 3. In a large mixing bowl, use an electric mixer to cream together the butter, sugar, and egg. 4. In increments, mix the flour mixture into the butter mixture. 5. Gently stir in the milk and berries, and then pour the batter into the basket. 6. Place a paper towel over it and then cover tightly with aluminum foil. 7. Add the water to the cooking pot, place the Cook & Crisp Basket on top of diffuser and press down firmly. 8. Install the pressure lid and turn the pressure release valve to the SEAL position. 9. Select PRESSURE COOK, set the cooking temperature to HI and adjust the cooking time to 35 minutes. 10. When cooked, let the unit naturally release pressure. Remove the aluminum foil and paper towel. 11. Use a fork to check to ensure that the cake is done. The fork's tines should come out clean. 12. If not, replace the paper towel and aluminum foil and return the basket to the pot, lock the lid back into place, and cook for a few more minutes. 13. Let the dish cool on a cooling rack for 10 minutes to cool. Run a knife around the edge of the cake and then invert it onto a plate. Allow the dish to cool completely before serving. 14. Open the container of frosting and scoop ½ cup of it into a microwave-safe container. Microwave it for 15 seconds. 15. Stir the frosting and drizzle over the cake, then cut into 8 slices. Warm and drizzle more frosting, if desired.
Per Serving: Calories 672; Fat 30.01g; Sodium 532mg; Carbs 96.62g; Fibre 1.9g; Sugar 59.29g; Protein 6.78g

Cheeses Egg Bites

Prep time: 10 minutes | Cook time: 8 minutes | Serves: 4

60g crumbled cooked bacon or sausage (optional)
4 large eggs

75g shredded Monterey Jack cheese
120g small-curd cottage cheese
60g heavy cream

½ teaspoon fine sea salt
240ml water, for steaming

1. Divide the crumbled bacon or sausage (optional) between the silicone egg bite molds. 2. In a medium mixing bowl, whisk together the eggs, shredded cheese, cottage cheese, cream, and salt. 3. Divide the egg mixture between the molds. Cover the molds with aluminum foil. 4. Add the water to the cooking pot, place the reversible rack in the pot in the lower position and drop the lower rack through the reversible rack handles. 5. Arrange the molds onto the rack. 6. Install the pressure lid and turn the pressure release valve to the SEAL position. 7. Select PRESSURE COOK, set the cooking temperature to HI and adjust the cooking time to 8 minutes. 8. When cooked, let the unit naturally release pressure. 9. Remove the silicone molds from the pot. Allow the eggs to rest in the mold for 2 minutes before removing.
Per Serving: Calories 202; Fat 16.1g; Sodium 548mg; Carbs 1.88g; Fibre 0g; Sugar 1.13g; Protein 12.24g

Simple Porridge

Prep time: 5 minutes | Cook time: 5 minutes | Serves: 4

160g rolled oats
1.2L water

1 tablespoon unsalted butter (optional)
½ teaspoon fine sea salt (optional)

1. Pour the rolled oats into the cooking pot. Add the water, butter (optional), and salt (optional) and stir them well. 2. Install the pressure lid and turn the pressure release valve to the SEAL position. 3. Select PRESSURE COOK, set the cooking temperature to LO and adjust the cooking time to 5 minutes. 4. When cooked, let the unit naturally release pressure. 5. Serve and enjoy.
Per Serving: Calories 133; Fat 5.23g; Sodium 300mg; Carbs 31.12g; Fibre 7.2g; Sugar 0.68g; Protein 8.25g

Granola with Cranberries

Prep time: 10 minutes | Cook time: 2 hours 30 minutes | Serves: 6

320g old-fashioned rolled oats
120g roasted almonds, roughly chopped
55g packed light brown sugar

½ teaspoon ground cinnamon
½ teaspoon salt
120ml olive oil

170g honey
1 teaspoon vanilla extract
60g dried cranberries

1. Spray inside of the cooking pot with cooking spray. 2. Pour in rolled oats, almonds, brown sugar, cinnamon, and salt. Mix them well. 3. In a small bowl, whisk together oil, honey, and vanilla. 4. Pour wet ingredients over dry ingredients in the pot and mix until fully combined. Cover partially with a glass lid, leaving 7.5cm of open air. 5. Install the pressure lid and turn the pressure release valve to the VENT position. 6. Press FUNCTION and turn the dial to select SLOW COOK. 7. Press TEMP and turn the dial to select HI, press TIME and turn the dial to set the cooking time to 2½ hours; press START/STOP to begin cooking. 8. Stir the mixture every 30 minutes during cooking time. 9. When done, mix in the cranberries. Remove granola from the cooking pot and spread onto a large baking pan. Let cool. 10. Pour cooled granola into an air-tight container. You can store the dish at room temperature for 5 to 7 days.
Per Serving: Calories 419; Fat 22.74g; Sodium 201mg; Carbs 68.54g; Fibre 9.8g; Sugar 26.9g; Protein 11.09g

Hard-Boiled Eggs

Prep time: 15 minutes | Cook time: 5 minutes | Serves: 2

240ml water, for steaming

1 or more large eggs

1. Add the water to the cooking pot, and place the eggs in it. 2. Install the pressure lid and turn the pressure release valve to the SEAL position. 3. Select PRESSURE COOK, set the cooking temperature to HI and adjust the cooking time to 3 (Soft-boiled) or 5 (Hard-boiled) minutes. 4. When cooked, let the unit naturally release pressure. 5. Add ice and cold water to a large bowl. Transfer the eggs to the ice bath and allow the eggs to rest in the ice bath for 5 minutes. 6. Once the eggs have cooled, you can peel and eat them immediately, or store them whole in the refrigerator. 7. Hard-boiled eggs will keep for up to 4 days. Soft-boiled eggs will keep for up to 2 days.
Per Serving: Calories 36; Fat 2.38g; Sodium 38mg; Carbs 0.18g; Fibre 0g; Sugar 0.09g; Protein 3.14g

Poblano Frittatas

Prep time: 10 minutes | Cook time: 30 minutes | Serves: 4

4 eggs
240ml whole milk
1 can diced green poblano

½ teaspoon salt
½ teaspoon ground cumin
100g Mexican blend shredded cheese

Tortillas or toast, for serving

1. Beat the eggs in a medium bowl, and then mix in the half and half, poblano, salt, cumin, and 50g cheese. 2. Spray the Cook & Crisp Basket with cooking spray and pour in the frittata mix. 3. Add 480 ml of water to the cooking pot, and place the Cook & Crisp Basket on top of diffuser and press down firmly. 4. Install the pressure lid and turn the pressure release valve to the SEAL position. 5. Select PRESSURE COOK, set the cooking temperature to HI and adjust the cooking time to 20 minutes. 6. When cooked, let the unit naturally release pressure. 7. Preheat your grill and add the remaining cheese to the top of the frittata and grill 5 minutes or until the cheese is golden brown. 8. Serve the dish with toast or tortillas.
Per Serving: Calories 248; Fat 14.05g; Sodium 884mg; Carbs 14.73g; Fibre 2.1g; Sugar 3.81g; Protein 16.05g

Chocolate Granola Bars

Prep time: 10 minutes | Cook time: 5 minutes | Serves: 8

120g old-fashioned rolled oats
55g packed light brown sugar
60g roasted whole almonds, chopped

¼ teaspoon salt
145g honey
55g unsalted butter

1 teaspoon vanilla extract
60g dried cranberries
125g mini chocolate chips, divided

1. Line a suitable baking pan with parchment paper and spray with cooking spray. Set aside. 2. In a medium bowl, mix together oats, brown sugar, almonds, and salt. 3. Add the honey and butter to the cooking pot; press FUNCTION and turn the dial to select SEAR/SAUTÉ. 4. Press TEMP and turn the dial to select HI, and press START/STOP to begin cooking. 5. Melt the mixture until it begins to bubble; let the mixture bubble for 2 minutes. 6. Stop the machine and mix in vanilla. 7. Pour wet mixture over the dry mixture in the bowl and mix them well. 8. Mix in cranberries. Mix in 85g chocolate chips. The chocolate chips will melt slightly, helping the bars to stick together. 9. Pour granola bar mixture into prepared baking pan. Firmly press granola bars into baking pan. 10. Pour remaining chocolate chips on top and press them into granola bars with a spatula. Refrigerate the food for 2 hours. 11. Once chilled, cut into rectangles using a sharp knife. You can store the dish in an air-tight container for 5 to 7 days.

Per Serving: Calories 201; Fat 10.42g; Sodium 99mg; Carbs 30.11g; Fibre 4g; Sugar 14.7g; Protein 5.18g

Vanilla Banana Bread

Prep time: 10 minutes | Cook time: 50 minutes | Serves: 4

6 tablespoons unsalted butter, melted, plus extra for greasing the pan
3 very ripe bananas
1 large egg, beaten

1 teaspoon vanilla extract
100g granulated sugar
1 teaspoon baking soda
Pinch fine sea salt

185g plain flour, divided
240ml water, for steaming

1. Grease the Cook & Crisp Basket with butter. 2. In a medium bowl, mash the bananas with a fork. 3. Add the butter, egg, and vanilla and mix them well. Stir in the sugar, baking soda, and salt. 4. In increments, add the flour to the mixture. Pour the batter into the basket. Place a paper towel over it, then cover tightly with aluminum foil. 5. Add the water to the cooking pot, place the Cook & Crisp Basket on top of diffuser and press down firmly. 6. Install the pressure lid and turn the pressure release valve to the SEAL position. 7. Select PRESSURE COOK, set the cooking temperature to HI and adjust the cooking time to 50 minutes. 8. When cooked, let the unit naturally release pressure. 9. Let the dish cool for 5 minutes on a cooling rack; slice the dish before serving.

Per Serving: Calories 441; Fat 17.53g; Sodium 366mg; Carbs 64.9g; Fibre 3.1g; Sugar 21.28g; Protein 6.99g

Baby Spinach Frittata

Prep time: 15 minutes | Cook time: 30 minutes | Serves: 4

Nonstick cooking spray
2 tablespoons olive oil
1 onion, chopped
60g baby spinach
2 garlic cloves, minced

8 large eggs
240g shredded mozzarella cheese, divided
150g canned diced tomatoes, drained
60ml milk
½ teaspoon fine sea salt

¼ teaspoon ground black pepper
240ml water, for steaming
Sour cream, for topping (optional)

1. Line a suitable pan with aluminum foil to keep the liquid from leaking, and then spray the foil with nonstick cooking spray. 2. Add the oil to the cooking pot; press FUNCTION and turn the dial to select SEAR/SAUTÉ. 3. Press TEMP and turn the dial to select MD, and press START/STOP to begin cooking. 4. Heat the oil, and then add the onion, spinach, and garlic, and sauté them for 3 minutes until the onion is almost translucent and the spinach is wilted. 5. Transfer the vegetables to a medium bowl. Rinse out the cooking pot to make sure there's no onion or garlic that may have stuck to the bottom. 6. Add the eggs, 120g of cheese, the tomatoes, milk, salt, and pepper to the bowl and whisk until well combined. 7. Pour the egg mixture into the prepared pan and cover with aluminum foil. 8. Add the water to the cooking pot, place the reversible rack in the pot in the lower position and drop the lower rack through the reversible rack handles. 9. Arrange the pan onto the rack. 10. Install the pressure lid and turn the pressure release valve to the SEAL position. 11. Select PRESSURE COOK, set the cooking temperature to HI and adjust the cooking time to 25 minutes. 12. When cooked, let the unit naturally release pressure. 13. Remove the foil. Gently dab a paper towel on top of the frittata to remove any moisture that may have built up. 14. As the frittata cools, it will begin to pull away from the edges. Run a knife around the edges to loosen it. 15. Place a plate over top of frittata and turn the pan upside down so that the frittata releases. Top the dish with the remaining cheese and sour cream, if desired.

Per Serving: Calories 311; Fat 16.77g; Sodium 781mg; Carbs 15.33g; Fibre 3.5g; Sugar 8.26g; Protein 26.57g

Whole Milk Yogurt

Prep time: 5 minutes | Cook time: 5 minutes | Serves: 16

3.8L whole milk

2 tablespoons yogurt (use only the kind

with live cultures)

1. Add milk to the cooking pot. 2. Install the pressure lid and turn the pressure release valve to the VENT position. 3. Press FUNCTION and turn the dial to select YOGURT. 4. Press TEMP and turn the dial to select FMNT, press TIME and turn the dial to set the cooking time to 10 hours; press START/STOP to begin pasteurization. 5. Unit will display BOIL while pasteurizing. Stir and whisk the milk occasionally to get it to heat evenly. 6. When pasteurization temperature is reached, the unit will beep and display COOL. 7. Once the milk has cooled, the unit will display ADD And STIR in succession and the incubation time. 8. Put the live culture yogurt in a small bowl and add some of the warm milk mixture; whisk together. Add the yogurt mixture to the rest of the milk in the inner cooking pot. 9. Install the pressure lid and press START/STOP to begin incubation process. 10. For a mild yogurt, incubate it for 6 to 8 hours. For a tangier yogurt, incubate for 8 to 10 hours. 11. When the cycle ends, remove the pot, keep it covered, and place it in the refrigerator for 6 to 8 hours. It should be thick enough for a spoon to stand upright in it.

Per Serving: Calories 209; Fat 7.13g; Sodium 102mg; Carbs 29.78g; Fibre 0g; Sugar 29.62g; Protein 6.9g

Egg Ham Burritos

Prep time: 5 minutes | Cook time: 35 minutes | Serves: 5

Nonstick cooking spray
275g frozen hash browns
65g diced ham (optional)
3 large eggs

2 tablespoons milk
2 tablespoons sour cream
25g shredded Cheddar cheese
⅛ teaspoon fine sea salt

⅛ teaspoon ground black pepper
240ml water, for steaming
5 flour tortillas

1. Grease a suitable heat-safe bowl with nonstick cooking spray. 2. Put the hash browns in the prepared bowl and top with the ham (optional). 3. In a medium bowl, whisk together the eggs, milk, sour cream, cheese, salt, and pepper. 4. Pour the egg mixture over the meat and hash browns. Cover the bowl tightly with aluminum foil. 5. Add the water to the cooking pot, place the reversible rack in the pot in the lower position and drop the lower rack through the reversible rack handles. 6. Arrange the bowl onto the rack. 7. Install the pressure lid and turn the pressure release valve to the SEAL position. 8. Select PRESSURE COOK, set the cooking temperature to HI and adjust the cooking time to 25 minutes. 9. When cooked, let the unit naturally release pressure. 10. Remove the bowl from the pot and remove the foil. Stir again, and then spoon the filling onto the tortillas. Wrap the tortillas around the filling, tucking in the edges.

Per Serving: Calories 290; Fat 12.75g; Sodium 456mg; Carbs 35.94g; Fibre 2.4g; Sugar 2.12g; Protein 8.31g

Giant Pancake with Berry Compote

Prep time: 10 minutes | Cook time: 50 minutes | Serves: 2-4

250g plain flour
2½ teaspoons baking powder
2 tablespoons granulated white sugar, plus
1 teaspoon for berry compote

2 large eggs
360ml milk
Butter, for serving
Maple syrup, for serving

130g of your favorite frozen berries, like strawberries and blueberries or mixed berries

1. Add eggs and milk to a large mixing bowl and whisk until completely blended. 2. Blend dry ingredients in another bowl. 3. Fold dry ingredients into the batter and whisk until there are only a few small lumps remaining. 4. Grease a suitable pan. 5. Pour the batter into the pan. 6. Add the water to the cooking pot, place the reversible rack in the pot in the lower position and drop the lower rack through the reversible rack handles. 7. Arrange the pan onto the rack. 8. Install the pressure lid and turn the pressure release valve to the SEAL position. 9. Select PRESSURE COOK, set the cooking temperature to HI and adjust the cooking time to 45 minutes. 10. When cooked, turn the pressure release valve to the VENT position to quick release the steam. 11. Insert a toothpick into the pancake; when toothpick removes cleanly, the pancake is done. 12. Add berries, 1 teaspoon sugar, and 240ml water to a small saucepan. Cover the saucepan and simmer the mixture on medium heat for 10 minutes. 13. Remove berry compote from stove top and stir with a spoon to make sure it's at the desired thickness. 14. Top pancake with butter, syrup and berry compote.

Per Serving: Calories 383; Fat 5.99g; Sodium 49mg; Carbs 71.03g; Fibre 2.4g; Sugar 20.37g; Protein 10.94g

Toast Casserole

Prep time: 5 minutes | Cook time: 5 minutes | Serves: 4

Butter or nonstick cooking spray
2 large eggs
240ml milk
2 teaspoons vanilla extract

1 teaspoon ground cinnamon
7 bread slices (cinnamon raisin, wheat, Italian—choose your favorite), cut into 2.5 cm cubes

240ml water, for steaming
Assorted toppings (butter, maple syrup, sliced fruit, chopped nuts, chocolate chips, etc)

1. Grease a suitable pan with the butter. 2. In a large mixing bowl, whisk together the eggs, milk, vanilla, and cinnamon. 3. Add the bread cubes to the egg mixture and mix to coat all the bread pieces with the egg mixture. 4. Pour the bread and egg mixture into the prepared pan. Cover the pan with aluminum foil. 5. Add the water to the cooking pot, place the reversible rack in the pot in the lower position and drop the lower rack through the reversible rack handles. 6. Arrange the pan onto the rack. 7. Install the pressure lid and turn the pressure release valve to the SEAL position. 8. Select PRESSURE COOK, set the cooking temperature to HI and adjust the cooking time to 15 minutes. 9. When cooked, let the unit naturally release pressure. 10. Let the casserole rest for 5 minutes. Top the dish with your favorite toppings.
Per Serving: Calories 319; Fat 4.79g; Sodium 74mg; Carbs 66.97g; Fibre 3.2g; Sugar 49.1g; Protein 7.4g

Banana Toast Casserole

Prep time: 15 minutes | Cook time: 10 minutes | Serves: 6

6 slices French bread
4 bananas
2 tablespoons brown sugar
60g cream cheese

3 eggs
60ml milk
1 tablespoon white sugar
1 teaspoon vanilla extract

½ teaspoon ground cinnamon
2 tablespoons butter
30g chopped pecans

1. Cut the bread into 2cm cubes and slice the bananas. 2. Place a layer of bread cubes on the bottom of a suitable pan. 3. Add sliced banana over the bread and sprinkle with a layer of brown sugar. 4. Melt the cream cheese in the microwave and then spread half of it over the brown sugar. 5. Repeat steps 2 to 4, creating another layer. 6. Add half the pecans on top of the second layer then slice the butter over the pecans. 7. Beat the eggs in a small bowl, and then mix in the sugar, vanilla, milk, and cinnamon. 8. Pour the egg mixture over the bread. 9. Add 180ml water to the cooking pot, place the reversible rack in the pot in the lower position and drop the lower rack through the reversible rack handles. 10. Arrange the pan onto the rack. 11. Install the pressure lid and turn the pressure release valve to the VENT position. 12. Select STEAM and adjust the cooking time to 5 minutes. 13. When cooked, let the unit naturally release pressure. 14. Allow the dish to cool for 5 minutes, then remove and top with remaining bananas and nuts before serving.
Per Serving: Calories 629; Fat 18.45g; Sodium 967mg; Carbs 96.25g; Fibre 5.6g; Sugar 21.4g; Protein 21.74g

Blueberry French Toast

Prep time: 10 minutes | Cook time: 60 minutes | Serves: 8

Non-stick cooking spray
8 large eggs
120g plain yogurt
80g sour cream

1 teaspoon vanilla extract
½ teaspoon ground cinnamon
240ml milk
115g maple syrup

1 loaf of French or Italian bread, cubed
120g fresh or frozen blueberries
300g cream cheese, cubed
Maple syrup, for serving

1. Add eggs, yogurt, sour cream, vanilla, and cinnamon to a large mixing bowl; stir to combine. Gradually whisk in milk and maple syrup until blended. 2. Grease a suitable pot with cooking spray. 3. Add half the cubed bread to the pot; layer with half of the blueberries, cream cheese, and egg mixture. 4. Add a second layer of bread cubes, then the other half of the blueberries, cream cheese, and egg mixture. 5. Cover the pot and refrigerate the food overnight. 6. Remove French toast mixture from the refrigerator and allow the toast to rest for 30 minutes before cooking. 7. Add the water to the cooking pot, place the reversible rack in the pot in the lower position and drop the lower rack through the reversible rack handles. 8. Arrange the pot onto the rack. 9. Install the pressure lid and turn the pressure release valve to the SEAL position. 10. Select PRESSURE COOK, set the cooking temperature to LO and adjust the cooking time to 60 minutes. 11. When cooked, let the unit naturally release pressure. 12. A knife inserted in the centre comes out clean. Serve the dish with maple syrup and enjoy!
Per Serving: Calories 318; Fat 19.69g; Sodium 310mg; Carbs 24.21g; Fibre 0.6g; Sugar 19.41g; Protein 11.53g

Coffee Egg Bites

Prep time: 10 minutes | Cook time: 18 minutes | Serves: 4

4 eggs
4 strips bacon
75g shredded cheddar cheese

120g cottage cheese
60g cream
2 tablespoons chives, chopped

½ teaspoon salt

1. Chop the bacon and cook them in the frying pan over medium heat. Crumble when cool enough to touch. 2. Evenly distribute the crumbled bacon into 4 mason jars. 3. Add the eggs, cheese, cottage cheese, cream and salt to a blender and blend until smooth. Mix in the chopped chives. 4. Pour the mixture into the mason jars and cover with foil. 5. Add 240 ml of water to the cooking pot, place the reversible rack in the pot in the lower position and drop the lower rack through the reversible rack handles. 6. Arrange the jars onto the rack. 7. Install the pressure lid and turn the pressure release valve to the VENT position. 8. Select STEAM and adjust the cooking time to 8 minutes. 9. When cooked, let the unit naturally release pressure. 10. Serve warm.
Per Serving: Calories 298; Fat 23.4g; Sodium 724mg; Carbs 2.82g; Fibre 0.2g; Sugar 1.66g; Protein 18.57g

Chocolate Cherry Porridge

Prep time: 5 minutes | Cook time: 6 hours 30 minutes | Serves: 4

160g steel cut oatmeal
1.4L water
240ml milk
2½ tablespoons cocoa powder,

unsweetened
4 tablespoons sugar
1 teaspoon cinnamon
1 teaspoon vanilla

250g bag frozen cherries
Cherries and/or chocolate chips for garnish

1. Mix all of the ingredients except the garnish in the cooking pot. 2. Install the pressure lid and turn the pressure release valve to the VENT position. 3. Press FUNCTION and turn the dial to select SLOW COOK. 4. Press TEMP and turn the dial to select HI, press TIME and turn the dial to set the cooking time to 6½ hours; press START/STOP to begin cooking. 5. Mix them well before transferring to serving bowls. Top the dish with cherries and chocolate chips to serve.
Per Serving: Calories 235; Fat 3.52g; Sodium 167mg; Carbs 47.75g; Fibre 4.5g; Sugar 31.19g; Protein 5.69g

Cinnamon Banana Porridge

Prep time: 20 minutes | Cook time: 5 minutes | Serves: 3

80g old fashioned oats
240ml milk

240ml water
2 bananas

2 teaspoons cinnamon
1 tablespoon brown sugar

1. Spray the bottom of the cooking pot with cooking spray and stir in the oatmeal, water, and milk. 2. Thinly slice one of the bananas and stir into the oatmeal along with the cinnamon and brown sugar. 3. Install the pressure lid and turn the pressure release valve to the SEAL position. 4. Select PRESSURE COOK, set the cooking temperature to HI and adjust the cooking time to 5 minutes. 5. When cooked, let the unit naturally release pressure. 6. Thinly slice the second banana. 7. Transfer the oatmeal to serving bowls and top with banana slices before serving.
Per Serving: Calories 197; Fat 3.74g; Sodium 126mg; Carbs 38.6g; Fibre 4.4g; Sugar 20.03g; Protein 5.22g

Southwest Breakfast Casserole

Prep time: 10 minutes | Cook time: 15 minutes | Serves: 3

4 eggs
900g red potatoes
1 yellow onion
1 jalapeño

150g ham
50g cheddar cheese or pepper jack, shredded
½ teaspoon salt

¼ teaspoon chili powder
¾ teaspoon taco seasoning

1. Dice the onion and jalapeños, and cube the ham and potatoes. 2. In a medium bowl, beat the eggs and mix in the seasonings and salt. Mix in the onions, potatoes, cheese, ham and jalapeño. 3. Transfer the mixture to a suitable greased casserole dish and cover with foil. 4. Add 240ml water to the cooking pot, place the reversible rack in the pot in the lower position and drop the lower rack through the reversible rack handles. 5. Arrange the casserole dish onto the rack. 6. Install the pressure lid and turn the pressure release valve to the SEAL position. 7. Select PRESSURE COOK, set the cooking temperature to HI and adjust the cooking time to 13 minutes. 8. When cooked, let the unit naturally release pressure. 9. Serve the dish with tortillas and a dollop of sour cream.
Per Serving: Calories 557; Fat 22.74g; Sodium 1538mg; Carbs 55.91g; Fibre 6.2g; Sugar 7.29g; Protein 33.33g

Homemade Huevos Rancheros

Prep time: 20 minutes | Cook time: 40 minutes | Serves: 6-8

1 tablespoon butter
10 eggs, beaten
240g whipping cream
150g Mexican blend cheese, shredded
½ teaspoon pepper

½ teaspoon chili powder
½ teaspoon garlic powder
½ teaspoon cumin powder
Pinch of nutmeg
1 (100g) can green chilies, drained

1 (250g) can red enchilada sauce
50g cheddar cheese, shredded
8 tortillas, warmed

1. Grease the Cook & Crisp Basket with the butter. 2. Combine eggs, cream, Mexican cheese, and spices in a large mixing bowl. 3. Fold in the chilies and pour into the basket. 4. Add the water to the cooking pot, place the Cook & Crisp Basket on top of diffuser and press down firmly. 5. Install the pressure lid and turn the pressure release valve to the SEAL position. 6. Select PRESSURE COOK, set the cooking temperature to HI and adjust the cooking time to 30 minutes. 7. When cooked, let the unit naturally release pressure. 8. Remove lid and top with enchilada sauce and cheddar cheese. Replace lid and cook the food for an additional 15 minutes or until cheese is melted. 9. Top tortillas with huevos rancheros and serve immediately with your favorite breakfast drink!
Per Serving: Calories 431; Fat 25.05g; Sodium 635mg; Carbs 29.54g; Fibre 1.7g; Sugar 4.44g; Protein 21.2g

Traditional Porridge

Prep time: 5 minutes | Cook time: 20 minutes | Serves: 1

40g rolled oats
240ml water
1 pinch sea salt

Milk or almond milk, for serving
Honey, for serving
Cinnamon, for serving

Sliced almonds, raisins, walnuts for
garnish

1. Add oats, water and salt to the cooking pot. 2. Install the pressure lid and turn the pressure release valve to the SEAL position. 3. Select PRESSURE COOK, set the cooking temperature to HI and adjust the cooking time to 20 minutes. 4. When cooked, let the unit naturally release pressure. 5. Open the lid and stir the oats. 6. Fold in milk, honey, and cinnamon, if desired, and serve while hot. 7. Garnish the dish with nuts and raisins if desired.
Per Serving: Calories 192; Fat 4.35g; Sodium 188mg; Carbs 48.73g; Fibre 10.7g; Sugar 12.89g; Protein 9.76g

Omelet Quiche

Prep time: 10 minutes | Cook time: 40 minutes | Serves: 4-6

6 large eggs, well beaten
80g half and half
⅛ teaspoon sea salt
⅛ teaspoon ground black pepper

⅛ teaspoon chili powder
⅛ teaspoon garlic powder
65g ham, diced
75g peppers, diced

30g sweet onion, diced
75g cheddar cheese, shredded

1. Add 360ml of water to the cooking pot. 2. Butter a suitable soufflé dish and set aside. 3. Whisk together the eggs, half and half, and spices in a large mixing bowl. 4. Add diced ham, peppers, onions, and cheese to the soufflé dish and stir to mix well. Pour egg mixture over the top of the veggies and ham and stir to combine. 5. Cover the soufflé dish with a silicone lid or aluminum foil loosely. Use the aluminum foil to create a sling. 6. Add the water to the cooking pot, place the reversible rack in the pot in the lower position and drop the lower rack through the reversible rack handles. 7. Arrange the dish onto the rack. 8. Install the pressure lid and turn the pressure release valve to the SEAL position. 9. Select PRESSURE COOK, set the cooking temperature to HI and adjust the cooking time to 30 minutes. 10. When cooked, let the unit naturally release pressure. 11. Open the lid, lift out the soufflé dish and remove the foil carefully. 12. Serve the dish immediately with an iced tea or cup of coffee!
Per Serving: Calories 162; Fat 10.87g; Sodium 366mg; Carbs 3.39g; Fibre 0.2g; Sugar 1.81g; Protein 12.4g

Vegetable & Wild Rice Soup

Prep time: 25 minutes | Cook time: 20 minutes | Serves: 12

1.4L reduced-sodium vegetable stock
2 cans fire-roasted diced tomatoes, undrained
2 celery ribs, sliced
2 medium carrots, chopped
175g baby Portobello mushrooms, sliced

1 medium onion, chopped
1 medium parsnip, peeled and chopped
1 medium sweet potato, peeled and cubed
1 medium green pepper, chopped
185g uncooked wild rice
2 garlic cloves, minced

¾ teaspoon salt
¼ teaspoon pepper
2 bay leaves
2 fresh thyme sprigs

1. Combine all of the ingredients in the cooking pot. 2. Install the pressure lid and turn the pressure release valve to the SEAL position. 3. Select PRESSURE COOK, set the cooking temperature to HI and adjust the cooking time to 20 minutes. 4. When cooked, let the unit naturally release pressure. 5. Discard the bay leaves and thyme sprigs before serving. If desired, serve the dish with additional thyme.
Per Serving: Calories 99; Fat 0.54g; Sodium 521mg; Carbs 21.64g; Fibre 4.1g; Sugar 5.99g; Protein 3.78g

Mexican Beef Wraps

Prep time: 20 minutes | Cook time: 50 minutes | Serves: 6

1 boneless beef chuck roast (900g–1.3kg), halved
½ teaspoon salt
½ teaspoon pepper
1 small onion, finely chopped
1 jalapeno pepper, seeded and minced

3 garlic cloves, minced
1 can (200g) tomato sauce
120ml water
60ml lime juice
1 tablespoon chili powder
1 teaspoon ground cumin

¼ teaspoon cayenne pepper
6 flour or whole wheat tortillas (15cm)
Optional toppings: Torn romaine, chopped tomatoes, sliced avocado and sour cream

1. Sprinkle roast with salt and pepper, and then place in the cooking pot; top them with onion, jalapeno pepper and garlic. 2. In a small bowl, mix tomato sauce, water, lime juice, chili powder, cumin and cayenne, and pour the sauce in the pot. 3. Install the pressure lid and turn the pressure release valve to the SEAL position. 4. Select PRESSURE COOK, set the cooking temperature to HI and adjust the cooking time to 50 minutes. 5. When cooked, let the unit naturally release pressure. 6. A thermometer inserted in beef should read at least 60°C. 7. Remove roast; cool slightly. Shred meat with 2 forks; return to pressure cooker. Serve beef on tortillas with the toppings of your choice.
Per Serving: Calories 336; Fat 13.01g; Sodium 571mg; Carbs 24.01g; Fibre 5.7g; Sugar 3.1g; Protein 31.98g

Garlic Black Bean Soup

Prep time: 20 minutes | Cook time: 5 minutes | Serves: 8

1 teaspoon olive oil
165g fresh or frozen corn
2 cans (375g each) black beans, rinsed and drained

360ml vegetable stock
1 medium onion, finely chopped
1 medium sweet red pepper, finely chopped

4 garlic cloves, minced
2 teaspoon ground cumin
Dash pepper
Minced fresh coriander

1. Cook the corn with oil in the cooking pot at MD for 4 to 6 minutes on SEAR/SAUTÉ mode, and sauté them until golden brown. 2. Stop the machine, remove the corn, and add beans, vegetable stock, onion, red pepper, garlic and cumin to the pot. 3. Install the pressure lid and turn the pressure release valve to the SEAL position. 4. Select PRESSURE COOK, set the cooking temperature to HI and adjust the cooking time to 5 minutes. 5. When cooked, let the unit naturally release pressure. 6. Puree soup using a stick blender, or cool soup slightly and puree in batches in a blender. 7. Return them to pressure cooker; heat through. Sprinkle soup with pepper. 8. Garnish the dish with reserved corn and coriander.
Per Serving: Calories 126; Fat 2.88g; Sodium 516mg; Carbs 21.72g; Fibre 3.8g; Sugar 4.3g; Protein 4.44g

Beef Sloppy Joes

Prep time: 35 minutes | Cook time: 5 minutes | Serves: 10

900g lean beef mince (90% lean)
4 medium carrots, shredded
1 medium yellow summer squash, shredded
1 medium courgette, shredded
1 medium sweet red pepper, finely chopped

2 medium tomatoes, seeded and chopped
1 small red onion, finely chopped
120g ketchup
60ml water
3 tablespoon minced fresh basil or 3 teaspoon dried basil
2 tablespoon cider vinegar

2 garlic cloves, minced
½ teaspoon salt
½ teaspoon pepper
3 tablespoon molasses
10 whole wheat hamburger buns split

1. Sauté the beef in the cooking pot at MD for 8 to 10 minutes on SEAR/SAUTÉ mode, breaking into crumbles. 2. Drain the beef and then return to the pot; add the carrots, summer squash, courgette, red pepper, tomatoes, onion, ketchup, water, basil, vinegar, garlic, salt and pepper to the pot, do not stir them. 3. Install the pressure lid and turn the pressure release valve to the SEAL position. 4. Select PRESSURE COOK, set the cooking temperature to HI and adjust the cooking time to 5 minutes. 5. When cooked, turn the pressure release valve to the VENT position to quick release the steam. 6. Stir in the molasses. Serve the beef mixture with the buns. 7. You can freeze the cooled meat mixture and juices in freezer containers. To use, partially thaw in refrigerator overnight. 8. Heat the food through in a saucepan, stirring occasionally and adding a little water if necessary.
Per Serving: Calories 304; Fat 10.96g; Sodium 400mg; Carbs 23.47g; Fibre 2.2g; Sugar 11.34g; Protein 27.06g

Greek Lentil Soup

Prep time: 20 minutes | Cook time: 15 minutes | Serves: 12

960ml water
960ml vegetable stock
400g dried lentils, rinsed
2 medium carrots, chopped
1 small onion, chopped
1 celery rib, chopped

2 garlic cloves, minced
1 teaspoon dried oregano
30g chopped fresh spinach
120g tomato sauce
60g sliced ripe olives, drained
3 tablespoon red wine vinegar

½ teaspoon salt
¼ teaspoon pepper
Optional toppings: Chopped red onion, chopped parsley and lemon wedges

1. Add the water, stock, lentils, carrots, onion, celery, garlic and oregano to the cooking pot. 2. Install the pressure lid and turn the pressure release valve to the SEAL position. 3. Select PRESSURE COOK, set the cooking temperature to HI and adjust the cooking time to 15 minutes. 4. When cooked, let the unit naturally release pressure. 5. Stir in spinach, tomato sauce, ripe olives, red wine vinegar, salt and pepper. If desired, serve with red onion, parsley and lemon wedges.
Per Serving: Calories 90; Fat 1.48g; Sodium 694mg; Carbs 16g; Fibre 2.6g; Sugar 3.41g; Protein 3.76g

Italian Beef Sandwiches

Prep time: 10 minutes | Cook time: 60 minutes | Serves: 12

1 jar (400g) sliced pepperoncini, undrained
1 can (360g) diced tomatoes, undrained
1 medium onion, chopped
120ml water

2 pkg. Italian salad dressing mix
1 teaspoon dried oregano
½ teaspoon garlic powder
1 beef rump roast or bottom round roast

(1.3kg– 1.8kg)
12 Italian rolls, split

1. Mix the pepperoncini, tomatoes, onion, water, salad dressing mix, oregano, and garlic powder in a bowl. 2. Halve the beef roast, and place in the cooking pot; pour the pepperoncini mixture over the food. 3. Install the pressure lid and turn the pressure release valve to the SEAL position. 4. Select PRESSURE COOK, set the cooking temperature to HI and adjust the cooking time to 60 minutes. 5. When cooked, let the unit naturally release pressure. 6. A thermometer inserted into beef should read at least 60°C. 7. Remove roast; cool slightly. Skim fat from cooking juices. Shred beef with 2 forks. Return beef and cooking juices to pressure cooker; heat through. 8. Serve on rolls. 9. In a large shallow freezer container, combine the first 7 ingredients. Add roast; cover and freeze. 10. To use, place freezer container in refrigerator 48 hours or until roast is completely thawed. Cook the food and serve as directed. 11. Freeze cooled, cooked beef mixture in freezer containers. To use, partially thaw in refrigerator overnight. 12. Heat through in a saucepan, stirring occasionally and adding a little water if necessary.
Per Serving: Calories 228; Fat 6.53g; Sodium 803mg; Carbs 24.87g; Fibre 1.8g; Sugar 5.44g; Protein 17.64g

Lean Turkey Chili

Prep time: 20 minutes | Cook time: 5 minutes | Serves: 12

455g lean turkey mince
360ml water
2 cans (360g each) diced tomatoes, undrained
1 jar (100g) meatless pasta sauce
1 can (400g) hot chili beans, undrained
1 can (400g) kidney beans, rinsed and drained
1 can (375g) pinto beans, rinsed and drained
90g chopped celery
95g chopped onion
105g chopped green pepper
80g frozen corn
2 tablespoon chili powder
1 teaspoon ground cumin
¼ teaspoon pepper
⅛ to ¼ teaspoon cayenne pepper
Optional toppings: Sour cream, cubed avocado, diced jalapeno peppers

1. Sauté the turkey in the cooking pot at MD for 6 to 8 minutes on SEAR/SAUTÉ mode, breaking up turkey into crumbles; drain the meat. 2. Add the water to the pot and cook for 1 minute, stirring to loosen browned bits from the pot. Return the turkey to the pot. Stir in tomatoes, pasta sauce, beans, celery, onion, green pepper, corn and seasonings. 3. Install the pressure lid and turn the pressure release valve to the SEAL position. 4. Select PRESSURE COOK, set the cooking temperature to HI and adjust the cooking time to 5 minutes. 5. When cooked, let the unit naturally release pressure. 6. If desired, serve with sour cream, avocado and jalapeno. 7. Freeze cooled chili in freezer containers. To use, partially thaw in refrigerator overnight. Heat the food through in a saucepan, stirring occasionally and adding a little water if necessary.
Per Serving: Calories 188; Fat 5.68g; Sodium 840mg; Carbs 22.72g; Fibre 6.4g; Sugar 7.3g; Protein 13.59g

Tandoori Onion Chicken Panini

Prep time: 25 minutes | Cook time: 20 minutes | Serves: 6

675g boneless skinless chicken breasts
120ml reduced-sodium chicken stock
2 garlic cloves, minced
2 teaspoon minced fresh gingerroot
1 teaspoon paprika
¼ teaspoon salt
¼ to ½ teaspoon cayenne pepper
¼ teaspoon ground turmeric
6 green onions, chopped
6 tablespoon chutney
6 naan flatbreads

1. Add the chicken breasts, chicken stock, garlic cloves, gingerroot, paprika, salt, cayenne pepper, and turmeric to the cooking pot. 2. Install the pressure lid and turn the pressure release valve to the SEAL position. 3. Select PRESSURE COOK, set the cooking temperature to HI and adjust the cooking time to 6 minutes. 4. When cooked, turn the pressure release valve to the VENT position to quick release the steam. 5. A thermometer inserted in chicken should read at least 75°C. 6. Remove chicken and shred with 2 forks. Return the meat to the pot. Stir in green onions; heat them through on the same settings. 7. Spread chutney over 1 side of each naan. 8. Top chutney side of 3 naan with chicken mixture; top them with remaining naan, chutney side down. 9. Cook the sandwiches on a panini maker or indoor grill for 6 to 8 minutes until golden brown. To serve, cut each sandwich in half. 10. Freeze the cooled meat mixture and juices in freezer containers. To use, partially thaw in refrigerator overnight. 11. Heat through in a saucepan, stirring occasionally and adding a little stock if necessary.
Per Serving: Calories 490; Fat 10.64g; Sodium 702mg; Carbs 60.2g; Fibre 6.9g; Sugar 12g; Protein 37.78g

Split Pea Soup

Prep time: 15 minutes | Cook time: 15 minutes | Serves: 8

1 meaty ham bone
960ml water
1 bottle (300ml) light beer
265g dried green split peas, rinsed
2 celery ribs, chopped
1 large carrot, chopped
1 sweet onion, chopped
1 tablespoon prepared English mustard
120ml low fat milk
10g minced fresh parsley
½ teaspoon salt
¼ teaspoon pepper
¼ teaspoon ground nutmeg

1. Add the ham bone, water, beer, peas, celery, carrot, onion and mustard to the cooking pot. 2. Install the pressure lid and turn the pressure release valve to the SEAL position. 3. Select PRESSURE COOK, set the cooking temperature to HI and adjust the cooking time to 15 minutes. 4. When cooked, let the unit naturally release pressure. 5. Remove bone from soup. Cool slightly, trim away fat and remove meat from bone; discard fat and bone. 6. Cut meat into bite-sized pieces; return to pressure cooker. Stir in remaining ingredients. If desired, top with additional minced parsley.
Per Serving: Calories 215; Fat 9.96g; Sodium 304mg; Carbs 13.4g; Fibre 3.9g; Sugar 4.7g; Protein 15.56g

Pulled Pork Sandwiches

Prep time: 20 minutes | Cook time: 45 minutes | Serves: 12

1 tablespoon fennel seed, crushed
1 tablespoon steak seasoning
1 teaspoon cayenne pepper, optional
1 boneless pork shoulder roast

1 tablespoon olive oil
2 medium green or sweet red peppers, thinly sliced
2 medium onions, thinly sliced

1 can (360g) diced tomatoes, undrained
120ml water
12 whole wheat hamburger buns split

1. In a small bowl, combine fennel seed, steak seasoning and cayenne if desired. Cut roast in half. Rub the seasoning mixture over pork. 2. Heat the oil in the cooking pot at MD on SEAR/SAUTÉ mode; when oil is hot, brown a roast half on all sides. Remove and do the same with remaining pork. 3. Stop the machine and add the cooked meat to the pot; add the peppers, onions, tomatoes and water to the pot. 4. Install the pressure lid and turn the pressure release valve to the SEAL position. 5. Select PRESSURE COOK, set the cooking temperature to HI and adjust the cooking time to 45 minutes. 6. When cooked, let the unit naturally release pressure. 7. A thermometer inserted in pork should read at least 60°C. 8. Remove pork roast; shred with 2 forks. Strain cooking juices; skim fat. Return cooking juices, vegetables and pork to the pot; heat the food through. Serve the pork mixture on buns. 9. Freeze the cooled meat mixture and juices in freezer containers. To use, partially thaw in refrigerator overnight. Heat through in a saucepan, stirring occasionally and adding a little water if necessary.

Per Serving: Calories 462; Fat 16.8g; Sodium 553mg; Carbs 21.07g; Fibre 2.4g; Sugar 5.15g; Protein 53.56g

Veggie Turkey Soup

Prep time: 30 minutes | Cook time: 5 minutes | Serves: 10

490g Italian turkey sausage links, casings removed
3 large tomatoes, chopped
1 can (375g) chickpeas, rinsed and drained
3 medium carrots, thinly sliced

150g cut fresh green beans (2.5cm pieces)
1 medium courgette, quartered lengthwise and sliced
1 large sweet red or green pepper, chopped
8 green onions, chopped

960ml chicken stock
1 can (300g) tomato paste
½ teaspoon seasoned salt
10g minced fresh basil

1. In a large bowl, whisk stock, tomato paste and seasoned salt. 2. Sauté the sausage in the cooking pot at MD for 6 to 8 minutes on SEAR/SAUTÉ mode, breaking the sausage into crumbles; drain the meat and return to the pot. 3. Stop the machine, and add tomatoes, beans, carrots, green beans, courgette, pepper and onions to the pot, and then pour the stock mixture over the food. 4. Install the pressure lid and turn the pressure release valve to the SEAL position. 5. Select PRESSURE COOK, set the cooking temperature to HI and adjust the cooking time to 5 minutes. 6. When cooked, let the unit naturally release pressure. 7. Just before serving, stir in basil. 8. Freeze cooled soup in freezer containers. To use, partially thaw in refrigerator overnight. 9. Heat through in a saucepan, stirring occasionally and adding a little stock if necessary.

Per Serving: Calories 596; Fat 14.9g; Sodium 733mg; Carbs 25.11g; Fibre 6.3g; Sugar 10.89g; Protein 88.02g

Onion Chicken Gyros

Prep time: 20 minutes | Cook time: 10 minutes | Serves: 8

2 medium onions, chopped
6 garlic cloves, minced
1 teaspoon lemon-pepper seasoning
1 teaspoon dried oregano

½ teaspoon ground allspice
120ml lemon juice
60ml red wine vinegar
2 tablespoon olive oil

900g boneless skinless chicken breasts
8 whole pita breads
Toppings: Tzatziki sauce, torn romaine and sliced tomato, cucumber and onion

1. Combine the onions, garlic cloves, lemon-pepper seasoning, oregano, allspice, lemon juice, red wine vinegar, and olive oil in the cooking pot, and then add the chicken to the pot. 2. Install the pressure lid and turn the pressure release valve to the SEAL position. 3. Select PRESSURE COOK, set the cooking temperature to HI and adjust the cooking time to 6 minutes. 4. When cooked, turn the pressure release valve to the VENT position to quick release the steam. 5. A thermometer inserted in chicken should read at least 75°C. 6. Remove chicken; shred with 2 forks. Return to the cooker. Using tongs, place chicken mixture on pita breads. Serve with toppings. 7. Freeze the cooled meat mixture and juices in freezer containers. To use, partially thaw in refrigerator overnight. 8. Heat through in a saucepan, stirring occasionally and adding a little water if necessary.

Per Serving: Calories 262; Fat 7.18g; Sodium 178mg; Carbs 20.49g; Fibre 2.8g; Sugar 2.09g; Protein 28.89g

Cream Cauliflower Soup

Prep time: 20 minutes | Cook time: 5 minutes | Serves: 14

1.4L water
795g Yukon Gold potatoes (about 4 medium), peeled and cut into 2.5cm cubes
1 medium head cauliflower (about 675g) cut into 2.5cm pieces
1 small onion, chopped

3 garlic cloves, minced
1 large bay leaf
3 teaspoon dried celery flakes
1½ teaspoon salt
1½ teaspoon adobo seasoning
¾ teaspoon ground mustard

¼ teaspoon cayenne pepper
90g nonfat dry milk powder
Optional toppings: Shredded cheddar cheese, sliced green onions and croutons

1. Add the water, vegetables and seasonings to the cooking pot. 2. Install the pressure lid and turn the pressure release valve to the SEAL position. 3. Select PRESSURE COOK, set the cooking temperature to HI and adjust the cooking time to 5 minutes. 4. When cooked, let the unit naturally release pressure. 5. Discard bay leaf. Stir in milk powder until dissolved. Puree soup using an immersion blender. 6. Or you can cool the dish slightly and puree soup in batches in a blender; return to pressure cooker and heat through. If desired, serve with toppings.
Per Serving: Calories 59; Fat 0.21g; Sodium 297mg; Carbs 12.71g; Fibre 1.8g; Sugar 1.95g; Protein 5.06g

Typical Beef Stew

Prep time: 30 minutes | Cook time: 35 minutes | Serves: 6

675g beef stew meat, cut into 2.5cm cubes
30g plain flour
1 teaspoon salt
1 teaspoon ground black pepper
3 tablespoons olive oil
2 tablespoons tomato paste

1 teaspoon dried thyme leaves
720ml beef stock
1 teaspoon Worcestershire sauce
3 cloves garlic, peeled and minced
1 (200g) container sliced button mushrooms

3 medium carrots, peeled and cut into 1cm pieces
1 medium yellow onion, peeled and roughly chopped
1 large russet potato, peeled and cut into 1cm cubes

1. Add beef, flour, salt, and pepper to a zip-top bag. Shake the bag to coat beef cubes evenly. 2. Heat the oil in the cooking pot at MD on SEAR/SAUTÉ mode. 3. Add half the beef to pot in an even layer, making sure there is space between beef cubes to prevent steam from forming. 4. Brown the beef for 3 minutes on each side. Remove the beef from pot and reserve on a plate. Do the same with remaining beef. 5. Add tomato paste and thyme to pot and cook for 30 seconds, then add stock and scrape pot to release any browned bits. 6. Stop the machine, and add beef cubes and the remaining ingredients to the pot. 7. Install the pressure lid and turn the pressure release valve to the SEAL position. 8. Select PRESSURE COOK, set the cooking temperature to HI and adjust the cooking time to 35 minutes. 9. When cooked, let the unit naturally release pressure. 10. Open the lid and stir the food well. 11. If you prefer a thicker stew, press the Sauté button and let stew reduce to desired thickness. 12. Serve hot.
Per Serving: Calories 258; Fat 10.28g; Sodium 933mg; Carbs 22g; Fibre 2.5g; Sugar 3.4g; Protein 20.68g

Guinness Veggie & Beef Stew

Prep time: 30 minutes | Cook time: 35 minutes | Serves: 8

900g boneless beef chuck steak, cubed
2 tablespoons plain flour
½ teaspoon salt
¼ teaspoon black pepper
2 tablespoons vegetable oil

1 medium onion, peeled and chopped
1 clove garlic, chopped
½ teaspoon dried thyme
240ml Guinness stout
240ml beef stock

1 bay leaf
2 large carrots, peeled and chopped
2 medium russet potatoes, chopped
10g chopped fresh flat-leaf parsley

1. In a medium bowl add the beef, flour, salt, and pepper. Toss meat with seasoned flour until thoroughly coated. Set aside. 2. Heat the oil in the cooking pot at MD on SEAR/SAUTÉ mode. 3. Add half the beef to pot in an even layer, making sure there is space between beef cubes to prevent steam from forming; brown the beef for 3 minutes on each side. Remove the beef from pot and reserve on a plate. Do the same with remaining beef. 4. Add the onion, garlic, and thyme to pot and cook them for 5 minutes until the onion is tender, then add half the Guinness and scrape off all the browned bits from the bottom of the pot. 5. Add the remaining Guinness, stock, bay leaf, carrots, potatoes, and the browned beef along with any juices that have accumulated on plate. 6. Cancel the cooking mode, and install the pressure lid and turn the pressure release valve to the SEAL position. 7. Select PRESSURE COOK, set the cooking temperature to HI and adjust the cooking time to 20 minutes. 8. When cooked, let the unit naturally release pressure. 9. Open the lid and stir the food well. 10. If you prefer a thicker stew, press the Sauté button and let stew reduce to desired thickness. 11. Discard the bay leaf, and serve hot with fresh parsley as a garnish.
Per Serving: Calories 302; Fat 12.16g; Sodium 326mg; Carbs 22.24g; Fibre 2.4g; Sugar 2.36g; Protein 27.2g

Chicken Thigh Stew

Prep time: 25 minutes | Cook time: 20 minutes | Serves: 6

455g boneless, skinless chicken thighs, cut into 2.5cm pieces
30g plain flour
1 teaspoon salt
1 teaspoon ground black pepper

3 tablespoons olive oil
2 cloves garlic, peeled and minced
1 teaspoon dried thyme leaves
½ teaspoon poultry seasoning
720ml chicken stock

3 medium carrots, peeled and diced
2 stalks celery, chopped
1 medium yellow onion, peeled and chopped
2 medium red potatoes cut into 1cm cubes

1. Add chicken, flour, salt, and pepper to a zip-top bag. Shake the bag to coat chicken evenly. 2. Heat the oil in the cooking pot at MD on SEAR/SAUTÉ mode. 3. Add half the chicken to pot in an even layer, making sure there is space between beef cubes to prevent steam from forming; brown the chicken for 3 minutes on each side. Remove the chicken from pot and reserve on a plate. Do the same with remaining chicken. 4. Add garlic, thyme, and poultry seasoning to pot and cook them for 30 seconds, then add stock and scrape pot to release any browned bits. 5. Stop the machine, and add the chicken pieces and the remaining ingredients to the cooking pot. 6. Install the pressure lid and turn the pressure release valve to the SEAL position. 7. Select PRESSURE COOK, set the cooking temperature to HI and adjust the cooking time to 20 minutes. 8. When cooked, let the unit naturally release pressure. 9. Open the lid and stir the food well. 10. If you prefer a thicker stew, press the Sauté setting and let stew reduce to desired thickness. Serve hot.
Per Serving: Calories 510; Fat 19.71g; Sodium 1132mg; Carbs 45.82g; Fibre 4.8g; Sugar 7.97g; Protein 36.46g

Easy Cioppino

Prep time: 15 minutes | Cook time: 15 minutes | Serves: 8

2 tablespoons unsalted butter
2 stalks celery, chopped
1 medium yellow onion, peeled and diced
1 medium red pepper, seeded and diced
3 cloves garlic, minced
1 teaspoon dried oregano
½ teaspoon Italian seasoning

½ teaspoon black pepper
½ teaspoon salt
2 tablespoons tomato paste
240ml white wine
1 (375g) can crushed tomatoes
960ml seafood stock
1 bay leaf

455g fresh mussels, scrubbed clean and beards removed
455g fresh clams, scrubbed clean
225g large prawns , peeled and deveined
225g fresh scallops
225g calamari rings
1 tablespoon lemon juice

1. Melt the butter in the cooking pot at MD on SEAR/SAUTÉ mode; add the celery, onion, and pepper, and sauté them for 8 minutes; add the garlic, oregano, Italian seasoning, black pepper, and salt and cook them for 30 seconds; add tomato paste and cook for 1 minutes, and then slowly pour in wine and scrape bottom of pot well. 2. Stop the machine, and stir in the tomatoes, stock, and bay leaf. 3. Install the pressure lid and turn the pressure release valve to the SEAL position. 4. Select PRESSURE COOK, set the cooking temperature to HI and adjust the cooking time to 5 minutes. 5. When cooked, turn the pressure release valve to the VENT position to quick release the steam. 6. Open lid and stir in mussels, clams, prawns , scallops, and calamari. 7. Allow soup to simmer for 10 minutes at LO on SEAR/SAUTÉ mode until the seafood is cooked through. 8. Discard bay leaf and stir in lemon juice. Serve hot.
Per Serving: Calories 278; Fat 9.3g; Sodium 1147mg; Carbs 30.39g; Fibre 3.9g; Sugar 8.48g; Protein 18.68g

Potato, Onion & Fish Potato Stew

Prep time: 15 minutes | Cook time: 20 minutes | Serves: 8

2 tablespoons unsalted butter
2 stalks celery, chopped
1 medium yellow onion, peeled and diced
1 medium carrot, peeled and diced
2 cloves garlic, peeled and minced
1 teaspoon Italian seasoning

¼ teaspoon dried thyme
¼ teaspoon ground black pepper
¼ teaspoon salt
240ml lager-style beer
1 (700g) can diced tomatoes
720ml Seafood Stock

1 bay leaf
2 large russet potatoes, peeled and diced
900g whitefish (haddock, cod, or catfish), cut into 2.5cm pieces
2 tablespoons lemon juice

1. Melt the butter in the cooking pot at MD on SEAR/SAUTÉ mode; add the celery, onion, and carrot, and sauté them for 8 minutes; add garlic, Italian seasoning, thyme, pepper, and salt and cook for 30 seconds; add beer and scrape bottom of the pot well. 2. Stop the machine, and stir in the tomatoes, stock, bay leaf, and potatoes. 3. Install the pressure lid and turn the pressure release valve to the SEAL position. 4. Select PRESSURE COOK, set the cooking temperature to HI and adjust the cooking time to 10 minutes. 5. When cooked, turn the pressure release valve to the VENT position to quick release the steam. 6. Open lid and stir in fish. 7. Allow soup to simmer at LO for 10 minutes on SEAR/SAUTÉ mode until seafood is cooked through. 8. Discard bay leaf and stir in lemon juice. Serve hot.
Per Serving: Calories 258; Fat 3.96g; Sodium 725mg; Carbs 28.02g; Fibre 4.5g; Sugar 5.34g; Protein 26.05g

Chicken and Dumplings

Prep time: 25 minutes | Cook time: 30 minutes | Serves: 8

165g plain flour
2 tablespoons unsalted butter
2 teaspoons baking powder
½ teaspoon salt
2 large eggs, beaten
60ml whole milk

900g boneless, skinless chicken breasts
cut into 2.5cm pieces
1 medium onion, peeled and chopped
2 stalks celery, chopped
1 medium carrot, peeled and chopped
½ teaspoon salt

½ teaspoon ground black pepper
½ teaspoon poultry seasoning
1 bay leaf
960ml chicken stock
120ml whole milk
50g frozen peas

1. In a large bowl combine flour, butter, baking powder, and salt. 2. Rub the butter into the flour mixture until it resembles coarse sand. 3. Add eggs and milk and mix until mixture forms into a dough ball. 4. Roll out to ½ cm thick and cut into 2.5cm strips. Cover the strips with a tea towel until ready to use. 5. Place chicken, onion, celery, carrot, salt, pepper, poultry seasoning, bay leaf, and stock in the cooking pot. 6. Install the pressure lid and turn the pressure release valve to the SEAL position. 7. Select PRESSURE COOK, set the cooking temperature to HI and adjust the cooking time to 5 minutes. 8. When cooked, let the unit naturally release pressure. 9. Open lid and stir in whole milk and peas. 10. Let the dish stay in the cooker on Keep Warm mode before serving.

Per Serving: Calories 869; Fat 23.17g; Sodium 999mg; Carbs 45.64g; Fibre 3.1g; Sugar 9.03g; Protein 112.49g

Delicious Pozole

Prep time: 30 minutes | Cook time: 35 minutes | Serves: 6

1.1kg boneless pork shoulder, cut into 5
cm pieces
1 teaspoon salt, divided
1 teaspoon ground black pepper, divided
2 tablespoons vegetable oil
2 medium yellow onions, peeled and
chopped
2 medium poblano peppers, seeded and

diced
1 chipotle pepper in adobo, minced
1 cinnamon stick
4 cloves garlic, peeled and minced
1 tablespoon smoked paprika
2 teaspoons chili powder
1 teaspoon ground cumin
1 teaspoon dried oregano

½ teaspoon ground coriander
1 (300ml) can lager-style beer
960ml chicken stock
2 (375g) cans hominy, drained and rinsed
1 tablespoon lime juice
15g chopped coriander

1. Season the pork pieces with ½ teaspoon salt and ½ teaspoon pepper. 2. Heat the oil in the cooking pot at MD on SEAR/ SAUTÉ mode; add half the pork to the pot in an even layer, making sure there is space between pieces to prevent steam from forming. Brown the meat for 3 minutes on each side. Remove the pork from pot and reserve on a plate. Do the same with remaining pork. 3. Add onions and poblano peppers to pot and cook them for 5 minutes until they are just tender; add the chipotle pepper, cinnamon, garlic, paprika, chili powder, cumin, oregano, and coriander, and cook them for 1 minute until spices and garlic are fragrant. Return pork to pot and turn to coat with spices. Stir in beer and stock, and stop the machine. 4. Install the pressure lid and turn the pressure release valve to the SEAL position. 5. Select PRESSURE COOK, set the cooking temperature to HI and adjust the cooking time to 35 minutes. 6. When cooked, let the unit naturally release pressure. 7. Open lid and stir the food well. 8. If you prefer a thicker stew, press the Sauté button and let stew reduce to desired thickness. 9. Season the dish with remaining salt and pepper, then stir in hominy, lime juice, and coriander. Serve hot.

Per Serving: Calories 672; Fat 23.43g; Sodium 1538mg; Carbs 27.21g; Fibre 5.3g; Sugar 4.88g; Protein 80.46g

Lentil Sausage Stew

Prep time: 15 minutes | Cook time: 25 minutes | Serves: 6

2 tablespoons vegetable oil
455g chicken sausage, sliced
3 stalks celery, cut into 1cm pieces
2 medium carrots, peeled and cut into 1cm
pieces

1 medium yellow onion, peeled and
roughly chopped
2 cloves garlic, peeled and minced
½ teaspoon salt
380g green lentils

1 large russet potato, peeled and cut into 1
cm pieces
10g chopped fresh flat-leaf parsley
960ml chicken stock

1. Add the oil to the cooking pot, and cook the sausage with the oil at MD on SEAR/SAUTÉ mode for 8 minutes until the edges are browned. Transfer the sausage to a plate and set aside. 2. Add celery, carrots, and onion to the pot, and sauté them for 3 minutes until they are tender; add garlic and salt, and cook them for 30 seconds until fragrant. 3. Stop the machine, and add sausage and the remaining ingredients to the pot. 4. Install the pressure lid and turn the pressure release valve to the SEAL position. 5. Select PRESSURE COOK, set the cooking temperature to HI and adjust the cooking time to 25 minutes. 6. When cooked, let the unit naturally release pressure. 7. Remove the lid and stir the food. 8. Serve warm.

Per Serving: Calories 230; Fat 7.24g; Sodium 899mg; Carbs 22.04g; Fibre 2.4g; Sugar 3g; Protein 20.8g

Chicken Thighs & Pinto Beans Stew

Prep time: 25 minutes | Cook time: 20 minutes | Serves: 6

455g boneless, skinless chicken thighs cut into 2.5cm pieces
30g plain flour
1 teaspoon salt
1 teaspoon ground black pepper
3 tablespoons olive oil
2 cloves garlic, peeled and minced
1 teaspoon ground cumin
½ teaspoon ground coriander
½ teaspoon chili powder
720ml chicken stock
2 medium carrots, peeled and diced
2 stalks celery, chopped
1 medium yellow onion, peeled and
chopped
1 (375g) can pinto beans, drained and rinsed
1 (250g) can diced tomatoes with green chilies, drained

1. Add chicken, flour, salt, and pepper to the zip-top bag. Shake the bag to coat beef cubes evenly. 2. Heat the oil in the cooking pot at MD on SEAR/SAUTÉ mode; add half the chicken to the pot in an even layer, making sure there is space between pieces to prevent steam from forming. Brown the meat for 3 minutes on each side. Remove the chicken from pot and reserve on a plate. Do the same with remaining chicken. 3. Add the garlic, cumin, coriander, and chili powder to pot and cook them for 30 seconds, and then add stock and scrape pot to release any browned bits. 4. Stop the machine, and add the chicken pieces and the remaining ingredients to the pot. 5. Install the pressure lid and turn the pressure release valve to the SEAL position. 6. Select PRESSURE COOK, set the cooking temperature to HI and adjust the cooking time to 20 minutes. 7. When cooked, let the unit naturally release pressure. 8. Open the lid and stir the food well. 9. If you prefer a thicker stew, press the Sauté button and let stew reduce to desired thickness. Serve hot.
Per Serving: Calories 299; Fat 12.03g; Sodium 1390mg; Carbs 36.21g; Fibre 5g; Sugar 6.71g; Protein 12.56g

Lean Lamb and Vegetable Stew

Prep time: 25 minutes | Cook time: 30 minutes | Serves: 6

900g lean, boneless lamb shoulder, cut into 2.5cm cubes
¼ teaspoon salt
¼ teaspoon ground black pepper
2 tablespoons olive oil
1 large onion, peeled and chopped
1 clove garlic, peeled and minced
60ml dry white wine
960ml chicken stock
1 bay leaf
1 teaspoon dried thyme
900g small red potatoes, scrubbed and
quartered
400g sliced button mushrooms
200g baby-cut carrots
200g frozen peas

1. Season the lamb cubes with salt and pepper. Cover the meat and refrigerate for 15 minutes. 2. Heat the oil in the cooking pot at MD on SEAR/SAUTÉ mode; add half the lamb to the pot in an even layer, making sure there is space between pieces to prevent steam from forming. Brown the meat for 3 minutes on each side. Remove the lamb from pot and reserve on a plate. Do the same with remaining lamb. 3. Add the onion and garlic to the cooking pot, and sauté them for 1 minute, then add wine and scrape any bits from bottom of pot. 4. Stop the machine, and add lamb, stock, bay leaf, thyme, potatoes, mushrooms, and carrots to the pot. 5. Install the pressure lid and turn the pressure release valve to the SEAL position. 6. Select PRESSURE COOK, set the cooking temperature to HI and adjust the cooking time to 20 minutes. 7. When cooked, let the unit naturally release pressure. 8. Open lid, discard bay leaf, stir in peas, and let stand on the Keep Warm setting. 9. Serve warm.
Per Serving: Calories 1285; Fat 34.93g; Sodium 1553mg; Carbs 84.08g; Fibre 8.9g; Sugar 21.26g; Protein 153g

Tomato Lamb Stew

Prep time: 25 minutes | Cook time: 30 minutes | Serves: 6

900g lamb shoulder, cut into 5cm cubes
¼ teaspoon salt
¼ teaspoon ground black pepper
2 tablespoons olive oil
1 large onion, peeled and chopped
4 cloves garlic, peeled and minced
2 tablespoons sweet paprika
120ml dry white wine
130g sliced roasted red peppers
2 Roma tomatoes, seeded and chopped
720ml chicken stock
240ml red wine
1 bay leaf
1 sprig fresh rosemary

1. Season the lamb should cubes with salt and pepper. 2. Heat the oil in the cooking pot at MD on SEAR/SAUTÉ mode; add half the lamb to the pot in an even layer, making sure there is space between pieces to prevent steam from forming. Brown the meat for 3 minutes on each side. Remove the lamb from pot and reserve on a plate. Do the same with remaining lamb. 3. Add the onion and garlic to the pot, and cook them for 1 minute, then add paprika and cook for 2 minutes until paprika is slightly darker in color; add white wine and scrape any bits from bottom of pot. 4. Stop the machine and add lamb along with the remaining ingredients to the pot. 5. Install the pressure lid and turn the pressure release valve to the SEAL position. 6. Select PRESSURE COOK, set the cooking temperature to HI and adjust the cooking time to 30 minutes. 7. When cooked, let the unit naturally release pressure. 8. Open lid and stir the food well. Discard bay leaf and rosemary. Serve warm.
Per Serving: Calories 864; Fat 32.35g; Sodium 719mg; Carbs 7.98g; Fibre 2g; Sugar 3.85g; Protein 130.27g

Pork Stewed in Beer

Prep time: 30 minutes | Cook time: 35 minutes | Serves: 6

2 tablespoons vegetable oil
900g boneless pork shoulder, cut into 5 cm pieces
1 medium yellow onion, peeled and chopped
1 medium carrot, peeled and chopped

1 stalk celery, chopped
1 Granny Smith apple, peeled, cored, and sliced
3 cloves garlic, peeled and minced
½ teaspoon dried thyme
2 tablespoons light brown sugar

720ml chicken stock
1 (300ml) bottle lager-style beer
½ teaspoon salt
½ teaspoon ground black pepper
450g cooked wide egg noodles

1. Heat the oil in the cooking pot at MD on SEAR/SAUTÉ mode; add half the pork to the pot in an even layer, making sure there is space between pieces to prevent steam from forming. Brown the meat for 3 minutes on each side. Remove the pork from pot and reserve on a plate. Do the same with remaining pork. 2. Add onion, carrot, celery, and apple, and cook them for 8 minutes until vegetables and apple are tender, stirring frequently; add garlic, thyme, and brown sugar and cook for 30 seconds. 3. Stop the machine, and stir in the browned pork, stock, and beer. 4. Install the pressure lid and turn the pressure release valve to the SEAL position. 5. Select PRESSURE COOK, set the cooking temperature to HI and adjust the cooking time to 35 minutes. 6. When cooked, let the unit naturally release pressure. 7. Open the lid and stir the food well. 8. If you prefer a thicker stew, press the Sauté button and let stew reduce to desired thickness. 9. Season the dish with salt and pepper. Serve hot over cooked egg noodles.
Per Serving: Calories 703; Fat 21.41g; Sodium 791mg; Carbs 51.6g; Fibre 3.4g; Sugar 5.78g; Protein 68.15g

Vegetable Chuck Roast Mix

Prep time: 45 minutes | Cook time: 40 minutes | Serves: 6

1.1kg boneless chuck roast or brisket, cut into 10cm pieces
1 teaspoon salt
1 teaspoon ground black pepper
1 tablespoon olive oil
2 medium yellow onions, peeled and chopped

2 medium red peppers, seeded and chopped
6 cloves garlic, peeled and minced
2 teaspoons dried oregano
2 teaspoons ground cumin
2 teaspoons smoked paprika
½ teaspoon cayenne pepper

120ml white wine
1 (360g) can diced tomatoes
1 bay leaf
90g halved Spanish olives
2 teaspoons distilled white vinegar

1. Season the meat with salt and pepper on all sides. 2. Heat the oil in the cooking pot at MD on SEAR/SAUTÉ mode; add half the meat and brown the meat for 7 minutes on each side. Transfer browned meat to a platter and set aside. Do the same with the remaining meat. 3. Add onions and peppers to pot, and cook for 5 minutes until vegetables are just tender; add garlic, oregano, cumin, paprika, and cayenne pepper, and cook for 1 minute until fragrant; add wine and cook for 2 minutes until liquid is reduced by half; add the tomatoes, bay leaf, and meat back to pot. 4. Stop the machine, and install the pressure lid and turn the pressure release valve to the SEAL position. 5. Select PRESSURE COOK, set the cooking temperature to HI and adjust the cooking time to 40 minutes. 6. When cooked, let the unit naturally release pressure. 7. Open lid and discard bay leaf. Stir in olives and vinegar, then shred meat with two forks. Serve hot.
Per Serving: Calories 431; Fat 20.1g; Sodium 711mg; Carbs 11.6g; Fibre 3.9g; Sugar 5.45g; Protein 52.45g

Black Bean & Bacon Stew

Prep time: 20 minutes | Cook time: 30 minutes | Serves: 6

2 tablespoons vegetable oil
8 slices thick-cut smoked bacon, chopped
1 medium green pepper, seeded and chopped
1 medium yellow onion, peeled and chopped

1 small jalapeño pepper, seeded and chopped
4 cloves garlic, peeled and minced
1 tablespoon light brown sugar
1 teaspoon ground cumin
½ teaspoon dried oregano

1 tablespoon white vinegar
270g dried black beans, soaked overnight in water to cover and drained
1.4L ham stock
1 teaspoon salt
1 teaspoon ground black pepper

1. Heat the oil in the cooking pot at MD on SEAR/SAUTÉ mode; add bacon and cook for 5 minutes until begins to render and edges begin to brown; add the pepper, onion, and jalapeño, and cook them for 8 minutes until they are tender, stirring frequently. 2. Add garlic, brown sugar, cumin, and oregano to pot and cook for 30 seconds, then add vinegar and scrape pot well. 3. Stop the machine, and stir in the beans and stock. 4. Install the pressure lid and turn the pressure release valve to the SEAL position. 5. Select PRESSURE COOK, set the cooking temperature to HI and adjust the cooking time to 30 minutes. 6. When cooked, let the unit naturally release pressure. Open lid and stir the food well. 7. If you prefer a thicker stew, press the Sauté button and let stew reduce to desired thickness. 8. Season the dish with salt and pepper. Serve hot.
Per Serving: Calories 385; Fat 19.52g; Sodium 1449mg; Carbs 35.46g; Fibre 8.3g; Sugar 3.39g; Protein 18.31g

Pork & Chickpea Stew

Prep time: 35 minutes | Cook time: 35 minutes | Serves: 6

2 tablespoons vegetable oil
900g boneless pork shoulder, cut into 5 cm pieces
455g Spanish chorizo, sliced
1 medium yellow onion, peeled and chopped

1 medium carrot, peeled and chopped
2 cloves garlic, peeled and minced
1 tablespoon smoked paprika
2 teaspoons hot paprika
2 (375g) cans chickpeas, drained and rinsed

960ml chicken stock
1 (375g) can crushed tomatoes
½ teaspoon salt
½ teaspoon ground black pepper

1. Heat the oil in the cooking pot at MD on SEAR/SAUTÉ mode; add half the pork to the pot in an even layer, making sure there is space between pieces to prevent steam from forming. Brown the meat for 3 minutes on each side. Remove the pork from pot and reserve on a plate. Do the same with remaining pork. 2. Add chorizo to pot and cook for 6 minutes until chorizo has rendered some fat and edges are browned. 3. Add onion, carrot, garlic, smoked paprika, and hot paprika, and cook them for 8 minutes until vegetables are tender, stirring frequently. 4. Add chickpeas, stock, and tomatoes and stir well, then add browned pork back to pot. 5. Stop the machine, and install the pressure lid and turn the pressure release valve to the SEAL position. 6. Select PRESSURE COOK, set the cooking temperature to HI and adjust the cooking time to 20 minutes. 7. When cooked, let the unit naturally release pressure. 8. Open lid and stir the food well. 9. If you prefer a thicker stew, press the Sauté button and let stew reduce to desired thickness. 10. Season the dish with salt and pepper. Serve hot.
Per Serving: Calories 485; Fat 14.4g; Sodium 1430mg; Carbs 44.29g; Fibre 9.2g; Sugar 9.02g; Protein 44.87g

Chinese Pork Belly Stew

Prep time: 25 minutes | Cook time: 30 minutes | Serves: 8

120ml soy sauce
60ml Chinese cooking wine
105g packed light brown sugar
900g pork belly, skinned and cut into

2.5cm cubes
3 tablespoons vegetable oil
2 spring onions , cut into 2.5cm pieces
3 cloves garlic, minced

2 tablespoons soy sauce
1 teaspoon Chinese five-spice powder
480ml vegetable stock
960ml cooked white rice

1. Add soy sauce, wine, and brown sugar to a zip-top bag and mix them well. Add pork and turn to coat evenly. Refrigerate the meat for at least 4 hours. Strain off marinade and reserve. Pat pork dry. 2. Heat the oil in the cooking pot at MD on SEAR/SAUTÉ mode; add half the pork to the pot in an even layer, making sure there is space between pieces to prevent steam from forming. Brown the meat for 3 minutes on each side. Remove the pork from pot and reserve on a plate. Do the same with remaining pork. 3. Stop the machine, and add remaining ingredients and browned pork to the pot with reserved marinade. 4. Install the pressure lid and turn the pressure release valve to the SEAL position. 5. Select PRESSURE COOK, set the cooking temperature to HI and adjust the cooking time to 20 minutes. 6. When cooked, let the unit naturally release pressure. 7. Open lid and stir the food well. 8. If you prefer a thicker stew, press the Sauté button and let stew reduce to desired thickness. 9. Serve hot over cooked rice.
Per Serving: Calories 850; Fat 70.39g; Sodium 663mg; Carbs 36.87g; Fibre 2.2g; Sugar 5.73g; Protein 16.32g

Potato Beef Stew

Prep time: 25 minutes | Cook time: 30 minutes | Serves: 6

900g beef stew meat, cut into 2.5cm cubes
60ml lemon juice
2 tablespoons soy sauce
1 teaspoon ground black pepper
3 tablespoons vegetable oil
3 cloves garlic, peeled and minced

2 medium carrots, peeled and sliced
1 medium yellow onion, peeled and roughly chopped
1 medium red pepper, seeded and chopped
240g tomato sauce
2 large russet potatoes, peeled and cut into

1 cm cubes
1 bay leaf
720ml beef stock
240ml water

1. Add beef, lemon juice, soy sauce, and black pepper to a zip-top bag. Turn to coat beef cubes evenly, then let stand for 20 minutes. Strain off marinade and reserve. Pat beef dry. 2. Heat the oil in the cooking pot at MD on SEAR/SAUTÉ mode; add half the beef to the pot in an even layer, making sure there is space between pieces to prevent steam from forming. Brown the meat for 3 minutes on each side. Remove the beef from pot and reserve on a plate. Do the same with remaining beef. 3. Add garlic, carrots, onion, and pepper to pot, and cook them for 3 minutes until they are just tender. 4. Stop the machine, and add beef and the remaining ingredients to the pot with marinade. Install the pressure lid and turn the pressure release valve to the SEAL position. 5. Select PRESSURE COOK, set the cooking temperature to HI and adjust the cooking time to 30 minutes. 6. When cooked, let the unit naturally release pressure. 7. Open lid, discard bay leaf, and stir the food well. 8. If you prefer a thicker stew, press the Sauté button and let stew reduce to desired thickness. 9. Serve hot.
Per Serving: Calories 435; Fat 14.42g; Sodium 1268mg; Carbs 37.43g; Fibre 5.3g; Sugar 8.51g; Protein 39.22g

Butter Carrots

Prep time: 5 minutes | Cook time: 5 minutes | Serves: 6

455g carrots, scrubbed, peeled, and large-diced

240ml water
2 tablespoons unsalted butter

½ teaspoon salt

1. Add carrots and water to the cooking pot. 2. Install the pressure lid and turn the pressure release valve to the SEAL position. 3. Select PRESSURE COOK, set the cooking temperature to HI and adjust the cooking time to 5 minutes. 4. When cooked, let the unit naturally release pressure. 5. Transfer the carrots to a serving dish. Toss with butter and salt. Serve warm.
Per Serving: Calories 54; Fat 2.75g; Sodium 248mg; Carbs 7.24g; Fibre 2.1; Sugar 3.58g; Protein 0.86g

Red Cabbage with Apples

Prep time: 10 minutes | Cook time: 5 minutes | Serves: 4

1 large head of red cabbage (approximately 900 g), cored and sliced into thin strips
2 large Granny Smith apples, peeled, cored, and diced

1 small sweet yellow onion, peeled and diced
½ teaspoon ground allspice
2 tablespoons light brown sugar

240ml water
60ml apple cider vinegar
2 tablespoons unsalted butter
½ teaspoon salt

1 Add the cabbage, apple, onion, allspice, brown sugar, water, and apple cider vinegar to the cooking pot. 2. Install the pressure lid and turn the pressure release valve to the SEAL position. 3. Select PRESSURE COOK, set the cooking temperature to HI and adjust the cooking time to 4 minutes. 4. When cooked, let the unit naturally release pressure. 5. Transfer the cabbage and apple mixture to a serving dish. Toss with butter and salt. Serve warm.
Per Serving: Calories 179; Fat 4.39g; Sodium 342mg; Carbs 34.12g; Fibre 6.7g; Sugar 22.41g; Protein 3.41g

Corn on the Cob

Prep time: 5 minutes | Cook time: 5 minutes | Serves: 6-8

240ml whole milk
120ml water

4 fresh ears of corn, shucked and halved
1 teaspoon salt

3 tablespoons unsalted butter, cut into several pats

1. Add milk, water, and corn to the cooking pot, and sprinkle them with salt and place butter pats on the corn. 2. Install the pressure lid and turn the pressure release valve to the SEAL position. 3. Select PRESSURE COOK, set the cooking temperature to HI and adjust the cooking time to 2 minutes. 4. Toss the food twice during cooking. 5. When cooked, let the unit naturally release pressure. 6. Transfer corn to a serving dish and serve warm.
Per Serving: Calories 115; Fat 4.67g; Sodium 317mg; Carbs 17.54g; Fibre 1.9g; Sugar 6.22g; Protein 3.38g

Basic Butter Polenta

Prep time: 5 minutes | Cook time: 10 minutes | Serves: 6

1.2L water
125g polenta

2 tablespoons unsalted butter
1 teaspoon salt

1. Stir all ingredients together in the cooking pot. 2. Install the pressure lid and turn the pressure release valve to the SEAL position. 3. Select PRESSURE COOK, set the cooking temperature to HI and adjust the cooking time to 10 minutes. 4. When cooked, let the unit naturally release pressure. 5. Whisk polenta in pot for 5 minutes until it thickens. 6. Transfer polenta to a serving dish and serve warm.
Per Serving: Calories 61; Fat 2.75g; Sodium 482mg; Carbs 8.06g; Fibre 0.4g; Sugar 0.16g; Protein 0.37g

Cheese Asparagus

Prep time: 5 minutes | Cook time: 1 minute | Serves: 4

240ml water
455g asparagus spears, woody ends
trimmed and discarded

2 teaspoons olive oil
1 tablespoon balsamic vinegar
2 tablespoons crumbled blue cheese

2 tablespoons crushed walnuts

1. Add water to the cooking pot, place the reversible rack in the pot in the lower position and drop the lower rack through the reversible rack handles. 2. Arrange the asparagus evenly onto the rack. 3. Install the pressure lid and turn the pressure release valve to the SEAL position. 4. Select PRESSURE COOK, set the cooking temperature to HI and adjust the cooking time to 1 minute. 5. When cooked, let the unit naturally release pressure. 6. Transfer asparagus to a serving dish and toss with oil and vinegar. Garnish with blue cheese and walnuts. Serve warm.
Per Serving: Calories 92; Fat 6.32g; Sodium 128mg; Carbs 6.12g; Fibre 2.6g; Sugar 3.33g; Protein 4.7g

Orange-Flavour Beetroot

Prep time: 10 minutes | Cook time: 10 minutes | Serves: 6

240ml water
6 medium beetroot, ends trimmed

Juice of 1 medium orange
2 teaspoons unsalted butter

1 teaspoon salt

1. Add the water to the cooking pot, place the reversible rack in the pot in the lower position and drop the lower rack through the reversible rack handles. 2. Arrange the beets onto the rack. 3. Install the pressure lid and turn the pressure release valve to the SEAL position. 4. Select PRESSURE COOK, set the cooking temperature to HI and adjust the cooking time to 10 minutes. 5. When cooked, let the unit naturally release pressure. 6. Let beets rest 5 minutes. Peel off their outer skin. Cut beets into quarters and transfer to a serving dish. 7. Add orange juice, butter, and salt to dish. Toss and serve warm.
Per Serving: Calories 53; Fat 1.02g; Sodium 453mg; Carbs 10.23g; Fibre 2.4g; Sugar 7.27g; Protein 1.51g

Green Beans with Almonds

Prep time: 10 minutes | Cook time: 5 minutes | Serves: 4

455g fresh green beans, rinsed and ends
trimmed

480ml chicken stock
1 teaspoon salt

2 tablespoons unsalted butter
30g slivered almonds

1. Add beans and stock to the cooking pot. 2. Install the pressure lid and turn the pressure release valve to the SEAL position. 3. Select PRESSURE COOK, set the cooking temperature to HI and adjust the cooking time to 3 minutes. 4. When cooked, let the unit naturally release pressure. 5. Add salt, butter, and almonds to pot and toss with the beans. 6. Transfer beans to a serving dish and serve warm.
Per Serving: Calories 68; Fat 4.68g; Sodium 1048mg; Carbs 5.46g; Fibre 2.2g; Sugar 1.42g; Protein 2.31g

Green Cabbage in Chicken Stock

Prep time: 5 minutes | Cook time: 6 minutes | Serves: 4

2 tablespoons unsalted butter
2 slices bacon, diced
240ml chicken stock

1 head green cabbage, chopped, hard
midsection removed
1 teaspoon apple cider vinegar

½ teaspoon salt

1. Melt the butter in the cooking pot at MD:HI for 30 seconds on SEAR/SAUTÉ mode; add bacon and sauté for 3 minute, stirring frequently to render fat from bacon. 2. Stop the machine and add stock to the pot, scraping any bits from the bottom and sides of pot, and then add the cabbage, vinegar, and salt. 3. Install the pressure lid and turn the pressure release valve to the SEAL position. 4. Select PRESSURE COOK, set the cooking temperature to HI and adjust the cooking time to 3 minutes. 5. When cooked, let the unit naturally release pressure. 6. Transfer cabbage to a serving dish. Serve warm.
Per Serving: Calories 94; Fat 9.2g; Sodium 600mg; Carbs 0.69g; Fibre 0.1g; Sugar 0.53g; Protein 2.33g

Simple Cinnamon Applesauce

Prep time: 10 minutes | Cook time: 10 minutes | Serves: 6

1.2kg apples (such as Fuji or McIntosh), peeled and sliced

½ teaspoon ground cinnamon
120ml water

1. Add the apples, cinnamon, and water to the cooking pot. 2. Install the pressure lid and turn the pressure release valve to the SEAL position. 3. Select PRESSURE COOK, set the cooking temperature to HI and adjust the cooking time to 10 minutes. 4. When cooked, let the unit naturally release pressure. 5. Use a potato masher or blender to puree the apples to the consistency of your choice. 6. Serve the applesauce warm, or transfer it to an airtight container and chill in the fridge until ready to serve. 7. Store the applesauce in the fridge for 1 week or in the freezer for 3 months.
Per Serving: Calories 118; Fat 0.39g; Sodium 3mg; Carbs 31.5g; Fibre 5.6g; Sugar 23.57g; Protein 0.6g

Chickpeas Hummus

Prep time: 5 minutes | Cook time: 50 minutes | Serves: 4-5

175g dried chickpeas (not soaked)
840ml water
65g tahini

2 tablespoons freshly squeezed lemon juice
2 cloves garlic, minced

1 teaspoon fine sea salt
1 teaspoon ground cumin
Freshly ground black pepper

1. Place the dried chickpeas in the cooking pot and add 720ml of the water. 2. Install the pressure lid and turn the pressure release valve to the SEAL position. 3. Select PRESSURE COOK, set the cooking temperature to HI and adjust the cooking time to 50 minutes. 4. When cooked, let the unit naturally release pressure. 5. Drain the cooked chickpeas in a colander. 6. To blend the hummus, you can either return the cooked chickpeas to the cooking pot and use an immersion blender, or add the chickpeas to a food processor or blender. 7. Add the tahini, the remaining water, the lemon juice, garlic, salt, cumin, and several grinds of black pepper and blend until smooth. Adjust the seasonings to your taste. 8. Serve the hummus right away or store it in an airtight container in the fridge for 7 days.
Per Serving: Calories 228; Fat 9g; Sodium 493mg; Carbs 29.02g; Fibre 6.2g; Sugar 4.52g; Protein 10.45g

Quick Cauliflower "Rice"

Prep time: 5 minutes | Cook time: 1 minutes | Serves: 4

1 head cauliflower, cut into florets

Fine sea salt

1. Add 240ml of water to the cooking pot, place the reversible rack in the pot in the lower position and drop the lower rack through the reversible rack handles. 2. Arrange the cauliflower florets onto the rack. 3. Install the pressure lid and turn the pressure release valve to the SEAL position. 4. Select PRESSURE COOK, set the cooking temperature to HI and adjust the cooking time to 20 minutes. 5. When cooked, let the unit naturally release pressure. 6. Use oven mitts to lift the steam basket out of the pot and pour out any water from the pot. 7. Add the cooked cauliflower back to the pot. Season generously with salt and use a potato masher to break up the cauliflower into a rice-like consistency. Serve warm. 8. Store the leftovers in an airtight container in the fridge for 5 days.
Per Serving: Calories 53; Fat 0.59g; Sodium 102mg; Carbs 10.44g; Fibre 4.2g; Sugar 4.01g; Protein 4.03g

Mashed Sweet Potatoes

Prep time: 10 minutes | Cook time: 8 minutes | Serves: 4

900g sweet potatoes, peeled and cut into 2.5cm chunks
1 teaspoon minced fresh thyme

½ teaspoon minced fresh rosemary
1 tablespoon extra-virgin olive oil (optional)

½ teaspoon fine sea salt
Freshly ground black pepper

1. Add the water to the cooking pot, place the reversible rack in the pot in the lower position and drop the lower rack through the reversible rack handles. 2. Arrange the sweet potatoes onto the rack. 3. Install the pressure lid and turn the pressure release valve to the SEAL position. 4. Select PRESSURE COOK, set the cooking temperature to HI and adjust the cooking time to 8 minutes. 5. When cooked, let the unit naturally release pressure. 6. Pour the water out of the pot. 7. Pour the drained sweet potatoes back into the pot and use a potato masher to mash the potatoes. Add the thyme, rosemary, olive oil, salt, and several grinds of pepper sind stir well to combine. 8. Taste and adjust the seasonings, then serve warm. 9. Store the leftovers in an airtight container in the fridge for 5 days.
Per Serving: Calories 189; Fat 1.71g; Sodium 334mg; Carbs 39.71g; Fibre 5g; Sugar 1.77g; Protein 4.61g

Pinto Beans

Prep time: 10 minutes | Cook time: 20 minutes | Serves: 4

180g dried pinto beans, soaked for 8 hours and drained
720ml water
½ yellow onion, chopped

2 cloves garlic, minced
1 teaspoon ground cumin
1 teaspoon chili powder
¼ teaspoon freshly ground black pepper

Pinch of cayenne pepper (optional)
½ to ¾ teaspoon fine sea salt
Chopped fresh coriander, for garnish
Lime wedges, for garnish

1. Combine the drained beans, water, onion, and garlic in the cooking pot. Stir them well, making sure the beans are submerged. 2. Install the pressure lid and turn the pressure release valve to the SEAL position. 3. Select PRESSURE COOK, set the cooking temperature to HI and adjust the cooking time to 20 minutes. 4. When cooked, let the unit naturally release pressure. 5. Drain the beans, reserving the liquid. Return the cooked beans to the cooking pot, and stir in 120ml of the reserved cooking liquid, along with the cumin, chili powder, black pepper, cayenne, and ½ teaspoon salt. 6. Use a potato masher to mash the cooked beans until smooth, leaving some texture if you like. 7. Taste and adjust the seasoning, adding more salt as needed, and serve warm with a garnish of coriander and a squeeze of lime juice. 8. Store the leftover beans in an airtight container in the fridge for 7 days.

Per Serving: Calories 191; Fat 2g; Sodium 322mg; Carbs 33.12g; Fibre 8.1g; Sugar 1.76g; Protein 10.78g

Lightened-Up Mashed Potatoes

Prep time: 10 minutes | Cook time: 10 minutes | Serves: 6

900g Yukon gold potatoes
1 yellow onion, chopped
100g cremini mushrooms, chopped
2 cloves garlic, minced

2 tablespoons soy sauce or tamari
Fine sea salt and freshly ground black pepper
240ml water

455g cauliflower, cut into florets
2 tablespoons chopped fresh chives
Cut the potatoes into 2.5cm chunks, reserving one cut-up potato for the gravy

1. Add the water to the cooking pot, place the Cook & Crisp Basket on top of diffuser and press down firmly, and then combine the onion, mushrooms, the reserved cut-up potato, the garlic, soy sauce, ¼ teaspoon salt, several grinds of black pepper, and the water in the basket; place the cauliflower florets and the remaining potatoes into the basket. 2. Install the pressure lid and turn the pressure release valve to the SEAL position. 3. Select PRESSURE COOK, set the cooking temperature to HI and adjust the cooking time to 10 minutes. 4. When cooked, let the unit naturally release pressure. 5. Transfer the cauliflower and potatoes to a large bowl. Use a potato masher to mash them and then season generously with salt and pepper to taste. Stir in the chives. 6. Use a blender to blend the gravy directly in the bottom of the cooking pot. Alternatively, you can pour the mixture into a blender and blend until smooth. Taste and adjust the seasonings. 7. Serve the mash immediately with the gravy on top. Store the leftovers in an airtight container in the fridge for 5 days.

Per Serving: Calories 276; Fat 3.14g; Sodium 121mg; Carbs 58.24g; Fibre 8.9g; Sugar 5.21g; Protein 8.21g

Vegetable Medley

Prep time: 5 minutes | Cook time: 5 minutes | Serves: 4

455g assorted non-starchy vegetables, such as cauliflower, carrots, and green beans

2 tablespoons extra-virgin olive oil
1 clove garlic, minced
Fine sea salt and freshly ground black

pepper
Chopped fresh parsley, for garnish

1. Add 240ml of water to the cooking pot, place the reversible rack in the pot in the lower position and drop the lower rack through the reversible rack handles. 2. Arrange the vegetables onto the rack. 3. Install the pressure lid and turn the pressure release valve to the SEAL position. 4. Select PRESSURE COOK, set the cooking temperature to HI and adjust the cooking time to 1 minute. 5. When cooked, let the unit naturally release pressure. 6. The vegetables should be tender, but with some tooth to them. Use oven mitts to remove the steamer basket full of vegetables, drain the water from the pot, then dry the pot and return it to the cooking pot. 7. Heat the oil in the cooking pot at MD on SEAR/SAUTÉ mode; once the oil is hot but not smoking, add the garlic and sauté for 30 seconds; add the steamed vegetables to the pot and stir well to coat them in the garlic-infused olive oil, cook them for 30 seconds. 8. Season the dish generously with salt and pepper, then serve warm with parsley on top. Store the leftover vegetables in an airtight container in the fridge for 1 week. They make for great toppings in a salad or grain bowl.

Per Serving: Calories 435; Fat 3.61g; Sodium 735mg; Carbs 37.43g; Fibre 5.3g; Sugar 0.03g; Protein 4.71g

Tasty Bulgur Pilaf

Prep time: 10 minutes | Cook time: 10 minutes | Serves: 4

1 tablespoon extra-virgin olive oil
½ red onion, diced
1 clove garlic, minced
1 teaspoon minced fresh ginger (about 1cm knob)
½ teaspoon turmeric

½ teaspoon ground cumin
150g bulgur
300ml water
½ teaspoon fine sea salt
65g finely diced celery
10g loosely packed chopped fresh mint

10g loosely packed chopped fresh flat-leaf parsley
2 tablespoons freshly squeezed lemon juice
60g finely chopped walnuts
80g golden raisins

1. Heat the oil in the cooking pot at MD on SEAR/SAUTÉ mode; once the oil is hot but not smoking, add the onion and sauté for 5 minutes; add the garlic, ginger, turmeric, and cumin, and sauté them for 1 minute. 2. Stop the machine, and stir in the bulgur, water, and salt, scraping the bottom of the pot to make sure nothing sticks. 3. Install the pressure lid and turn the pressure release valve to the SEAL position. 4. Select PRESSURE COOK, set the cooking temperature to HI and adjust the cooking time to 1 minute. 5. When cooked, let the unit naturally release pressure. 6. Fluff the bulgur with a fork. 7. Stir in the celery, mint, parsley, and lemon juice and serve warm topped with the walnuts and raisins. 8. Store the leftovers in an airtight container for 1 week.
Per Serving: Calories 195; Fat 8.42g; Sodium 346mg; Carbs 29.53g; Fibre 4.4g; Sugar 13.56g; Protein 4.4g

Cooked Beans

Prep time: 8 hours | Cook time: 10 minutes | Serves: 2

455g dried beans

2.9L water

1. Pour the beans in a large bowl and add 1.45L of the water. Let the beans soak on the counter for roughly 8 hours, or place them in the fridge to soak overnight. Drain the soaked beans in a colander and rinse with fresh water. 2. Add the drained beans to the cooking pot along with the remaining water. 3. Install the pressure lid and turn the pressure release valve to the SEAL position. 4. Select PRESSURE COOK, set the cooking temperature to HI and adjust the cooking time to 10 minutes. 5. When cooked, let the unit naturally release pressure. 6. Make sure the beans are tender by mashing one against the side of the pot with a fork. If they are not yet tender, secure the lid and cook for 5 minutes more at high pressure until done. 7. Drain the beans in a colander and use them right away, or store them in portions to replace a can of beans in recipes that call for precooked ones. Store cooked beans in an airtight container in the fridge for 7 days or in the freezer for 3 months.
Per Serving: Calories 50; Fat 1.04g; Sodium 33mg; Carbs 9.8g; Fibre 4.3g; Sugar 1.77g; Protein 2.57g

Apple Squash Porridge

Prep time: 10 minutes | Cook time: 10 minutes | Serves: 2-4

1 squash, peeled and chopped
3 apples, cored and chopped

2 tablespoons cinnamon powder
2 tablespoons maple syrup

180ml water
Salt to taste

1. Combine all of the ingredients in the cooking pot. 2. Install the pressure lid and turn the pressure release valve to the SEAL position. 3. Select PRESSURE COOK, set the cooking temperature to HI and adjust the cooking time to 8 minutes. 4. When cooked, let the unit naturally release pressure. 5. Stir the porridge and serve.
Per Serving: Calories 150; Fat 0.39g; Sodium 46mg; Carbs 39.93g; Fibre 7g; Sugar 20.31g; Protein 1.38g

Onion Turnips Mash

Prep time: 15 minutes | Cook time: 5 minutes | Serves: 4

4 turnips, peeled and cubed
1 yellow onion, chopped

120ml chicken stock
Salt and ground black pepper to the taste

60g sour cream

1. Add the turnips, onion, and chicken stock to the cooking pot. 2. Install the pressure lid and turn the pressure release valve to the SEAL position. 3. Select PRESSURE COOK, set the cooking temperature to HI and adjust the cooking time to 5 minutes. 4. When cooked, let the unit naturally release pressure. 5. In an electric beater, slowly blend sour cream into turnips until smooth and creamy. 6. Season the dish with salt and pepper. Serve.
Per Serving: Calories 95; Fat 4.37g; Sodium 139mg; Carbs 12g; Fibre 2.7g; Sugar 6.1g; Protein 2.62g

Butternut Apple Smooth

Prep time: 20 minutes | Cook time: 10 minutes | Serves: 4-6

240ml water
1 butternut squash, peeled, deseeded and cut into medium chunks

1 yellow onion, thinly sliced
2 apples, peeled and sliced
2 tablespoon brown butter

Salt to taste
½ teaspoon apple pie spice

1. Add the water to the cooking pot, place the reversible rack in the pot in the lower position and drop the lower rack through the reversible rack handles. 2. Arrange the squash, onion, and apples onto the rack. 3. Install the pressure lid and turn the pressure release valve to the SEAL position. 4. Select PRESSURE COOK, set the cooking temperature to HI and adjust the cooking time to 8 minutes. 5. When cooked, let the unit naturally release pressure.
Pour the water into the cooking pot and insert a steamer basket. 6. Transfer the squash, onion, and apples to a bowl. Using a potato masher or electric beater, mash them until smooth.
Add the butter, salt and apple pie spice. Mix them well and serve.
Per Serving: Calories 94; Fat 4.03g; Sodium 60mg; Carbs 15.65g; Fibre 2.7g; Sugar 8.12g; Protein 0.87g

Turnips with Alfredo Sauce

Prep time: 10 minutes | Cook time: 5 minutes | Serves: 4

240ml water
3 medium turnips, peeled and cubed

240g vegan alfredo sauce
½ teaspoon garlic salt

10g chives, chopped

1. Add the water and turnip to the cooking pot. 2. Install the pressure lid and turn the pressure release valve to the SEAL position. 3. Select PRESSURE COOK, set the cooking temperature to HI and adjust the cooking time to 5 minutes. 4. When cooked, let the unit naturally release pressure. 5. Use a potato masher to mash the turnips. Add the alfredo sauce, garlic salt and chives, and mix them well. 6. Serve the dish with veggies or pasta.
Per Serving: Calories 46; Fat 0.21g; Sodium 521mg; Carbs 10.54g; Fibre 2.9g; Sugar 6.04g; Protein 1.91g

Carrots Turnips Mix

Prep time: 15 minutes | Cook time: 10 minutes | Serves: 2-4

1 tablespoon olive oil
1 small onion, chopped
3 medium carrots, sliced

2 medium turnips, peeled and sliced
1 teaspoon ground cumin
1 teaspoon lemon juice

Salt and ground black pepper to the taste
240ml water

1. Heat the oil in the cooking pot at MD:HI for 30 seconds on SEAR/SAUTÉ mode; add onion and sauté for 2 minutes until fragrant; add the carrots, turnips, cumin, and lemon juice, and sauté them for 1 minute more. 2. Season them with salt and pepper. 3. Stop the machine and pour the water in the pot. 4. Install the pressure lid and turn the pressure release valve to the SEAL position. 5. Select PRESSURE COOK, set the cooking temperature to HI and adjust the cooking time to 7 minutes. 6. When cooked, let the unit naturally release pressure. 7. Taste the dish for seasoning. Serve.
Per Serving: Calories 59; Fat 3.6g; Sodium 45mg; Carbs 6.46g; Fibre 1.7g; Sugar 3.21g; Protein 0.92g

Honey Carrot Puree

Prep time: 20 minutes | Cook time: 5 minutes | Serves: 2-4

240ml water
675g carrots, peeled and sliced into 2.5cm pieces

1 tablespoon honey
1 tablespoon soy butter, softened
½ teaspoon salt

Brown sugar, optional

1. Add the water to the cooking pot, place the reversible rack in the pot in the lower position and drop the lower rack through the reversible rack handles. 2. Arrange the carrots onto the rack. 3. Install the pressure lid and turn the pressure release valve to the SEAL position. 4. Select PRESSURE COOK, set the cooking temperature to HI and adjust the cooking time to 4 minutes. 5. When cooked, let the unit naturally release pressure. 6. Using a potato masher or electric beater, slowly blend the carrots until smooth and creamy. 7. Add the honey and butter and stir well. Season the dish with salt and stir. 8. If desired, add sugar to taste. Serve.
Per Serving: Calories 101; Fat 3.19g; Sodium 414mg; Carbs 18.31g; Fibre 5.1g; Sugar 10.18g; Protein 1.34g

Sweet Potato & Carrot Medley

Prep time: 10 minutes | Cook time: 10 minutes | Serves: 6-8

2 tablespoons extra-virgin olive oil
1 medium onion, chopped

900g baby carrots, halved
900g sweet potatoes, peeled and cubed

240ml veggie stock
Salt and ground black pepper to taste

1. Heat the oil in the cooking pot at MD:HI for 30 seconds on SEAR/SAUTÉ mode; add onion and sauté for 5 minute until softened. 2. Stop the machine, add the carrots, sweet potatoes and stock, stir them well and season them with salt and pepper. 3. Install the pressure lid and turn the pressure release valve to the SEAL position. 4. Select PRESSURE COOK, set the cooking temperature to HI and adjust the cooking time to 8 minutes. 5. When cooked, let the unit naturally release pressure. 6. Serve warm.
Per Serving: Calories 167; Fat 2.31g; Sodium 262mg; Carbs 33.89g; Fibre 6.6g; Sugar 5.89g; Protein 4.09g

Glazed Carrots

Prep time: 30 minutes | Cook time: 10 minutes | Serves: 4-6

160ml water
900g carrots, sliced into 1 cm diagonal
pieces

50g raisins
1 tablespoon maple syrup
1 tablespoon butter

Salt and ground black pepper to taste

1. Add the water, carrots and raisins to the cooking pot. 2. Install the pressure lid and turn the pressure release valve to the SEAL position. 3. Select PRESSURE COOK, set the cooking temperature to HI and adjust the cooking time to 4 minutes. 4. When cooked, let the unit naturally release pressure. 5. Transfer the carrots to a bowl. 6. Completely dry the pot before replacing it. 7. Press FUNCTION and turn the dial to select SEAR/SAUTÉ. 8. Press TEMP and turn the dial to select HI, and press START/STOP to begin cooking. 9. Heat the butter and maple syrup in the cooking pot; add the carrots and sauté them until they are fully coated with butter. 10. Season the dish with salt and pepper. Serve.
Per Serving: Calories 89; Fat 2.3g; Sodium 121mg; Carbs 16.98g; Fibre 4.3g; Sugar 9.2g; Protein 1.47g

Honey Glazed Baby Carrots

Prep time: 15 minutes | Cook time: 5 minutes | Serves: 2-4

160ml water
675g baby carrots
4 tablespoon butter

170g honey
1½ teaspoon dry dill
1 teaspoon dry thyme

Salt to taste

1. Add the water to the cooking pot, place the reversible rack in the pot in the lower position and drop the lower rack through the reversible rack handles. 2. Arrange the carrots onto the rack. 3. Install the pressure lid and turn the pressure release valve to the SEAL position. 4. Select PRESSURE COOK, set the cooking temperature to HI and adjust the cooking time to 20 minutes. 5. When cooked, let the unit naturally release pressure. 6. Transfer the carrots to a plate. Completely dry the pot before replacing it. 7. Melt the butter in the cooking pot at MD on SEAR/SAUTÉ mode; add the honey, dill, and thyme, and mix them well; add the carrots and sauté them for 1 minute more. 8. Taste for seasoning and add more salt if needed. Enjoy.
Per Serving: Calories 292; Fat 11.77g; Sodium 266mg; Carbs 49.31g; Fibre 5.2g; Sugar 42.91g; Protein 1.43g

Garlic Aubergine Dish

Prep time: 15 minutes | Cook time: 10 minutes | Serves: 2-4

1 tablespoon olive oil
3 cloves garlic, minced
320g aubergine , cubed

Salt and ground black pepper to taste
1 tablespoon garlic powder
240g marinara sauce

120ml water

1. Heat the oil in the cooking pot at MD on SEAR/SAUTÉ mode; add garlic and sauté for 2 minutes. 2. Stop the machine and add the aubergine, salt, pepper, marinara sauce and garlic powder; stir them to combine well. 3. Install the pressure lid and turn the pressure release valve to the SEAL position. 4. Select PRESSURE COOK, set the cooking temperature to HI and adjust the cooking time to 8 minutes. 5. When cooked, let the unit naturally release pressure. 6. Serve the dish with pasta.
Per Serving: Calories 82; Fat 3.68g; Sodium 463mg; Carbs 12.06g; Fibre 4g; Sugar 5.54g; Protein 2.41g

Savoy Cabbage

Prep time: 10 minutes | Cook time: 15 minutes | Serves: 2-4

1 medium onion, chopped	¼ teaspoon nutmeg	1 bay leaf
225g bacon, chopped	480ml bone stock	240ml coconut milk
1 medium savoy cabbage head, chopped	Salt and ground black pepper to taste	2 tablespoons parsley, chopped

1. Add the onion and bacon to the cooking pot; press FUNCTION and turn the dial to select SEAR/SAUTÉ. 2. Press TEMP and turn the dial to select HI, and press START/STOP to begin cooking. 3. Cook them for about 2 to 5 minutes or until the bacon is crispy. 4. Stop the cooker, and add the cabbage, nutmeg, stock, salt, pepper, and bay leaf; mix them well. 5. Install the pressure lid and turn the pressure release valve to the SEAL position. 6. Select PRESSURE COOK, set the cooking temperature to HI and adjust the cooking time to 10 minutes. 7. Add the milk and parsley halfway through cooking. 8. When cooked, let the unit naturally release pressure. 9. Taste the dish for seasoning and add more salt if needed. Serve.
Per Serving: Calories 190; Fat 13.72g; Sodium 743mg; Carbs 10.2g; Fibre 2.2g; Sugar 5.24g; Protein 9.35g

Spiced Aubergine Cubes

Prep time: 15 minutes | Cook time: 10 minutes | Serves: 4

1 tablespoon olive oil	1 teaspoon sea salt	120ml coconut milk
240g aubergine , peeled and cubed	½ teaspoon ground black pepper	180ml vegetable stock
30g fresh spinach, torn	1 tablespoon five spice powder	Fresh spring onions , chopped

1. Heat the oil in the cooking pot at MD on SEAR/SAUTÉ mode; add aubergine cubes and sauté them for 2 minutes; stir in the spinach. 2. Stop the cooker, and sprinkle them with salt, pepper and five spice powder; stir in the coconut milk and stock. 3. Install the pressure lid and turn the pressure release valve to the SEAL position. 4. Select PRESSURE COOK, set the cooking temperature to HI and adjust the cooking time to 4 minutes. 5. When cooked, let the unit naturally release pressure. 6. Top the dish with fresh spring onions and serve.
Per Serving: Calories 156; Fat 11.42g; Sodium 833mg; Carbs 12.66g; Fibre 3.7g; Sugar 4.45g; Protein 2.98g

Rice Mix Stuffed Peppers

Prep time: 15 minutes | Cook time: 15 minutes | Serves: 2-4

200g white rice, cooked	455g beef mince	4 peppers, tops and seeds removed
120ml milk	2 onions, chopped	240ml water
1 egg, beaten	Salt and ground black pepper to the taste	250g canned tomato soup

1. In a large bowl, combine the rice, milk, egg, beef, onions, salt and pepper. Fill each pepper to the top of the meat mixture. 2. Add the water and tomato soup to the cooking pot, place the reversible rack in the pot in the lower position and drop the lower rack through the reversible rack handles. 3. Arrange the stuffed peppers onto the rack. 4. Install the pressure lid and turn the pressure release valve to the SEAL position. 5. Select PRESSURE COOK, set the cooking temperature to HI and adjust the cooking time to 15 minutes. 6. When cooked, let the unit naturally release pressure. 7. Transfer the stuffed peppers to a serving bowl and drizzle with tomato sauce. Enjoy.
Per Serving: Calories 521; Fat 16.59g; Sodium 200mg; Carbs 52.41g; Fibre 4.4g; Sugar 8.71g; Protein 38.83g

Cheese Beetroot

Prep time: 10 minutes | Cook time: 20 minutes | Serves: 4-6

240ml water	Salt and ground black pepper to taste
6 medium beetroot, trimmed	25g cheese (by choice), crumbled

1. Add the water to the cooking pot, place the reversible rack in the pot in the lower position and drop the lower rack through the reversible rack handles. 2. Arrange the beetroot onto the rack. 3. Install the pressure lid and turn the pressure release valve to the SEAL position. 4. Select PRESSURE COOK, set the cooking temperature to HI and adjust the cooking time to 20 minutes. 5. When cooked, let the unit naturally release pressure. 6. Transfer the beets to a bowl and let them cool. Season with salt and pepper and add the blue cheese. Enjoy.
Per Serving: Calories 59; Fat 1.82g; Sodium 98mg; Carbs 8.59g; Fibre 2.4g; Sugar 5.95g; Protein 2.82g

Beetroot Salad with Parsley

Prep time: 35 minutes | Cook time: 20 minutes | Serves: 4

240ml water
4 medium beetroot, trimmed
1 clove garlic, chopped

10g parsley, chopped
Salt and ground black pepper to taste
2 tablespoons capers

1 tablespoon extra-virgin olive oil
2 tablespoons balsamic vinegar

1. Add the water to the cooking pot, place the reversible rack in the pot in the lower position and drop the lower rack through the reversible rack handles. 2. Arrange the beets onto the rack. 3. Install the pressure lid and turn the pressure release valve to the SEAL position. 4. Select PRESSURE COOK, set the cooking temperature to HI and adjust the cooking time to 20 minutes. 5. When cooked, let the unit naturally release pressure. 6. In a medium bowl, combine the garlic, parsley, salt, pepper, capers, and olive oil. 7. Transfer the beets to a plate and let them cool. 8. Peel and slice the beets, arrange them on a platter. 9. Drizzle the beetroot with the vinegar and sprinkle with parsley, and enjoy with the garlic mixture.
Per Serving: Calories 64; Fat 1.74g; Sodium 202mg; Carbs 11.04g; Fibre 2.8g; Sugar 7.38g; Protein 1.89g

Buttery Beetroot

Prep time: 20 minutes | Cook time: 25 minutes | Serves: 4-6

240ml water
795g medium beetroot, trimmed

2 tablespoons butter, melted
Salt and freshly ground black pepper to

taste
2 tablespoons fresh parsley, chopped

1. Add the water to the cooking pot, place the reversible rack in the pot in the lower position and drop the lower rack through the reversible rack handles. 2. Arrange the beets onto the rack. 3. Install the pressure lid and turn the pressure release valve to the SEAL position. 4. Select PRESSURE COOK, set the cooking temperature to HI and adjust the cooking time to 24 minutes. 5. When cooked, let the unit naturally release pressure. 6. Transfer the beets to a plate and let them cool. 7. Peel and into wedges the beets and put in the bowl. 8. Add the butter, salt and pepper. Gently stir to coat the beets with the butter. 9. Sprinkle the dish with parsley and serve.
Per Serving: Calories 92; Fat 4.09g; Sodium 135mg; Carbs 12.98g; Fibre 3.8g; Sugar 8.96g; Protein 2.25g

Tomatoes with Tofu Cubes

Prep time: 10 minutes | Cook time: 5 minutes | Serves: 4

100g firm tofu, cubed
150g diced tomatoes

2 tablespoon jarred banana pepper rings
120ml vegetable or chicken stock

2 teaspoon Italian seasoning
1 tablespoon olive oil

1. Combine the tofu, tomatoes, banana pepper rings, and stock in the cooking pot, and season them with Italian seasoning and oil. 2. Install the pressure lid and turn the pressure release valve to the SEAL position. 3. Select PRESSURE COOK, set the cooking temperature to HI and adjust the cooking time to 4 minutes. 4. When cooked, let the unit naturally release pressure. 5. Serve warm.
Per Serving: Calories 204; Fat 12.98g; Sodium 181mg; Carbs 8.6g; Fibre 3.3g; Sugar 1.92g; Protein 16.82g

Kale and Sweet Potatoes with Tofu

Prep time: 20 minutes | Cook time: 10 minutes | Serves: 4-6

1 tablespoon tamari sauce
240ml vegetable stock

100g tofu, cubed
60g kale, chopped

2 medium sweet potatoes, cubed

1. Add the ½ tablespoon of tamari sauce and 2 tablespoon of stock to the cooking pot; add the tofu cubes and cook them at MD for 3 minutes on SEAR/SAUTÉ mode. 2. Stop the cooker, add the kale, sweet potatoes, the remaining tamari sauce and stock to the pot, and mix them well. 3. Install the pressure lid and turn the pressure release valve to the SEAL position. 4. Select PRESSURE COOK, set the cooking temperature to HI and adjust the cooking time to 4 minutes. 5. When cooked, let the unit naturally release pressure. 6. Serve.
Per Serving: Calories 165; Fat 6.53g; Sodium 257mg; Carbs 16.8g; Fibre 3.6g; Sugar 3.8g; Protein 12.39g

Aubergine Spread

Prep time: 15 minutes | Cook time: 15 minutes | Serves: 4-6

4 tablespoon olive oil
900g aubergine , sliced
4 cloves garlic, sliced
1 teaspoon salt

240ml water
1 lemon, juiced
1 tablespoon tahini
1 teaspoon extra virgin olive oil

35g black olives, pitted and sliced
2 sprigs of thyme

1. Heat the oil in the cooking pot at MD on SEAR/SAUTÉ mode; add aubergine slices and sauté them for 3 minutes on both sides; add the garlic and sauté for 1 to 2 minutes more until fragrant; sprinkle them with salt. 2. Stop the cooker and pour the water in the pot. 3. Install the pressure lid and turn the pressure release valve to the SEAL position. 4. Select PRESSURE COOK, set the cooking temperature to HI and adjust the cooking time to 6 minutes. 5. When cooked, let the unit naturally release pressure. 6. Place the mixture in a blender or food processor; add the lemon juice and tahini. Blend them until the texture is smooth. 7. Transfer the food to a serving bowl and drizzle with extra virgin olive oil. 8. Serve the dish with olives and thyme.
Per Serving: Calories 140; Fat 10.97g; Sodium 402mg; Carbs 10.7g; Fibre 4.9g; Sugar 5.57g; Protein 2.08g

Delectable Cabbage Wedges

Prep time: 10 minutes | Cook time: 15 minutes | Serves: 4

1 tablespoon olive oil
1 cabbage cut into 6-8 wedges
360ml + 2 teaspoons water

60ml apple cider vinegar
1 teaspoon brown sugar
½ teaspoon red pepper flakes

½ teaspoon cayenne pepper
1 big carrot, grated
2 teaspoons cornflour

1. Heat the oil in the cooking pot at MD on SEAR/ SAUTÉ mode; add the cabbage wedges and sauté them for 3 minutes on one side. 2. Stop the cooker, and stir in 360ml of water, vinegar, sugar, pepper flakes, cayenne pepper and carrot. 3. Install the pressure lid and turn the pressure release valve to the SEAL position. 4. Select PRESSURE COOK, set the cooking temperature to HI and adjust the cooking time to 5 minutes. 5. When cooked, let the unit naturally release pressure. 6. Transfer the cabbage and carrot to a serving bowl. 7. Mix together the cornflour and 2 teaspoon of water. Add the mixture to the pot. 8. Cook the sauce at MD:HI on SEAR/ SAUTÉ mode until thickened enough. 9. Pour the sauce over cabbage. Enjoy.
Per Serving: Calories 159; Fat 4.03g; Sodium 105mg; Carbs 30.48g; Fibre 7.8g; Sugar 16.17g; Protein 5.17g

Onion Courgette Casserole

Prep time: 20 minutes | Cook time: 10 minutes | Serves: 2-4

120ml vegetable stock
2 courgettes cut into 1cm slices
4 stalks celery, chopped

1 large onions, chopped
4 eggs, beaten
1 package Italian seasoning

Salt and ground black pepper to taste

1. Add the stock, courgettes, celery, onion, and eggs to the cooking pot; sprinkle them with Italian seasoning, salt, and pepper. 2. Install the pressure lid and turn the pressure release valve to the SEAL position. 3. Select PRESSURE COOK, set the cooking temperature to HI and adjust the cooking time to 4 minutes. 4. When cooked, let the unit naturally release pressure. 5. Serve warm.
Per Serving: Calories 325; Fat 31.54g; Sodium 233mg; Carbs 6.09g; Fibre 1.4g; Sugar 2.34g; Protein 6.27g

Mushroom Stroganoff

Prep time: 15 minutes | Cook time: 10 minutes | Serves: 2

1 tablespoon butter
4 cloves garlic, chopped
200g baby Bella mushrooms, quartered

240ml vegetable or chicken stock
1½ teaspoon flour
1 teaspoon Dijon mustard

Salt and ground black pepper to taste
120g sour cream

1. Melt the butter in the cooking pot at MD:HI on SEAR/SAUTÉ mode; add the garlic and mushrooms, and sauté them for 4 to 5 minutes until softened. 2. Stop the cooker, and mix in the stock, flour, Dijon mustard, salt and pepper. 3. Install the pressure lid and turn the pressure release valve to the SEAL position. 4. Select PRESSURE COOK, set the cooking temperature to HI and adjust the cooking time to 2 minutes. 5. When cooked, let the unit naturally release pressure. 6. Select the SEAR/SAUTÉ setting, pour the sour cream in the pot and stir them for 2 minutes at MD. 7. Serve warm.
Per Serving: Calories 214; Fat 13.39g; Sodium 762mg; Carbs 14.03g; Fibre 1.8g; Sugar 4.26g; Protein 11.86g

BBQ Tofu Cubes

Prep time: 15 minutes | Cook time: 11 minutes | Serves: 4-6

2 tablespoon olive oil
1 medium yellow onion, chopped
3 cloves garlic, minced
1 celery stalk, chopped

1 green pepper, chopped
1 red pepper, chopped
Salt to taste
⅛ teaspoon curry powder

700g firm tofu, cubed
360g BBQ sauce

1. Heat the oil in the cooking pot at MD on SEAR/ SAUTÉ mode; add the onion, garlic, celery and peppers, and sauté them for 1 minute; season them with salt and curry powder, and sauté them for 1 minute more; add the tofu cubes and cook them for 4 minutes longer. 2. Stop the cooker and stir in the BBQ sauce. 3. Install the pressure lid and turn the pressure release valve to the SEAL position. 4. Select PRESSURE COOK, set the cooking temperature to HI and adjust the cooking time to 5 minutes. 5. When cooked, let the unit naturally release pressure. 6. Serve warm.
Per Serving: Calories 267; Fat 16.23g; Sodium 507mg; Carbs 13.71g; Fibre 4.9g; Sugar 4.17g; Protein 22.49g

Savory Bok Choy

Prep time: 15 minutes | Cook time: 10 minutes | Serves: 2-4

1 tablespoon olive oil
½ teaspoon ginger, grated
1 clove garlic, minced

900g bok choy, trimmed tough ends
180ml water
1 teaspoon extra virgin olive oil

1 teaspoon soy sauce
Salt and ground black pepper to taste

1. Heat the oil in the cooking pot at MD on SEAR/SAUTÉ mode; add garlic and ginger, and sauté them for 3 to 4 minutes until they start to brown. 2. Stop the cooker, and add the bok choy and water to the pot. 3. Install the pressure lid and turn the pressure release valve to the SEAL position. 4. Select PRESSURE COOK, set the cooking temperature to HI and adjust the cooking time to 5 minutes. 5. When cooked, let the unit naturally release pressure. 6. Transfer the food to a serving plate. 7. In a small bowl, whisk together the liquid from the pot, extra virgin olive oil, soy sauce, salt and pepper. 8. Drizzle the bok choy with the sauce and serve.
Per Serving: Calories 70; Fat 4.57g; Sodium 178mg; Carbs 5.93g; Fibre 2.5g; Sugar 2.95g; Protein 3.61g

Red Cabbage with Onion

Prep time: 15 minutes | Cook time: 15 minutes | Serves: 2-4

1 tablespoon olive oil
70g yellow onion, chopped
3 cloves garlic, chopped

540g red cabbage, chopped
1 tablespoon apple cider vinegar
240g applesauce

Salt and ground black pepper to taste
240ml water

1. Heat the oil in the cooking pot at MD for on SEAR/SAUTÉ mode; add onion and sauté for about 4 minutes until softened; add the garlic and sauté for 1 minute more. 2. Stop the cooker, and add the cabbage, apple cider vinegar, applesauce, salt, pepper, and water to the pot. 3. Install the pressure lid and turn the pressure release valve to the SEAL position. 4. Select PRESSURE COOK, set the cooking temperature to HI and adjust the cooking time to 10 minutes. 5. When cooked, let the unit naturally release pressure. 6. Stir the dish. Taste for seasoning and add more salt, pepper or vinegar, if needed. Enjoy.
Per Serving: Calories 117; Fat 4.85g; Sodium 41mg; Carbs 18.71g; Fibre 3.9g; Sugar 11.36g; Protein 2.32g

Cabbage with Bacon Slices

Prep time: 15 minutes | Cook time: 10 minutes | Serves: 2-4

3 bacon slices, chopped
55g butter

1 green cabbage head, chopped
Salt and ground black pepper to taste

480ml chicken stock

1. Sauté the bacon slices in the cooking pot at MD for 5 minutes on SEAR/ SAUTÉ mode until they begin to render some fat but are not yet crispy; add butter and cook until it melts. 2. Stop the cooker, and stir in the cabbage, salt, pepper, and stock. 3. Install the pressure lid and turn the pressure release valve to the SEAL position. 4. Select PRESSURE COOK, set the cooking temperature to HI and adjust the cooking time to 3 minutes. 5. When cooked, let the unit naturally release pressure. 6. Serve warm.
Per Serving: Calories 195; Fat 19.56g; Sodium 661mg; Carbs 2.08g; Fibre 0.3g; Sugar 1.43g; Protein 3.65g

Cabbage & Carrots

Prep time: 25 minutes | Cook time: 10 minutes | Serves: 2-4

2 tablespoons coconut oil
2 small onions, sliced
2 cloves garlic, chopped
Salt to taste

1 tablespoon curry powder
1 jalapeño pepper, deseeded and chopped
1 head cabbage, shredded
2 carrots, sliced

240ml water
2 tablespoons fresh lemon juice
45g desiccated unsweetened coconut

1. Heat the oil in the cooking pot at MD on SEAR/ SAUTÉ mode; add the onion and sauté for about 4 minutes until softened; add garlic, salt, curry powder, and jalapeño pepper, stir and sauté them for 1 minute more. 2. Stop the cooker, and add cabbage, carrots, water, lemon juice, and coconut to the pot. 3. Install the pressure lid and turn the pressure release valve to the SEAL position. 4. Select PRESSURE COOK, set the cooking temperature to HI and adjust the cooking time to 5 minutes. 5. When cooked, let the unit naturally release pressure. 6. Taste the dish for seasoning and add more salt if needed. Enjoy.
Per Serving: Calories 136; Fat 7.39g; Sodium 114mg; Carbs 17.94g; Fibre 5g; Sugar 8.59g; Protein 3.21g

Courgettes and Tomatoes Mix

Prep time: 15 minutes | Cook time: 10 minutes | Serves: 2-4

1 tablespoon olive oil
2 yellow onions, chopped
6 courgettes, roughly chopped

455g cherry tomatoes cut into halves
240g tomato puree
Salt and ground black pepper to taste

1 bunch basil, chopped
2-3 cloves garlic, minced
1 teaspoon extra virgin olive oil, optional

1. Heat the oil in the cooking pot at MD on SEAR/ SAUTÉ mode; add the onion and sauté for 5 minutes until softened. 2. Stop the cooker, and stir in the courgettes, tomatoes, tomato puree, salt and pepper. 3. Install the pressure lid and turn the pressure release valve to the SEAL position. 4. Select PRESSURE COOK, set the cooking temperature to HI and adjust the cooking time to 5 minutes. 5. When cooked, let the unit naturally release pressure. 6. Add the basil and garlic to the pot and stir well. 7. If desired, drizzle with extra virgin olive oil before serving.
Per Serving: Calories 195; Fat 9.01g; Sodium 33mg; Carbs 28.71g; Fibre 4.7g; Sugar 19.49g; Protein 3.3g

Baby Bella Mushrooms

Prep time: 5 minutes | Cook time: 10 minutes | Serves: 2-4

1 can (375g) baby Bella mushrooms, chopped
300g tomatoes, diced

2 stalks celery, chopped
1 teaspoon Mexican spicy seasoning
1 tablespoon cumin

Salt to taste

1. Combine the mushrooms, tomatoes, celery, spicy seasoning, cumin and salt in the cooking pot. 2. Install the pressure lid and turn the pressure release valve to the SEAL position. 3. Select PRESSURE COOK, set the cooking temperature to HI and adjust the cooking time to 10 minutes. 4. When cooked, let the unit naturally release pressure. 5. Stir the dish and serve.
Per Serving: Calories 27; Fat 0.72g; Sodium 58mg; Carbs 4.82g; Fibre 1.3g; Sugar 2.15g; Protein 1.3g

Mushroom Ham Scramble Mug

Prep time: 15 minutes | Cook time: 5 minutes | Serves: 2-4

3 large eggs
1 teaspoon extra virgin olive oil
240ml + 1 tablespoon water
½ teaspoon ground red pepper

50g mushrooms, chopped
25g deli ham, sliced and chopped
1 tablespoon parsley, minced
⅛ teaspoon cumin

Salt and ground black pepper to taste
2 tablespoon Swiss cheese, shredded

1. Whisk together the eggs, oil, 1 tablespoon of water, and red pepper in a bowl. 2. Add the mushrooms and ham, mix well. 3. Add the parsley, cumin, salt, pepper and cheese. Stir them to combine. 4. Pour the mixture into three heatproof ramekins and top them with cheese. 5. Add 240ml of water to the cooking pot, place the reversible rack in the pot in the lower position and drop the lower rack through the reversible rack handles. 6. Arrange the ramekins onto the rack. Install the pressure lid and turn the pressure release valve to the SEAL position. 7. Select PRESSURE COOK, set the cooking temperature to HI and adjust the cooking time to 5 minutes. 8. When cooked, let the unit naturally release pressure. 9. Serve warm.
Per Serving: Calories 96; Fat 5.93g; Sodium 254mg; Carbs 2.84g; Fibre 0.4g; Sugar 1.23g; Protein 7.82g

Cherry Salad

Prep time: 30 minutes | Cook time: 10 minutes | Serves: 4

285g farro, rinsed
720ml water
80g dried cherries, chopped
280g fresh cherries, pitted and halved

8 mint leaves, minced
10g chives, minced
1 teaspoon lemon juice
1 tablespoon apple cider vinegar

¼ teaspoon salt
1½ tablespoon extra-virgin olive oil

1. Combine the farro and water in the cooking pot. 2. Install the pressure lid and turn the pressure release valve to the SEAL position. 3. Select PRESSURE COOK, set the cooking temperature to HI and adjust the cooking time to 10 minutes. 4. When cooked, let the unit naturally release pressure. 5. Transfer the farro to a salad bowl and let it cool for a few minutes. 6. Add the remaining ingredients, except for the fresh cherries, and stir to combine. 7. Allow the faro totally cool; add the fresh cherries, stir and serve.
Per Serving: Calories 120; Fat 2.99g; Sodium 346mg; Carbs 21.11g; Fibre 1.7g; Sugar 11.64g; Protein 3.89g

Vegan Pizza

Prep time: 15 minutes | Cook time: 5 minutes | Serves: 2

360ml water
1 pizza crust, store-bought

60g vegan Alfredo sauce
50g vegan cheese, shredded

1 teaspoon oregano, chopped

1. Line a baking dish that can fit into the pot with parchment paper. 2. Place the pizza crust inside the baking dish and spread the Alfredo sauce over the food. 3. Sprinkle the cheese over the crust and top with oregano. 4. Add the water to the cooking pot, place the reversible rack in the pot in the lower position and drop the lower rack through the reversible rack handles. 5. Arrange the molds onto the rack. 6. Install the pressure lid and turn the pressure release valve to the SEAL position. 7. Select PRESSURE COOK, set the cooking temperature to HI and adjust the cooking time to 5 minutes. 8. When cooked, let the unit naturally release pressure. 9. Serve warm.
Per Serving: Calories 833; Fat 38.12g; Sodium 1771mg; Carbs 83.5g; Fibre 9.1g; Sugar 12.32g; Protein 39.17g

Spiced Okra & Onions

Prep time: 15 minutes | Cook time: 10 minutes | Serves: 4-6

2 tablespoons olive oil
1 teaspoon cumin seeds
6 cloves garlic, chopped
2 medium onions, sliced

120ml vegetable stock
900g okra, cut into 2.5cm pieces
2 medium tomatoes, chopped
Salt and ground black pepper to taste

½ teaspoon ground turmeric
½ teaspoon red chili powder
1 teaspoon ground coriander
1 teaspoon lemon juice

1. Heat the oil in the cooking pot at MD on SEAR/ SAUTÉ mode; add the cumin and garlic and sauté for 1 minute; add the onion and sauté for 4 minutes more; add the stock, okra, tomatoes, salt, pepper, turmeric, chili powder, coriander and lemon juice, stir them well and cook them for 1 minute. 2. Cancel the cooking progress, and install the pressure lid and turn the pressure release valve to the SEAL position. 3. Select PRESSURE COOK, set the cooking temperature to HI and adjust the cooking time to 2 minutes. 4. When cooked, let the unit naturally release pressure. 5. Serve warm.
Per Serving: Calories 108; Fat 5.02g; Sodium 67mg; Carbs 15.13g; Fibre 5.7g; Sugar 3.7g; Protein 3.66g

Saucy Chicken Thighs

Prep time: 15 minutes | Cook time: 10 minutes | Serves: 6

6 boneless skinless chicken thighs (about 675g)
½ teaspoon poultry seasoning
1 medium onion, chopped
1 can (360g) diced tomatoes, undrained

1 can (200g) tomato sauce
120g barbecue sauce
60ml water
60ml orange juice
1 teaspoon garlic powder

¾ teaspoon dried oregano
½ teaspoon hot pepper sauce
¼ teaspoon pepper
Hot cooked brown rice, optional

1. Mix the tomato sauce, barbecue sauce, water, orange juice and seasonings in a small bowl. 2. Place the chicken in the cooking pot and sprinkle with poultry seasoning; top the meat with onion and tomatoes, and then pour the sauce over them. 3. Install the pressure lid and turn the pressure release valve to the SEAL position. 4. Select PRESSURE COOK, set the cooking temperature to HI and adjust the cooking time to 10 minutes. 5. When cooked, let the unit naturally release pressure. 6. A thermometer inserted in chicken should read at least 75°C. 7. If desired, serve with rice. 8. Place cooked chicken mixture in freezer containers. Cool and freeze. To use, partially thaw in refrigerator overnight. 9. Microwave, covered, on high in a microwave-safe dish until heated through, gently stirring and adding a little water if necessary.
Per Serving: Calories 211; Fat 3.46g; Sodium 437mg; Carbs 17.27g; Fibre 2.8g; Sugar 12.55g; Protein 27.02g

Lemon Chicken Breast Halves

Prep time: 10 minutes | Cook time: 10 minutes | Serves: 4

4 boneless skinless chicken breast halves (150g each)

2 medium lemons
1 bunch fresh basil leaves

480ml chicken stock

1. Finely grate enough zest from lemons to measure 4 teaspoon. Cut lemons in half and squeeze juice. 2. Place the chicken in the cooking pot and add zest and juice. 3. Tear fresh basil leaves directly into the pot; add chicken stock. 4. Install the pressure lid and turn the pressure release valve to the SEAL position. 5. Select PRESSURE COOK, set the cooking temperature to HI and adjust the cooking time to 6 minutes. 6. When cooked, let the unit naturally release pressure. 7. A thermometer inserted in chicken should read at least 75°C. 8. When cool enough to handle, shred meat with 2 forks; return to pressure cooker. If desired, stir in additional lemon zest and chopped basil. Serve with a slotted spoon. 9. Place chicken and cooking liquid in freezer containers. Cool and freeze. To use, partially thaw in the refrigerator overnight. 10. Microwave, covered, on high in a microwave-safe dish until heated through, stirring gently.
Per Serving: Calories 217; Fat 4.78g; Sodium 539mg; Carbs 2.21g; Fibre 0.1g; Sugar 1.14g; Protein 39.16g

Ginger Chicken Pieces

Prep time: 15 minutes | Cook time: 35 minutes | Serves: 4-6

1 chicken cut into pieces
2 tablespoons olive oil
60ml soy sauce

1 large onion, finely diced
2.5cm ginger, finely grated
60ml dry sherry

60ml water
Salt and ground black pepper to taste

1. Heat the oil in the cooking pot at MD on SEAR/SAUTÉ mode; add the chicken pieces and sauté until the chicken has turned light brown. 2. Add the soy sauce, onion, ginger, sherry, and water to the pot, and mix them just until combined. 3. Install the pressure lid and turn the pressure release valve to the SEAL position. 4. Select PRESSURE COOK, set the cooking temperature to HI and adjust the cooking time to 10 minutes. 5. When cooked, let the unit naturally release pressure. 6. Season the dish with salt and pepper to taste. Serve.
Per Serving: Calories 268; Fat 10.77g; Sodium 284mg; Carbs 7.76g; Fibre 1.1g; Sugar 5.18g; Protein 33.45g

Chipotle Chicken

Prep time: 15 minutes | Cook time: 10 minutes | Serves: 6

120ml plus 2 tablespoon cold water, divided
120ml thawed orange juice concentrate
60g barbecue sauce

1 chipotle pepper in adobo sauce
¼ teaspoon salt
¼ teaspoon garlic powder
6 boneless skinless chicken breast halves

(150g each)
40g chopped red onion
4 teaspoon cornflour
Grated orange zest

1. Add 120ml water, orange juice concentrate, barbecue sauce, chipotle pepper, salt and garlic powder to a blender, and process them until blended. 2. Place chicken and onion in the pot, and top them with the juice mixture. 3. Install the pressure lid and turn the pressure release valve to the SEAL position. 4. Select PRESSURE COOK, set the cooking temperature to HI and adjust the cooking time to 6 minutes. 5. When cooked, let the unit naturally release pressure. 6. A thermometer inserted in chicken should read at least 75°C. Remove the chicken from pressure cooker; keep warm. 7. In a small bowl, mix cornflour and remaining 2 tablespoons of water until smooth; gradually stir into the pot. 8. Simmer the food at LO on SEAR/SAUTÉ mode for 1 to 2 minutes until thickened. 9. Spoon the sauce over the chicken and top them with orange zest. 10. Place chicken in freezer containers; top with sauce. Cool and freeze. To use, partially thaw in refrigerator overnight. 11. Heat through in a covered saucepan, stirring gently and adding a little water if necessary.
Per Serving: Calories 180; Fat 3.1g; Sodium 272mg; Carbs 10.44g; Fibre 0.4g; Sugar 6.49g; Protein 26g

Chicken & Veggie Mix

Prep time: 15 minutes | Cook time: 15 minutes | Serves: 4

4 boneless skinless chicken breast halves (100g each)
1 can (375g) no-salt-added black beans, rinsed and drained

1 can (360g) Mexican stewed tomatoes, undrained
1 jar (300g) roasted sweet red peppers, drained and cut into strips

1 large onion, chopped
120ml water
Pepper to taste
Hot cooked rice

1. In a bowl, combine beans, tomatoes, red peppers, onion, water and pepper. 2. Place chicken in the pot, and top the meat with bean mixture. 3. Install the pressure lid and turn the pressure release valve to the SEAL position. 4. Select PRESSURE COOK, set the cooking temperature to HI and adjust the cooking time to 5 minutes. 5. When cooked, let the unit naturally release pressure. 6. A thermometer inserted in chicken should read at least 75°C. Remove the chicken and keep warm. 7. Simmer the juices in the pot at LO on SEAR/SAUTÉ mode for 8 to 10 minutes until thickened. 8. Serve with rice and chicken. 9. Place chicken and bean mixture in freezer containers; top with cooking juices. Cool and freeze. To use, partially thaw in refrigerator overnight. 10. Microwave the food on high in a microwave-safe dish until heated through, stirring gently and adding a little stock or water if necessary.
Per Serving: Calories 339; Fat 5.7g; Sodium 377mg; Carbs 29.21g; Fibre 5.1g; Sugar 8.66g; Protein 42.33g

Country Chicken Thighs

Prep time: 25 minutes | Cook time: 10 minutes | Serves: 8

1 large onion, chopped
1 medium sweet red pepper, chopped
2 garlic cloves, minced
1.3kg boneless skinless chicken thighs
120ml chicken stock

1 tablespoon brown sugar
1 tablespoon curry powder
1 teaspoon ground ginger
1 teaspoon ground cinnamon
1 teaspoon dried thyme

1 can (360g) diced tomatoes, undrained
75g golden raisins or raisins
Hot cooked rice
Chopped fresh parsley, optional

1. Whisk stock, brown sugar and seasonings in a small bowl. 2. Place onion, red pepper and garlic in the pot; place the chicken on them and pour the stock mixture over them; top them with tomatoes and raisins. 3. Install the pressure lid and turn the pressure release valve to the SEAL position. 4. Select PRESSURE COOK, set the cooking temperature to HI and adjust the cooking time to 6 minutes. 5. When cooked, let the unit naturally release pressure. 6. A thermometer inserted in chicken should read at least 75°C. 7. Thicken cooking juices if desired. Serve with rice and if desired, parsley. 8. Place chicken and vegetables in freezer containers; top with cooking juices. Cool and freeze. To use, partially thaw in refrigerator overnight. 9. Heat through in a covered saucepan, stirring gently and adding a little stock if necessary.
Per Serving: Calories 319; Fat 5.91g; Sodium 204mg; Carbs 21.66g; Fibre 2.7g; Sugar 9.93g; Protein 43.39g

Chicken Thighs & Veggie Mix

Prep time: 20 minutes | Cook time: 5 minutes | Serves: 9

675g boneless skinless chicken thighs cut into 5cm pieces
225g sliced fresh mushrooms
2 celery ribs, sliced
1 medium onion, chopped
1 can (1100g) bean sprouts, rinsed and drained
1 can (200g) bamboo shoots, drained
1 can (200g) sliced water chestnuts, drained
65g frozen shelled edamame
360ml reduced-sodium chicken stock
120ml reduced-sodium soy sauce
1 tablespoon minced fresh gingerroot
¼ teaspoon crushed red pepper flakes
30g cornflour
60ml cold water
Hot cooked rice

1. Combine the stock, soy sauce, ginger and pepper flakes in a small bowl. 2. Place the chicken in the pot, top the chicken with celery, onion, bean sprouts, bamboo shoots, water chestnuts and edamame, and then pour the stock mixture over them. 3. Install the pressure lid and turn the pressure release valve to the SEAL position. 4. Select PRESSURE COOK, set the cooking temperature to HI and adjust the cooking time to 3 minutes. 5. When cooked, let the unit naturally release pressure. 6. A thermometer inserted in chicken should read at least 75°C. 7. In a small bowl, mix cornflour and water until smooth; stir the mixture into the chicken mixture. 8. Simmer them at LO on SEAR/SAUTÉ mode for 1 to 2 minutes until thickened. 9. Serve the dish with rice.
Per Serving: Calories 747; Fat 36.42g; Sodium 2284mg; Carbs 33.34g; Fibre 3.4g; Sugar 2.17g; Protein 68.82g

Classic Tso'S Stew

Prep time: 10 minutes | Cook time: 10 minutes | Serves: 6

240ml tomato juice
120ml water
60g pickled cherry peppers, chopped
2 tablespoons soy sauce
2 tablespoons hoisin sauce
1 tablespoon peanut oil
1 to 2 teaspoons crushed red pepper flakes
455g boneless skinless chicken breast halves
160g chopped onion
90g chopped fresh broccoli
35g chopped green onions
1 teaspoon sesame seeds, toasted

1. Combine the tomato juice, water, cherry peppers, soy sauce, hoisin sauce, peanut oil, and red pepper flakes in the pot; place in the chicken, onion and broccoli. 2. Install the pressure lid and turn the pressure release valve to the SEAL position. 3. Select PRESSURE COOK, set the cooking temperature to HI and adjust the cooking time to 6 minutes. 4. When cooked, let the unit naturally release pressure. 5. A thermometer inserted in chicken should read at least 75°C. 6. Remove chicken and shred with 2 forks. Return to the cooker and simmer on SEAR/SAUTÉ mode at LO until heat through. 7. Top with green onions and sesame seeds to serve. 8. Freeze cooled stew in freezer containers. To use, partially thaw in refrigerator overnight. Heat through in a saucepan, stirring occasionally and adding a little water if necessary.
Per Serving: Calories 171; Fat 6.27g; Sodium 256mg; Carbs 9.47g; Fibre 2.2g; Sugar 5.78g; Protein 18.73g

Smoke Whole Chicken

Prep time: 20 minutes | Cook time: 25 minutes | Serves: 6

2 tablespoons extra-virgin olive oil
1 tablespoon salt
1½ teaspoons smoked paprika
1 teaspoon freshly ground black pepper
½ teaspoon herbes de Provence
¼ teaspoon cayenne pepper
1 (1.6kg) whole chicken, rinsed and patted dry, giblets removed
1 large lemon, halved
6 garlic cloves, peeled and crushed with the flat side of a knife
1 large onion, cut into 8 wedges, divided
240ml chicken bone stock, low-sodium store-bought chicken stock, or water
2 large carrots, each cut into 4 pieces
2 celery stalks, each cut into 4 pieces

1. Combine the olive oil, salt, paprika, pepper, herbes de Provence, and cayenne in a small bowl. 2. Place the chicken on a cutting board and rub the olive oil mixture under the skin and all over the outside. Stuff the cavity with the lemon halves, garlic cloves, and 3 to 4 wedges of onion. 3. Pour the stock into the cooking pot; add the remaining onion wedges, carrots, and celery. 4. Place the reversible rack in the pot in the lower position and drop the lower rack through the reversible rack handles. 5. Arrange the chicken on the rack. 6. Install the pressure lid and turn the pressure release valve to the SEAL position. 7. Select PRESSURE COOK, set the cooking temperature to HI and adjust the cooking time to 21 minutes. 8. When cooked, let the unit naturally release pressure. 9. Carefully remove the chicken to a clean cutting board. Remove the skin and cut the chicken into pieces or shred/chop the meat, and serve.
Per Serving: Calories 246; Fat 8.29g; Sodium 1482mg; Carbs 7.26g; Fibre 1.6g; Sugar 2.58g; Protein 34.34g

Firecracker Chicken Meatballs

Prep time: 15 minutes | Cook time: 30 minutes | Serves: 6

For the Sauce
120g hot sauce
2 tablespoons honey

2 tablespoons low-sodium soy sauce or tamari

For the Meatballs
455g chicken or turkey mince
110g Panko breadcrumbs (whole wheat, if possible)

1 large egg, slightly beaten
1½ teaspoons garlic pepper
1 teaspoon onion powder

¼ teaspoon salt
2 tablespoons avocado oil, divided

1. Whisk together the hot sauce, honey, and soy sauce in a measuring cup to make the sauce. 2. In a large bowl, combine the chicken, Panko, egg, garlic pepper, onion powder, and salt. 3. Pinch off about a tablespoon of the meat mixture and roll it into a ball. (A 4cm cookie scoop makes the job easy.) Do the same with the remaining meat. 4. Heat 1 tablespoon of avocado oil in the cooking pot at MD on SEAR/SAUTÉ mode; add half of the meatballs around the edge of the pot and brown them for 3 to 5 minutes. 5. Flip the meatballs over and brown the other side for 3 to 5 minutes. Transfer to a paper towel–lined plate and do the same with the remaining 1 tablespoon of avocado oil and meatballs. 6. Stop the cooker, place the meatballs back to the pot and pour in the sauce mixture; stir to coat all sides of the meatballs with sauce, and then arrange them in a single layer. 7. Install the pressure lid and turn the pressure release valve to the SEAL position. 8. Select PRESSURE COOK, set the cooking temperature to HI and adjust the cooking time to 6 minutes. 9. When cooked, let the unit naturally release pressure. 10. Stir them to evenly distribute the sauce. Serve as an appetizer or as a main dish.
Per Serving: Calories 223; Fat 11.45g; Sodium 822mg; Carbs 14.04g; Fibre 1g; Sugar 6.82g; Protein 17.37g

Buffalo Chicken

Prep time: 10 minutes | Cook time: 20 minutes | Serves: 8

2 tablespoons avocado oil
60g finely chopped onion
1 celery stalk, finely chopped

1 large carrot, chopped
80g mild hot sauce
½ tablespoon apple cider vinegar

¼ teaspoon garlic powder
2 bone-in, skin-on chicken breasts (about 900g)

1. Heat the avocado oil in the cooking pot at MD on SEAR/SAUTÉ mode; add the onion, celery, and carrot, and sauté them for 3 to 5 minutes until the onion begins to soften. 2. Stop the cooker, and stir in the hot sauce, vinegar, and garlic powder; place in the chicken breasts with meat-side down. 3. Install the pressure lid and turn the pressure release valve to the SEAL position. 4. Select PRESSURE COOK, set the cooking temperature to HI and adjust the cooking time to 20 minutes. 5. When cooked, let the unit naturally release pressure. 6. Transfer the chicken breasts to a cutting board. 7. When the chicken is cool enough to handle, remove the skin, shred the chicken and return it to the pot. Let the chicken soak in the sauce for at least 5 minutes. 8. Serve immediately.
Per Serving: Calories 237; Fat 14.04g; Sodium 155mg; Carbs 2.5g; Fibre 0.6g; Sugar 1.28g; Protein 24g

Beer-Braised Chicken

Prep time: 20 minutes | Cook time: 20 minutes | Serves: 8

For the Chicken
240ml brown ale
1 teaspoon white wheat flour
2 bone-in, skin-on chicken breasts (about

900 g)
Salt
Freshly ground black pepper

1 tablespoon coarse-grain mustard

For the Slaw
60ml cider vinegar
2 tablespoons extra-virgin olive oil
1 tablespoon honey
1 tablespoon coarse-grain mustard

Salt
Freshly ground black pepper
¼ head purple or red cabbage, thinly sliced
300g seedless green grapes, halved

1 medium apple, cut into matchstick-size slices

1. In a small jar with a screw-top lid, combine the vinegar, olive oil, honey, and mustard. Shake well, then season with salt and pepper, and shake again. 2. In a large bowl, toss together the cabbage, grapes, and apple. Add the dressing and mix well. Let the mixture sit at room temperature while the chicken cooks. 3. Whisk together the ale and flour in a small bowl and then pour in the cooking pot. 4. Sprinkle the chicken breasts with salt and pepper. Place them in the pot with meat-side down. 5. Install the pressure lid and turn the pressure release valve to the SEAL position. 6. Select PRESSURE COOK, set the cooking temperature to HI and adjust the cooking time to 20 minutes. 7. When cooked, let the unit naturally release pressure. 8. Remove the chicken breasts to a cutting board, and bring the liquid in the cooking pot to a boil at HI on SEAR/SAUTÉ mode, scraping up any brown bits on the bottom of the pot; stir the sauce for 5 minutes or until the sauce has reduced in volume by about a third. 9. Stop the cooker and stir in the mustard. 10. When the chicken is cool enough to handle, remove the skin, shred the meat, and return it to the pot. 11. Let the chicken soak in the sauce for at least 5 minutes. 12. Serve and enjoy.
Per Serving: Calories 351; Fat 12.93g; Sodium 172mg; Carbs 31.86g; Fibre 2.2g; Sugar 11.31g; Protein 26.27g

Teriyaki Chicken Thighs

Prep time: 10 minutes | Cook time: 15 minutes | Serves: 4

3 tablespoons low-sodium gluten-free tamari or soy sauce
55g canned crushed pineapple
2 tablespoons dark brown sugar

2 tablespoons minced garlic
1 tablespoon peeled and minced fresh ginger
2 spring onions , both white and green

parts, thinly sliced, divided
675g boneless, skinless chicken thighs
Sesame seeds, for garnish

1. Combine the tamari, pineapple, brown sugar, garlic, ginger, and white parts of the spring onions in the cooking pot. 2. Dip the chicken thighs in the sauce to coat all sides, then nestle each piece in the sauce in a single layer. 3. Install the pressure lid and turn the pressure release valve to the SEAL position. 4. Select PRESSURE COOK, set the cooking temperature to HI and adjust the cooking time to 15 minutes. 5. When cooked, let the unit naturally release pressure. 6. Simmer the food at LO on SEAR/SAUTÉ mode for 5 minutes until the sauce has thickened. 7. Shred or chop the chicken, if desired. Remove the chicken to serving plates or a platter, sprinkle with the green parts of the spring onions and sesame seeds. 8. Serve immediately.
Per Serving: Calories 331; Fat 10.18g; Sodium 840mg; Carbs 42.35g; Fibre 3.1g; Sugar 13.12g; Protein 17.37g

Cheese Chicken Fajitas

Prep time: 10 minutes | Cook time: 10 minutes | Serves: 4-6

For the Fajitas
675g boneless, skinless chicken breasts cut into long thin strips
1 medium onion, chopped
120g canned crushed tomatoes
For Serving
Flour tortillas
Sour cream

60ml freshly squeezed lime juice
2 tablespoons vegetable oil
2 teaspoons ground cumin
1 teaspoon chili powder

Guacamole
Cheddar cheese

1 teaspoon smoked paprika
½ teaspoon dried oregano
½ teaspoon cayenne pepper (optional)
3 peppers, any color, sliced

1. Combine the chicken, onion, tomatoes, lime juice, oil, cumin, chili powder, smoked paprika, oregano, and cayenne (optional) in the cooking pot. 2. Place a vegetable steamer on top of the chicken and add the peppers. 3. Install the pressure lid and turn the pressure release valve to the SEAL position. 4. Select PRESSURE COOK, set the cooking temperature to HI and adjust the cooking time to 7 minutes. 5. When cooked, let the unit naturally release pressure. Remove the peppers and set aside. 6. Select SEAR/SAUTÉ and cook the chicken and onion mixture at MD for about 3 minutes to thicken. 7. Add the peppers and toss them in the seasonings. 8. Set out the tortillas, chicken fajita mixture, sour cream, guacamole, and Cheddar for people to assemble their own fajitas.
Per Serving: Calories 308; Fat 13.52g; Sodium 407mg; Carbs 34.11g; Fibre 3.3g; Sugar 9.05g; Protein 13.41g

Chicken Lettuce Wraps

Prep time: 10 minutes | Cook time: 20 minutes | Serves: 4

For the Chicken
2 teaspoons peanut oil
80ml low-sodium gluten-free tamari or soy sauce
1 tablespoon honey
2 tablespoons rice vinegar
For the Lettuce Wraps
Large lettuce leaves

2 teaspoons Sriracha sauce
1 tablespoon minced garlic
2 teaspoons peeled and minced fresh ginger
80ml chicken bone stock or water

90g broccoli slaw or shredded cabbage

2 spring onions , both white and green parts, thinly sliced, divided
1 bone-in, skin-on chicken breast (about 455g)

30g chopped cashews, toasted

1. Whisk the peanut oil, tamari, honey, rice vinegar, Sriracha, garlic, ginger, and stock in the cooking pot; stir in the white parts of the spring onions. 2. Place the chicken breast in the sauce with meat-side down. 3. Install the pressure lid and turn the pressure release valve to the SEAL position. 4. Select PRESSURE COOK, set the cooking temperature to HI and adjust the cooking time to 20 minutes. 5. When cooked, let the unit naturally release pressure. 6. Transfer the chicken breast to a cutting board. When the chicken is cool enough to handle, remove the skin, shred the chicken, and return it to the pot. 7. Let the chicken soak in the sauce for at least 5 minutes. 8. Spoon some of the chicken and sauce into the lettuce leaves. 9. Sprinkle with the broccoli slaw, the green parts of the spring onions , and the cashews. 10. Serve immediately.
Per Serving: Calories 430; Fat 25.27g; Sodium 1102mg; Carbs 22.83g; Fibre 4.1g; Sugar 12.85g; Protein 30.61g

Mexican Turkey Tenderloin with Cheese

Prep time: 5 minutes | Cook time: 25 minutes | Serves: 6

250g low-sodium salsa or bottled salsa
1 teaspoon chili powder
½ teaspoon ground cumin

¼ teaspoon dried oregano
675g unseasoned turkey tenderloin or
boneless turkey breast, cut into 6 pieces

Freshly ground black pepper
50g shredded Monterey Jack cheese or
Mexican cheese blend

1. In a small bowl or measuring cup, combine the salsa, chili powder, cumin, and oregano. Pour half of the mixture into the cooking pot. 2. Nestle the turkey into the sauce. Grind some pepper onto each piece of turkey. Pour the remaining salsa mixture on top. 3. Install the pressure lid and turn the pressure release valve to the SEAL position. 4. Select PRESSURE COOK, set the cooking temperature to HI and adjust the cooking time to 8 minutes. 5. When cooked, let the unit naturally release pressure. 6. Sprinkle the cheese on top, and put the lid back on for a few minutes to let the cheese melt. 7. Serve immediately.
Per Serving: Calories 251; Fat 5.85g; Sodium 200mg; Carbs 11.62g; Fibre 0.4g; Sugar 8.6g; Protein 37.41g

Herbed Turkey Breast

Prep time: 10 minutes | Cook time: 30 minutes | Serves: 12

3 tablespoons extra-virgin olive oil
1½ tablespoons herbes de Provence or
poultry seasoning
2 teaspoons minced garlic

1 teaspoon lemon zest (from 1 small
lemon)
1 tablespoon salt
1½ teaspoons freshly ground black pepper

1 (2.7kg) bone-in, skin-on whole turkey
breast, rinsed and patted dry

1. Whisk the olive oil, herbes de Provence, garlic, lemon zest, salt, and pepper in a small bowl. 2. Rub the outside of the turkey and under the skin with the olive oil mixture. 3. Add 240ml of water to the cooking pot, place the reversible rack in the pot in the lower position and drop the lower rack through the reversible rack handles. 4. Arrange the turkey onto the rack with skin-side up. 5. Install the pressure lid and turn the pressure release valve to the SEAL position. 6. Select PRESSURE COOK, set the cooking temperature to HI and adjust the cooking time to 30 minutes. 7. When cooked, let the unit naturally release pressure. 8. Carefully transfer the turkey to a cutting board. Remove the skin, slice, and serve.
Per Serving: Calories 350; Fat 6.27g; Sodium 836mg; Carbs 0.73g; Fibre 0.1g; Sugar 0.03g; Protein 68.46g

Turkey Meatballs

Prep time: 5 minutes | Cook time: 10 minutes | Serves: 6

1 recipe (about 22) frozen turkey sausage
meatballs
200g whole grain thin spaghetti

(uncooked), broken in half
1 tablespoon extra-virgin olive oil
1 (600g) jar pasta sauce

Freshly grated Parmesan cheese, for
serving (optional)

1. In the cooking pot, arrange the frozen meatballs in a single layer. 2. Place the broken spaghetti on top of the meatballs in an even layer. Drizzle them with the olive oil all over the spaghetti. 3. Pour in 720ml water and the pasta sauce. If the spaghetti is not completely covered, add a bit more water. Do not stir them. 4. Install the pressure lid and turn the pressure release valve to the SEAL position. 5. Select PRESSURE COOK, set the cooking temperature to HI and adjust the cooking time to 10 minutes. 6. When cooked, let the unit naturally release pressure. 7. Serve with Parmesan cheese (optional).
Per Serving: Calories 245; Fat 6.1g; Sodium 1073mg; Carbs 34.83g; Fibre 6.1g; Sugar 4.62g; Protein 15.83g

Tropical Chicken Breasts

Prep time: 5 minutes | Cook time: 10 minutes | Serves: 4

900g boneless, skinless chicken breasts
235g garden salsa
260g frozen pineapple chunks (no need to

thaw)
260g frozen mango chunks (no need to
thaw)

120ml water
1 tablespoon chopped fresh coriander, for
garnish

1. In the cooking pot, combine the chicken, salsa, pineapple, mango, and water. 2. Install the pressure lid and turn the pressure release valve to the SEAL position. 3. Select PRESSURE COOK, set the cooking temperature to HI and adjust the cooking time to 10 minutes. 4. When cooked, let the unit naturally release pressure. 5. Transfer the chicken to a serving platter. Spoon the salsa and fruit on top of each piece of chicken and garnish with coriander.
Per Serving: Calories 519; Fat 13.14g; Sodium 1067mg; Carbs 78.95g; Fibre 5.9g; Sugar 40.57g; Protein 22.52g

Chicken Andouille Sausage and Prawns

Prep time: 10 minutes | Cook time: 20 minutes | Serves: 4

3 tablespoons avocado oil, divided
½ large onion, halved and then cut into ½ cm-thick slices
200g okra, cut into 1cm -thick slices
¼ teaspoon salt
¼ teaspoon freshly ground black pepper
3 garlic cloves, minced
1 teaspoon dried oregano
1 (700g) carton or can chopped tomatoes
2 links precooked chicken andouille
sausage, cut into ½cm -thick slices (about 150g)
200g raw prawns (26 to 35 count), peeled and deveined
Fresh parsley, chopped

1. Heat 1½ tablespoons of avocado oil in the cooking pot at MD on SEAR/SAUTÉ mode; add the onion and sauté for 3 to 5 minutes or until just soften. 2. Add the remaining 1½ tablespoons of olive oil and okra to the pot, and sprinkle them with salt and pepper, and then sauté them for 2 to 3 minutes or until the okra begins to brown a little bit. 3. Stop the cooker, and add the garlic, oregano, tomatoes and their juices, and 240ml of water to the pot. 4. Install the pressure lid and turn the pressure release valve to the SEAL position. 5. Select PRESSURE COOK, set the cooking temperature to HI and adjust the cooking time to 20 minutes. 6. When cooked, let the unit naturally release pressure. 7. Add the sausage and prawns to the pot and sauté the food at MD for 5 minutes or until the prawns is opaque and the sausage is hot. 8. Sprinkle the dish with the parsley and serve.
Per Serving: Calories 266; Fat 13.22g; Sodium 926mg; Carbs 15.22g; Fibre 6.8g; Sugar 7.15g; Protein 23.81g

Lemon Chicken Thighs

Prep time: 15 minutes | Cook time: 20 minutes | Serves: 4

1 tablespoon butter
1 tablespoon olive oil
4 garlic cloves, minced
1 tablespoon capers
1 teaspoon Italian seasoning
6 boneless, skinless chicken thighs
120ml water
120ml white wine or water
80ml freshly squeezed lemon juice
1 to 2 teaspoons cornflour

1. Add the butter, olive oil, garlic, capers, Italian seasoning, and chicken thighs to the pot, and sear the chicken thighs at MD on SEAR/SAUTÉ mode for 2 minutes or until they are browned on each side. 2. Stop the cooker, and add the water, wine, and lemon juice to the pot. 3. Install the pressure lid and turn the pressure release valve to the SEAL position. 4. Select PRESSURE COOK, set the cooking temperature to HI and adjust the cooking time to 12 minutes. 5. When cooked, let the unit naturally release pressure. 6. Transfer the chicken thighs to a serving dish. 7. Stir in the cornflour and cook them at MD on SEAR/SAUTÉ mode for 5 minutes to thicken the sauce. 8. Drizzle the sauce over the chicken thighs and serve.
Per Serving: Calories 709; Fat 54.42g; Sodium 362mg; Carbs 4.25g; Fibre 0.3g; Sugar 0.63g; Protein 48.2g

Chicken Sauce & Polenta Dumplings

Prep time: 10 minutes | Cook time: 25 minutes | Serves: 4-6

For the Polenta Dumplings
125g plain flour
120g polenta
2 tablespoons sugar
For the Creamy Chicken
1 tablespoon butter or olive oil
½ onion, finely chopped
60g chopped celery
2 garlic cloves, minced
1 tablespoon herbes de Provence
½ teaspoon baking powder
½ teaspoon baking soda
½ teaspoon sea salt

675g boneless, skinless chicken breasts, cut into 2.5cm chunks
1 (300g) bag frozen mixed vegetables (no need to thaw)
2 carrots, cut into 2.5cm chunks
120ml whole milk
1 tablespoon melted butter or olive oil

720ml chicken stock
240ml whole milk
1 tablespoon cornflour

1. In a large bowl, mix the flour, polenta, sugar, baking powder, baking soda, and salt until blended. 2. Add the milk and melted butter, and stir them until a thick batter forms. Set aside. 3. Add the butter, onion, celery, garlic, and herbes de Provence to the cooking pot, and sauté them at MD on SEAR/SAUTÉ mode for 2 minutes until the onions are translucent. 4. Stop the cooker, add the chicken, frozen vegetables, carrots, chicken stock, and milk to the pot; place the reversible rack in the pot in the lower position and drop the lower rack through the reversible rack handles. 5. Arrange the dumplings onto the rack. 6. Install the pressure lid and turn the pressure release valve to the SEAL position. 7. Select PRESSURE COOK, set the cooking temperature to HI and adjust the cooking time to 15 minutes. 8. When cooked, let the unit naturally release pressure. 9. Remove the racks with dumplings and select SEAR/SAUTÉ. 10. Add the cornflour in the pot and stir them well, and then cook them at MD for 5 minutes to thicken the sauce. 11. Serve the dumplings with the dish.
Per Serving: Calories 515; Fat 13.56g; Sodium 1122mg; Carbs 80.19g; Fibre 4.1g; Sugar 19.87g; Protein 17.51g

Chicken, Bacon, and Ranch Casserole

Prep time: 5 minutes | Cook time: 15 minutes | Serves: 4

3 bacon slices, chopped
½ onion, chopped
455g boneless, skinless chicken breasts, cut into 2.5cm chunks

1 (300g) bag mixed frozen vegetables (no need to thaw)
600ml chicken stock, store-bought or homemade

180g raw long-grain white rice
1 (25g) packet ranch dressing and seasoning mix
100g shredded Cheddar cheese

1. Add the bacon and onion and sauté them at MD on SEAR/SAUTÉ mode for about 2 minutes or until the bacon is halfway crispy and the onions are translucent. 2. Stop the cooker, and add the chicken, frozen vegetables, chicken stock, rice, and ranch seasoning. 3. Install the pressure lid and turn the pressure release valve to the SEAL position. 4. Select PRESSURE COOK, set the cooking temperature to HI and adjust the cooking time to 12 minutes. 5. When cooked, let the unit naturally release pressure. 6. Stir in the Cheddar cheese while the mixture is still piping hot. 7. Serve as soon as the cheese is melted.
Per Serving: Calories 708; Fat 27.52g; Sodium 1162mg; Carbs 81.46g; Fibre 6.8g; Sugar 12.46g; Protein 30.74g

Turkey Loaf with Mashed Potatoes

Prep time: 10 minutes | Cook time: 25 minutes | Serves: 4-6

For the Meat Loaf
455g turkey mince
100g Italian seasoned bread crumbs
For the Glaze
120g ketchup
1 tablespoon light brown sugar
2 tablespoons Worcestershire sauce

50g grated Parmesan cheese
1 small onion, finely chopped

For the Mashed Potatoes
240ml water
900g Yukon Gold potatoes, peeled and

1 large egg
2 tablespoons whole milk

quartered
2 tablespoons butter
Sea salt

1. In a medium bowl, mix together the turkey mince, bread crumbs, Parmesan, onion, egg, and milk. 2. In a medium bowl, mix the ketchup, brown sugar, and Worcestershire sauce until blended. 3. Shape the meat mixture into a loaf and centre it on a suitable sheet of heavy-duty aluminum foil. Scrunch up the foil to form a wall around the meat loaf, creating a makeshift loaf pan. Spoon the glaze over the meat loaf. 4. Pour the water into the pressure cooker pot. Place the potatoes in the water and place the reversible rack in the pot in the lower position and drop the lower rack through the reversible rack handles. 5. Arrange the sheet onto the rack. 6. Install the pressure lid and turn the pressure release valve to the SEAL position. 7. Select PRESSURE COOK, set the cooking temperature to HI and adjust the cooking time to 25 minutes. 8. When cooked, let the unit naturally release pressure. 9. Lift out the meat loaf and racks and transfer it to a serving dish. 10. Add the butter and salt to the potatoes, mash them with a fork, and transfer them to a serving bowl. 11. Slice the meat loaf and serve hot with the mashed potatoes. 12. You can refrigerate the leftover in an airtight container for up to 5 days.
Per Serving: Calories 617; Fat 41.2g; Sodium 532mg; Carbs 39.87g; Fibre 3.7g; Sugar 8.54g; Protein 22.02g

Peanut Turkey Rice Bowls

Prep time: 15 minutes | Cook time: 20 minutes | Serves: 4

For the Turkey
360ml water
125g peanut butter
½ onion, chopped
2 garlic cloves, minced
For the Rice
360ml water
For the Bowls
Peanuts
Coriander

2 tablespoons soy sauce
1 tablespoon sesame oil
1 teaspoon curry powder
1 teaspoon ground ginger

180g raw long-grain white rice

Freshly squeezed lime juice
Sriracha

455g turkey mince
3 carrots, cut into chunks
1 (200g) can sliced water chestnuts

1. Combine the water, peanut butter, onion, garlic, soy sauce, sesame oil, curry powder, and ground ginger in the cooking pot; add the turkey mince, carrots, and water chestnuts, and cook them at MD on SEAR/SAUTÉ mode for 5 minutes, breaking the turkey up. 2. In a suitable stainless steel bowl, mix the water and rice. 3. Place the reversible rack in the pot in the lower position and drop the lower rack through the reversible rack handles. 4. Arrange the bowl onto the rack. 5. Install the pressure lid and turn the pressure release valve to the SEAL position. 6. Select PRESSURE COOK, set the cooking temperature to HI and adjust the cooking time to 12 minutes. 7. When cooked, let the unit naturally release pressure. 8. Remove the bowl of rice and the trivet. 8. Select SEAR/SAUTÉ and cook the food in the pot for 3 minutes to thicken the turkey mixture. 9. Scoop the rice into bowls; top the rice with the turkey mixture and garnish with peanuts, coriander, lime juice, and sriracha. Enjoy.
Per Serving: Calories 969; Fat 62.69g; Sodium 690mg; Carbs 69.75g; Fibre 6.1g; Sugar 9.83g; Protein 29.48g

French Mustard Chicken

Prep time: 5 minutes | Cook time: 10 minutes | Serves: 4

2 tablespoons butter
3 shallots or 1 small onion, chopped
2 garlic cloves, minced
240ml chicken stock, store-bought or

homemade
3 tablespoons Dijon mustard
2 teaspoons herbes de Provence
4 (200g) boneless, skinless chicken breasts

Sea salt
Freshly ground black pepper
120g heavy cream or whole milk

1. Add the butter, shallots, garlic, chicken stock, mustard, and herbes de Provence in a bowl and stir to make a sauce. 2. Season the chicken breasts with salt and pepper and add them to the pot. 3. Install the pressure lid and turn the pressure release valve to the SEAL position. 4. Select PRESSURE COOK, set the cooking temperature to HI and adjust the cooking time to 10 minutes. 5. When cooked, let the unit naturally release pressure. 6. Stir in the cream, and serve.
Per Serving: Calories 237; Fat 15.13g; Sodium 604mg; Carbs 18.99g; Fibre 2.4g; Sugar 6.08g; Protein 7.19g

Maple-Soy Chicken Thighs

Prep time: 15 minutes | Cook time: 20 minutes | Serves: 4

85g maple syrup
2 tablespoons soy sauce
2 garlic cloves, minced

1 teaspoon sesame oil
1 teaspoon ground ginger
6 boneless, skinless chicken thighs

240ml water
1 to 2 teaspoons cornflour

1. Add the maple syrup, soy sauce, garlic, sesame oil, ginger, and chicken thighs to the cooking pot, and sauté them at MD on SEAR/SAUTÉ mode for 2 minutes or until the chicken thighs are lightly browned on both sides. 2. Stop the cooker and add the water. 3. Install the pressure lid and turn the pressure release valve to the SEAL position. 4. Select PRESSURE COOK, set the cooking temperature to HI and adjust the cooking time to 12 minutes. 5. When cooked, let the unit naturally release pressure. 6. Transfer the chicken thighs to a serving dish. 7. Stir in the cornflour and cook them at MD on SEAR/SAUTÉ mode for 5 minutes to thicken the sauce. 8. Drizzle the sauce on top of the chicken thighs and serve.
Per Serving: Calories 730; Fat 50.69g; Sodium 359mg; Carbs 17.35g; Fibre 0.3g; Sugar 13.48g; Protein 48.54g

Sticky Chicken Wings

Prep time: 5 minutes | Cook time: 15 minutes | Serves: 4-6

240ml water
240g sweet and smoky barbecue sauce
85g honey

1 small onion, chopped
1 garlic clove, minced
1 teaspoon Worcestershire sauce

900g chicken whole wings (tips cut off)
1 tablespoon cornflour

1. In the cooking pot, combine the water, barbecue sauce, honey, onion, garlic, and Worcestershire sauce and whisk together. 2. Place the reversible rack in the pot in the lower position and drop the lower rack through the reversible rack handles. 3. Arrange the chicken onto the rack. 4. Install the pressure lid and turn the pressure release valve to the SEAL position. 5. Select PRESSURE COOK, set the cooking temperature to HI and adjust the cooking time to 10 minutes. 6. When cooked, let the unit naturally release pressure. Remove the racks and chicken. 7. Select SEAR/SAUTÉ mode and whisk the cornflour into the pot and whisk for about 5 minutes to thicken the sauce. 8. Return the chicken to the pot and toss to coat with the sticky barbecue sauce. Serve.
Per Serving: Calories 337; Fat 5.57g; Sodium 501mg; Carbs 36.42g; Fibre 0.9g; Sugar 30.62g; Protein 33.88g

Easy Chimichurri Chicken Drumsticks

Prep time: 5 minutes | Cook time: 15 minutes | Serves: 4

8 chicken drumsticks (about 900g total)   240ml water   130g chimichurri

1. Combine the chicken, water, and chimichurri in the cooking pot. 2. Install the pressure lid and turn the pressure release valve to the SEAL position. 3. Select PRESSURE COOK, set the cooking temperature to HI and adjust the cooking time to 15 minutes. 4. When cooked, let the unit naturally release pressure. 5. Remove the drumsticks and place them on a serving platter. Drizzle the sauce over the chicken and serve. 6. You can refrigerate the leftover in an airtight container for up to 5 days or freeze for up to 6 months.
Per Serving: Calories 422; Fat 24.03g; Sodium 1038mg; Carbs 0.79g; Fibre 0.1g; Sugar 0.36g; Protein 47.15g

Caesar Chicken Sandwiches

Prep time: 5 minutes | Cook time: 15 minutes | Serves: 4-6

For the Caesar dressing
480g mayonnaise
4 garlic cloves, minced
60ml freshly squeezed lemon juice

2 teaspoons Dijon mustard
2 teaspoons Worcestershire sauce
½ teaspoon sea salt

½ teaspoon freshly ground black pepper
1 teaspoon anchovy paste (optional)

For the Chicken
675g boneless, skinless chicken breasts

240ml water

100g grated Parmesan cheese

For the Sandwiches
4 to 6 white sandwich buns

Tomato slices, for serving

Lettuce leaves, for serving

1. In a large bowl, combine the mayonnaise, garlic, lemon juice, mustard, Worcestershire sauce, sea salt, pepper, and anchovy paste (optional). 2. In the cooking pot, combine the chicken breasts, Caesar salad dressing, and water. 3. Install the pressure lid and turn the pressure release valve to the SEAL position. 4. Select PRESSURE COOK, set the cooking temperature to HI and adjust the cooking time to 15 minutes. 5. When cooked, let the unit naturally release pressure. 6. Remove the chicken, place it in a bowl, and shred it using two forks. Return the chicken to the pot an stir in the Parmesan. 7. Pile the chicken on the buns and top with tomato and lettuce. Serve.
Per Serving: Calories 593; Fat 39.64g; Sodium 1770mg; Carbs 32.88g; Fibre 3g; Sugar 7.84g; Protein 25.81g

Coconut Chicken Breasts

Prep time: 5 minutes | Cook time: 40 minutes | Serves: 4

1 tablespoon coconut oil
1 yellow onion
3 tablespoons curry powder
2 cloves garlic

1 can diced tomatoes
1 can tomato sauce
120ml chicken stock
2 tablespoons sugar

900g chicken breasts
Salt and pepper, to taste
1 can coconut milk

1. Chop the onion and garlic and drain the tomatoes. 2. Heat the coconut oil in the cooking pot at MD on SEAR/SAUTÉ mode; add the onion and sauté for 2 minutes; mix in the garlic and 2 tablespoons curry powder and continue to cook for another 2 minutes. 3. Stop the process, and stir in the tomatoes, tomato sauce, chicken stock, and sugar. 4. Poke holes in the chicken and season with salt, pepper, and remaining curry powder. Add the chicken to the pot. 5. Install the pressure lid and turn the pressure release valve to the SEAL position. 6. Select PRESSURE COOK, set the cooking temperature to HI and adjust the cooking time to 10 minutes. 7. When cooked, let the unit naturally release pressure. 8. Transfer the chicken to a bowl and shred it. 9. Return the chicken to the pot and return the pot. 10. Select SEAR/SAUTÉ, and cook them for 3 minutes by stirring continuously. 11. Turn the pot to Keep Warm function and pour in the coconut milk and cook them for another 10 minutes before serving. Serve over rice.
Per Serving: Calories 541; Fat 27.53g; Sodium 477mg; Carbs 16.25g; Fibre 5.6g; Sugar 9.79g; Protein 56.13g

Teriyaki Chicken and Vegetables

Prep time: 15 minutes | Cook time: 30 minutes | Serves: 3-4

1½ tablespoons sesame oil
1 medium boneless skinless chicken
breast, cut into cubes
Sea salt
Black pepper
Teriyaki Sauce
80ml soy sauce
60ml rice wine vinegar
85g honey

2 cloves garlic, minced
½ teaspoon minced ginger
55g red peppers, chopped
40g carrot, shredded
300g Jasmine rice, rinsed and drained

1½ tablespoons Mirin
1 teaspoon cornflour
3 tablespoons water, plus more as needed

thoroughly
240ml water
90g broccoli florets
55g shelled edamame beans
Sesame seeds, for garnish

to thin out the sauce

1. Whisk soy sauce, vinegar, honey, Mirin and starch in a mixing bowl. Pour into a saucepan and heat on medium high heat. 2. Slowly add water and bring to a boil, until thickened; transfer to a heat-safe bowl. 3. Heat the sesame oil in the pot for 1 minute; when oil is hot, add the chicken and season with sea salt and pepper, and then cook the chicken for 2 minutes until golden brown; add the garlic and ginger and cook for another 20 seconds. 4. Stop the cooker, and stir in 120ml of the teriyaki sauce, rice, peppers, carrots, broccoli, edamame, and water. 5. Add the water to the cooking pot, place the Cook & Crisp Basket on top of diffuser and press down firmly, and then place in the ingredients. 6. Install the pressure lid and turn the pressure release valve to the VENT position. 7. Select STEAM and set the cooking time to 10 minutes. 8. When cooked, let the unit naturally release pressure. 9. Drizzle with additional teriyaki sauce, top with sesame seeds, and serve.
Per Serving: Calories 316; Fat 13.36g; Sodium 398mg; Carbs 37.82g; Fibre 6.4g; Sugar 22.51g; Protein 18.83g

Thyme Turkey Breast

Prep time: 15 minutes | Cook time: 30 minutes | Serves: 4-6

1 (675g) boneless or bone-in turkey breast
½ teaspoon sea salt
½ teaspoon freshly ground black pepper

2 tablespoons butter
8 shallots, chopped
1 garlic clove, minced

1 teaspoon dried thyme
480ml water
3 tablespoons cornflour

1. Season the turkey breast with the salt and pepper. 2. Add the butter, shallots, garlic, and thyme to the pot, and sauté them at MD on SEAR/SAUTÉ mode until just to melt the butter. 3. Add the water to the cooking pot, place the reversible rack in the pot in the lower position and drop the lower rack through the reversible rack handles. 4. Arrange the turkey breast onto the rack. Install the pressure lid and turn the pressure release valve to the SEAL position. 5. Select PRESSURE COOK, set the cooking temperature to HI and adjust the cooking time to 25 minutes. 6. When cooked, let the unit naturally release pressure. 7. Transfer the turkey to a serving dish and remove the trivet from the pot. 8. Select SEAR/SAUTÉ and whisk the cornflour into the pot, and then cook them for about 5 minutes to thicken the gravy. 9. Slice the turkey. Serve the slices drizzled with gravy or pass the gravy separately in a gravy boat. 10. You can refrigerate the leftover in an airtight container for up to 5 days.
Per Serving: Calories 227; Fat 6.22g; Sodium 340mg; Carbs 6.22g; Fibre 0.5g; Sugar 1.06g; Protein 34.61g

Tso's Chicken

Prep time: 15 minutes | Cook time: 45 minutes | Serves: 2-4

3 garlic cloves, minced
1 teaspoon fresh ginger, roughly chopped
1 tablespoon rapeseed oil
10 dried Chinese red chilies
General Tso's Sauce:
60ml dark soy sauce
2 tablespoons Shaoxing rice wine
2 tablespoons distilled white vinegar

5 boneless skinless chicken thighs
1 stalk green onion, green part finely chopped for garnish, white part cut into 4 cm pieces

75g sugar or sugar substitute
1 teaspoon sesame oil
2 tablespoons cornflour

1 tablespoon honey
8-10 pieces of bib lettuce or romaine

2 tablespoons water

1. Whisk together the General Tso's Sauce ingredients in a glass mixing bowl until well-combined and set aside. 2. Heat the grapeseed oil in the cooking pot at MD on SEAR/SAUTÉ mode for 2 minutes; add garlic and ginger and sauté them for 3 minutes until translucent and softened; add the dried Chinese red chilies, the whites of the green onions, and sauté them for 3 minutes until fragrant. 3. Stop the process, and add the sauce and chicken thighs to the pot. 4. Install the pressure lid and turn the pressure release valve to the SEAL position. 5. Select PRESSURE COOK, set the cooking temperature to HI and adjust the cooking time to 25 minutes. 6. When cooked, let the unit naturally release pressure. 7. Remove the chicken from the cooking pot and shred with a fork. 8. Remove the Chinese red chili. Add honey to the pot and bring the sauce back to a boil on STEAM mode. 9. Mix the cornflour and water in a small mixing bowl. Fold into the sauce one third at a time until desired thickness. 10. Fold shredded chicken into the sauce and replace the lid; let the food stand on Keep Warm for 5 minutes. 11. Assemble lettuce leaves on a plate, spoon in the desired amount of dish and garnish with green onion. Enjoy.
Per Serving: Calories 677; Fat 46.4g; Sodium 786mg; Carbs 22.29g; Fibre 3.8g; Sugar 11.13g; Protein 43.69g

Chipotle Chicken with Coriander Rice

Prep time: 8 minutes | Cook time: 50 minutes | Serves: 4

140g quinoa, rinsed and drained
240ml water
⅛ teaspoon salt
½ teaspoon ground cumin
Pinch black pepper
1 tablespoon chipotle paste

225g medium salsa
455g boneless, skinless chicken thighs
1 (375g) black beans
¼ teaspoon sea salt
1 lime, juiced
2 teaspoons olive oil

2 tablespoons chopped coriander
150g halved cherry tomatoes, for serving
1 avocado, sliced, for serving
4 lime wedges, for garnish

1. Add quinoa and water to the cooking pot. 2. Install the pressure lid and turn the pressure release valve to the SEAL position. 3. Select PRESSURE COOK, set the cooking temperature to HI and adjust the cooking time to 22 minutes. 4. When cooked, let the unit naturally release pressure. 5. Fluff the quinoa with a fork; transfer the quinoa to a bowl and stir with the lime juice, olive oil, and coriander; cover the bowl and set aside. 6. Combine the salt, cumin black pepper, chipotle, and salsa in a medium mixing bowl. 7. Add the chicken to the cooking pot and pour the salsa mixture over the chicken. 8. Install the pressure lid and turn the pressure release valve to the SEAL position. 9. Select PRESSURE COOK, set the cooking temperature to HI and adjust the cooking time to 22 minutes. 10. After 20 minutes of cooking time, add the black beans. 11. When cooked, let the unit naturally release pressure. 12. Transfer chicken and beans to a bowl. 13. Equally distribute quinoa, chicken, and beans to each bowl. 14. Top the dish with cherry tomatoes and sliced avocado. Serve with lime wedges and enjoy.
Per Serving: Calories 558; Fat 21.22g; Sodium 999mg; Carbs 76.35g; Fibre 11.9g; Sugar 17.68g; Protein 20.72g

Braised Chicken with Tomatillos

Prep time: 10 minutes | Cook time: 4 hours | Serves: 6

2 tablespoons olive oil
Salt and pepper, to taste
1.1kg assorted chicken pieces
1 yellow onion

480ml chicken stock
6 cloves garlic
675g tomatillos
3 tablespoons coriander

2 teaspoon ground cumin
1 tablespoon lime juice

1. Remove the husks from the tomatillos and wash them. 2. Mince the garlic and chop the onion and coriander. 3. Heat the olive oil in the cooking pot at MD on SEAR/SAUTÉ mode; add the onion and cumin, and sauté them for about 5 minutes; add the garlic and tomatillos and continue cooking until the tomatillos begin to soften; add the remaining ingredients to the pot and stir to ensure the chicken is coated. 4. Stop the process, install the pressure lid and turn the pressure release valve to the VENT position. 5. Press FUNCTION and turn the dial to select SLOW COOK. 6. Press TEMP and turn the dial to select HI, press TIME and turn the dial to set the cooking time to 4 hours; press START/STOP to begin cooking. 7. Serve with tortillas, rice and sour cream.
Per Serving: Calories 228; Fat 9.04g; Sodium 439mg; Carbs 7.66g; Fibre 1.7g; Sugar 3.99g; Protein 28.62g

Chicken Breast with Spinach and Artichoke

Prep time: 5 minutes | Cook time: 15 minutes | Serves: 6

1 tablespoon olive oil
455g boneless, skinless, chicken breast
60g spinach
1 can artichoke hearts

120g heavy cream
25g parmesan
60g shredded mozzarella
1 teaspoon garlic powder

1 teaspoon onion powder
Salt and pepper, to taste

1. Cube the chicken and drain and chop the artichokes and spinach. 2. Heat the oil in the cooking pot at MD on SEAR/SAUTÉ mode; add the chicken and brown the chicken, and then add the artichokes, garlic powder, onion powder, salt, and pepper and cook them for another 3 minutes. 3. Turn the cooker to Keep Warm and stir in the remaining ingredients. 4. Cover and allow the cheeses to melt, stirring every few minutes until blended evenly.
Per Serving: Calories 233; Fat 10.53g; Sodium 377mg; Carbs 22.37g; Fibre 3.2g; Sugar 5.4g; Protein 12.94g

Buffalo Chicken Breast Wraps

Prep time: 5 minutes | Cook time: 15 minutes | Serves: 4

570g boneless, skinless chicken breast
2 stalks celery

1 onion
1 medium carrot

240g buffalo sauce
12 bib lettuce leaves

1. Dice the carrot, onion, and celery. 2. Combine all of the ingredients except for the lettuce in the pot and mix to coat the chicken. 3. Install the pressure lid and turn the pressure release valve to the SEAL position. 4. Select PRESSURE COOK, set the cooking temperature to HI and adjust the cooking time to 15 minutes. 5. When cooked, let the unit naturally release pressure. 6. Shred the chicken then return it to the pot and stir it in. 7. Serve the mixture in the lettuce leaves.
Per Serving: Calories 165; Fat 4.29g; Sodium 670mg; Carbs 24.29g; Fibre 3.6g; Sugar 8.87g; Protein 8.34g

Apricot Chicken

Prep time: 5 minutes | Cook time: 15 minutes | Serves: 4

900g boneless, skinless chicken thighs cut into strips
240ml water
255g apricot preserves

2 tablespoons sesame oil
2 tablespoons soy sauce
2 tablespoons rice vinegar
2 teaspoons ground ginger

1 to 2 teaspoons sriracha
1 teaspoon red pepper flakes
2 teaspoons cornflour

1. In the cooking pot, combine the chicken, water, apricot preserves, sesame oil, soy sauce, rice vinegar, ground ginger, sriracha, and red pepper flakes. 2. Install the pressure lid and turn the pressure release valve to the SEAL position. 3. Select PRESSURE COOK, set the cooking temperature to HI and adjust the cooking time to 8 minutes. 4. When cooked, let the unit naturally release pressure. 5. Select SEAR/SAUTÉ, and whisk the cornflour into the pot and whisk them for about 5 minutes until the sauce thickens and becomes sticky. 6. Serve hot. 7. You can refrigerate the leftover in an airtight container for up to 5 days.
Per Serving: Calories 547; Fat 21.34g; Sodium 731mg; Carbs 66.75g; Fibre 5.9g; Sugar 26.96g; Protein 22.55g

Harissa Chicken Breasts

Prep time: 5 minutes | Cook time: 20 minutes | Serves: 4

455g boneless, skinless chicken breasts
1 onion, chopped
1 carrot, chopped

240ml chicken stock
½ teaspoon ground cumin
¼ teaspoon garlic powder

Salt and pepper, to taste
240g mild Harissa sauce

1. In a small bowl, mix together the cumin, garlic, salt and pepper. 2. Sprinkle the spice mix over both sides of the chicken then transfer the chicken to the pot. 3. Pour the Harissa sauce over the chicken and stir to make sure the chicken is well coated. Add remaining ingredients and stir. 4. Install the pressure lid and turn the pressure release valve to the SEAL position. 5. Select PRESSURE COOK, set the cooking temperature to HI and adjust the cooking time to 20 minutes. 6. When cooked, let the unit naturally release pressure. 7. Transfer the chicken to a bowl and shred. Stir back into sauce and serve over couscous.
Per Serving: Calories 355; Fat 10.88g; Sodium 1064mg; Carbs 33.93g; Fibre 4g; Sugar 11.34g; Protein 25.17g

Turkey Bolognese

Prep time: 10 minutes | Cook time: 11 minutes | Serves: 4

3 tablespoons olive oil
1 small onion, chopped
3 garlic cloves, minced

1 teaspoon dried basil
455g turkey mince
1 (700g) can crushed tomatoes

3 carrots, chopped
240ml water
120ml dry red wine

1. Add the olive oil, onion, garlic, and basil and sauté them at MD on SEAR/SAUTÉ mode for about 2 minutes or until the onion is translucent. 2. Stop the cooker, and add the turkey, tomatoes, carrots, water, and red wine to the pot. 3. Install the pressure lid and turn the pressure release valve to the SEAL position. 4. Select PRESSURE COOK, set the cooking temperature to HI and adjust the cooking time to 5 minutes. 5. When cooked, let the unit naturally release pressure. 6. Select SEAR/SAUTÉ and sauté them for 3 to 4 minute more to thicken the sauce. 7. You can refrigerate the leftover in an airtight container for up to 5 days or freeze for up to 6 months.
Per Serving: Calories 705; Fat 61.2g; Sodium 328mg; Carbs 14.21g; Fibre 5.7g; Sugar 8.29g; Protein 24.05g

Sun-Dried Tomato & Turkey Breast

Prep time: 5 minutes | Cook time: 25 minutes | Serves: 4

675g turkey breast tenderloin
½ teaspoon sea salt
½ teaspoon freshly ground black pepper

240ml water
15g dry-pack sun-dried tomatoes, sliced
45g chopped kalamata olives

2 tablespoons dried basil
1 tablespoon olive oil

1. Season the turkey with the salt and pepper. 2. In the cooking pot, combine the turkey, water, sun-dried tomatoes, olives, basil, and oil. 3. Install the pressure lid and turn the pressure release valve to the SEAL position. 4. Select PRESSURE COOK, set the cooking temperature to HI and adjust the cooking time to 25 minutes. 5. When cooked, let the unit naturally release pressure. 6. Remove the turkey breast and cut it into slices. 7. Serve the turkey with the juices spooned over it. 8. You can refrigerate the leftover in an airtight container for up to 5 days.
Per Serving: Calories 305; Fat 8.8g; Sodium 540mg; Carbs 2.36g; Fibre 0.8g; Sugar 0.01g; Protein 51.74g

Courgette Chicken

Prep time: 15 minutes | Cook time: 20 minutes | Serves: 3

8 boneless chicken thighs
1 tablespoon smoked paprika
1 tablespoon unsalted butter, divided
1 teaspoon olive oil
3 cloves garlic, minced

240g chicken stock
25g Parmesan, shaved
1 lemon, juiced
1 teaspoon dried thyme
15g baby spinach, chopped

250g courgette slices or spiralized noodles
Sea salt and freshly ground black pepper, to taste

1. Combine all ingredients to the cooking pot. 2. Install the pressure lid and turn the pressure release valve to the SEAL position. 3. Select PRESSURE COOK, set the cooking temperature to HI and adjust the cooking time to 20 minutes. 4. When cooked, let the unit naturally release pressure. 5. Remove the food and transfer to plates. 6. Season the dish with sea salt and black pepper. Serve immediately as a main course.
Per Serving: Calories 1381; Fat 90.8g; Sodium 1014mg; Carbs 41.6g; Fibre 1.9g; Sugar 1.3g; Protein 94.67g

Curry Chicken Breasts

Prep time: 10 minutes | Cook time: 40 minutes | Serves: 3

3 chicken breasts
½ yellow onion
½ teaspoon ground ginger
2 tablespoons garlic powder

2 teaspoons curry powder
2 teaspoons ground cumin
¼ teaspoon ground cloves
1 tablespoon apple cider vinegar

1 tablespoon lemon juice
240ml chicken stock

1. Dice the onion then add all of the ingredients in the pot and mix around to coat the chicken. 2. Turn the pot to the Meat/Stew setting, seal and cook for 40 minutes. 3. Manually release the pressure, then transfer chicken to a bowl and shred with a fork. 4. Stir the chicken back into the sauce before serving.
Per Serving: Calories 556; Fat 27.64g; Sodium 503mg; Carbs 11.32g; Fibre 2g; Sugar 3.51g; Protein 63g

Garlic Chicken Drumsticks

Prep time: 5 minutes | Cook time: 25 minutes | Serves: 4-6

8 chicken drumsticks
60ml water
1 teaspoon sesame oil

120ml dark soy sauce
2 tablespoons honey
2 tablespoons mirin

2 garlic cloves, minced
1 teaspoon fresh ginger, minced
½ sweet onion, chopped

1. Add the water to the cooking pot, place the Cook & Crisp Basket on top of diffuser and press down firmly, and then place in all of the ingredients. 2. Install the pressure lid and turn the pressure release valve to the VENT position. 3. Select STEAM and set the cooking time to 30 minutes. 4. When cooked, let the unit naturally release pressure. 5. Let chicken rest on KEEP WARM mode before opening the pot. 6. Transfer the drumsticks to a cookie sheet lined with parchment paper. 7. Grill the chicken drumsticks in the air fryer on High for 2 minutes on each side. 8. Transfer chicken to a platter and serve with leftover sauce from the cooker; you can serve the dish with salad.
Per Serving: Calories 330; Fat 16.79g; Sodium 952mg; Carbs 9.67g; Fibre 0.4g; Sugar 7.31g; Protein 33.6g

Bourbon Chicken

Prep time: 5 minutes | Cook time: 20 minutes | Serves: 4

4-5 boneless skinless chicken thighs
½ teaspoon garlic powder
240ml water

2 teaspoons ground chili paste
180g tomato sauce
170g honey

60ml bourbon
2 tablespoons potato starch
1 head broccoli, chopped

1. Combine the water, tomato sauce, honey, bourbon, chili paste, and garlic in the cooking pot. 2. Add the chicken and coat with the honey mixture well. 3. Install the pressure lid and turn the pressure release valve to the SEAL position. 4. Select PRESSURE COOK, set the cooking temperature to HI and adjust the cooking time to 10 minutes. 5. When cooked, let the unit naturally release pressure. 6. Remove some sauce and transfer to a glass measuring cup. Whisk in potato starch until dissolved. 7. Fold into the pot with chicken. 8. Place the reversible rack in the pot in the lower position and drop the lower rack through the reversible rack handles. 9. Arrange the broccoli onto the rack, and resume cooking them for 10 minutes more. 10. Serve and enjoy!
Per Serving: Calories 813; Fat 36.63g; Sodium 917mg; Carbs 79.07g; Fibre 7.9g; Sugar 41.78g; Protein 41.57g

Massaman Chicken Thighs

Prep time: 20 minutes | Cook time: 1 hour 10 minutes | Serves: 4

160g massaman curry paste
240ml unsweetened coconut milk, from a can
4 chicken thighs, diced into 2.5cm pieces
120ml Belgian wheat beer

120ml low sodium chicken stock
225g potato, chopped
65g onion, chopped
1 tablespoon tamarind paste
1½ tablespoons palm sugar

2-3 bay leaves
25g roast cardamom
30g roast peanuts, chopped, for garnish

1. Pour the coconut milk and massaman curry paste into the cooking pot. Mix them thoroughly. 2. Install the pressure lid and turn the pressure release valve to the VENT position. 3. Select STEAM, set the cooking time to 15 minutes. 4. When cooked, let the unit naturally release pressure. 5. Add the rest of the ingredients to the cooking pot and stir well to combine. 6. STEAM them for 60 minutes, stirring them after 25 minutes and 50 minutes of cooking time. 7. Chicken should fall apart with the touch of a fork and be very tender. 8. Top the dish with roast peanuts, and enjoy!
Per Serving: Calories 672; Fat 41.58g; Sodium 204mg; Carbs 35.92g; Fibre 12.6g; Sugar 6.51g; Protein 42.34g

Chicken Tacos

Prep time: 10 minutes | Cook time: 35 minutes | Serves: 4-6

4 boneless, skinless chicken thighs
1 tablespoon chili powder
1 tablespoon ground cumin
1 teaspoon smoked paprika
1 teaspoon dried oregano

1 teaspoon garlic powder
1 teaspoon sea salt
2 limes, juiced
240ml chicken stock
6 corn tortillas

Lettuce, shredded for serving
Guacamole, for serving
Sour cream, for serving
Hot sauce, for serving
Feta cheese, for serving

1. Add the water to the cooking pot, place the Cook & Crisp Basket on top of diffuser and press down firmly, and then add chicken, spices, chicken stock and lime juice to the cooking pot. 2. Install the pressure lid and turn the pressure release valve to the VENT position. 3. Select STEAM and set the cooking time to 25 minutes. 4. When cooked, let the unit naturally release pressure. 5. Remove chicken and shred meat off the bone by using a fork. Transfer chicken back to pot and cook for an additional 5 to 10 minutes. 6. Remove chicken and discard unused stock. 7. Top tortillas with guacamole, chicken, lettuce, sour cream, cheese and hot sauce to serve.
Per Serving: Calories 422; Fat 25.59g; Sodium 730mg; Carbs 14.93g; Fibre 2.6g; Sugar 0.97g; Protein 32.13g

Dijon Chicken with Mushrooms

Prep time: 15 minutes | Cook time: 1 hour 20 minutes | Serves: 4

6 boneless chicken thighs, with the fat trimmed off
1 teaspoon olive oil
For Marinade
1 teaspoon garlic powder
Pinch of nutmeg
80ml balsamic vinegar

2 shallots, minced
100g mushrooms, diced
190g farro

1 teaspoon olive oil
1 tablespoon Dijon mustard
Pinch of sea salt

360ml low-sodium chicken or vegetable stock

Pinch of ground black pepper

1. Add all marinade ingredients to a plastic, resealable bag. Add chicken, turning to make sure each thigh is well-coated with marinade; refrigerate until needed. 2. Add 1 teaspoon olive oil to the cooking pot. Add shallots, stirring to coat, then lock lid. 3. Cook them at LO on SEAR/SAUTÉ mode for 5 minutes until shallots have softened. 4. Open pressure cooker and add mushrooms and cook them for 8 minutes. 5. Stop the cooker, and stir in farro and stock. 6. Place the chicken on top of farro mixture; discard any remaining marinade. 7. Install the pressure lid and turn the pressure release valve to the SEAL position. 8. Select PRESSURE COOK, set the cooking temperature to HI and adjust the cooking time to 30 minutes. 9. When cooked, let the unit naturally release pressure. 10. A thermometer inserted in beef should read at least 75°C. 11. Transfer portions to plates and serve hot with your favorite side.
Per Serving: Calories 885; Fat 51.73g; Sodium 1002mg; Carbs 46.51g; Fibre 1.4g; Sugar 4.93g; Protein 55.32g

Tangy Chicken Breasts

Prep time: 5 minutes | Cook time: 20 minutes | Serves: 8

2 slices bacon
900g boneless, skinless chicken breasts
2 tablespoons apple cider vinegar
240ml water
1 tablespoon dried chives

1½ teaspoons garlic powder
1½ teaspoons onion powder
1 teaspoon crushed red pepper flakes
1 teaspoon dried dill
¼ teaspoon salt

¼ teaspoon black pepper
50g shredded cheddar
1 spring onion

1. Chop the bacon and scallion. 2. Cook the bacon in the cooking pot at MD on SEAR/SAUTÉ mode until browned. 3. Remove the bacon and stop the cooker. 4. Combine the chicken, water, vinegar, chives, garlic powder, onion powder, crushed red pepper flakes, dill, salt, and pepper in the pot. 5. Install the pressure lid and turn the pressure release valve to the SEAL position. 6. Select PRESSURE COOK, set the cooking temperature to HI and adjust the cooking time to 15 minutes. 7. When cooked, let the unit naturally release pressure. 8. Shred the chicken then return it to the pot and mix in the cheddar. 9. Top the chicken with bacon and chopped scallion before serving.
Per Serving: Calories 262; Fat 11.85g; Sodium 461mg; Carbs 24.65g; Fibre 1.9g; Sugar 6.26g; Protein 13.48g

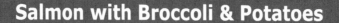

Salmon with Broccoli & Potatoes

Prep time: 25 minutes | Cook time: 5 minutes | Serves: 2-4

2 salmon fillets
Salt and ground black pepper to taste
Fresh herbs, optional

240ml water
455g new potatoes
90g broccoli, chopped

½ tablespoon butter

1. In a bowl, season the potatoes with salt, pepper and fresh herbs. 2. Add the water to the cooking pot, place the reversible rack in the pot in the lower position and drop the lower rack through the reversible rack handles. 3. Arrange the potatoes onto the rack. 4. Install the pressure lid and turn the pressure release valve to the SEAL position. 5. Select PRESSURE COOK, set the cooking temperature to HI and adjust the cooking time to 2 minutes. 6. When cooked, let the unit naturally release pressure. 7. In a bowl, season the broccoli and salmon with salt and pepper. 8. Place the broccoli and salmon on the steam rack along with the potatoes. 9. Resume cooking the food on PRESSURE COOK mode at HI for 2 minutes more. 10. Let the unit naturally release pressure. 11. Transfer the potatoes to a separate bowl and add the butter. Gently stir to coat the potatoes with the butter. 12. Serve the cooked fish with potatoes and broccoli.
Per Serving: Calories 309; Fat 8.61g; Sodium 143mg; Carbs 21.16g; Fibre 2.9g; Sugar 1.5g; Protein 35.44g

Pecan-Coated Salmon

Prep time: 15 minutes | Cook time: 10 minutes | Serves: 2-4

2 salmon fillets
120ml olive oil
½ teaspoon salt

30g flour
1 egg, beaten
30g pecans, finely chopped

240ml water

1. Season the fillets with salt. 2. Dip the fillets in the flour, then in whisked egg, then in pecans. 3. Heat the oil in the cooking pot at MD on SEAR/SAUTÉ mode; brown the fillets on both sides. 4. Remove the salmon from the pot, and place the reversible rack in the pot in the lower position and drop the lower rack through the reversible rack handles. 5. Pour in the water and place the fillets on the rack. Install the pressure lid and turn the pressure release valve to the SEAL position. 6. Select PRESSURE COOK, set the cooking temperature to HI and adjust the cooking time to 4 minutes. 7. When cooked, let the unit naturally release pressure. 8. Serve and enjoy.
Per Serving: Calories 544; Fat 40.94g; Sodium 437mg; Carbs 7.08g; Fibre 0.86g; Sugar 0.43g; Protein 36.21g

Salmon Fillets with Lemon Sauce

Prep time: 10 minutes | Cook time: 5 minutes | Serves: 2-4

455g salmon fillets
60ml olive oil
1 tablespoon red wine vinegar
1 clove garlic, minced

1 tablespoon lemon juice
¼ teaspoon dried oregano
Salt and ground black pepper to taste
1 tablespoon feta cheese, crumbled

240ml water
2 slices lemon
2 sprigs fresh rosemary

1. Combine the olive oil, vinegar, garlic, lemon juice, oregano, salt, pepper, and cheese in a bowl. 2. Add the water to the cooking pot, place the reversible rack in the pot in the lower position and drop the lower rack through the reversible rack handles. 3. Arrange the salmon onto the rack, pour the mixture over the salmon fillets and top with the lemon slices and rosemary. 4. Install the pressure lid and turn the pressure release valve to the SEAL position. 5. Select PRESSURE COOK, set the cooking temperature to HI and adjust the cooking time to 5 minutes. 6. When cooked, let the unit naturally release pressure. 7. Serve the salmon with the sauce.
Per Serving: Calories 317; Fat 22.54g; Sodium 556mg; Carbs 3.63g; Fibre 0.3g; Sugar 1.57g; Protein 24.4g

Salmon with Mayonnaise Sauce

Prep time: 10 minutes | Cook time: 15 minutes | Serves: 4-6

900g salmon fillet
120g mayonnaise
1 tablespoon lemon juice

4 cloves garlic, minced
1 teaspoon dry basil leaves
Salt and ground pepper to taste

2 tablespoon olive oil
Green onion, chopped

1. In a bowl, combine the mayonnaise, lemon juice, garlic, and basil. 2. Season the salmon with salt and pepper. 3. Heat the oil in the cooking pot at MD on SEAR/SAUTÉ mode; add the fillets and brown on both sides for 10 minutes; add the mayonnaise mixture to the pot and coat the fillets and cook for 5 minutes more, flip the salmon from time to time. 4. Transfer to a serving plate and top with chopped green onion.
Per Serving: Calories 346; Fat 21.79g; Sodium 812mg; Carbs 2.89g; Fibre 0.6g; Sugar 1.1g; Protein 32.81g

Poached Salmon with Skin

Prep time: 15 minutes | Cook time: 5 minutes | Serves: 2-4

2 salmon fillets with skin
Salt and ground black pepper to taste
480ml chicken stock

120ml dry white wine
1 teaspoon lemon zest
10g fresh dill

½ teaspoon fennel seeds
4 spring onions , chopped
1 bay leaf

1. Add the stock and wine to the cooking pot, place the reversible rack in the pot in the lower position and drop the lower rack through the reversible rack handles. 2. Arrange the salmon fillets onto the rack. Sprinkle the fish with lemon zest, fresh dill, fennel seeds, and spring onions . Add the bay leaf. 3. Install the pressure lid and turn the pressure release valve to the SEAL position. 4. Select PRESSURE COOK, set the cooking temperature to HI and adjust the cooking time to 5 minutes. 5. When cooked, let the unit naturally release pressure. 6. Serve the salmon fillets with sauce.
Per Serving: Calories 272; Fat 10.79g; Sodium 730mg; Carbs 3.27g; Fibre 0.7g; Sugar 1.13g; Protein 38.58g

Sockeye Salmon

Prep time: 15 minutes | Cook time: 15 minutes | Serves: 4

4 wild sockeye salmon fillets
2 tablespoon assorted chili pepper

seasoning
Salt and ground black pepper to taste

60ml lemon juice
240ml water

1. Season the salmon fillets with chili pepper, salt, pepper, and lemon juice. 2. Add the water to the cooking pot, place the reversible rack in the pot in the lower position and drop the lower rack through the reversible rack handles. 3. Arrange the fillets onto the rack. 4. Install the pressure lid and turn the pressure release valve to the SEAL position. 5. Select PRESSURE COOK, set the cooking temperature to HI and adjust the cooking time to 5 minutes. 6. When cooked, let the unit naturally release pressure. 7. Serve warm.
Per Serving: Calories 579; Fat 22.32g; Sodium 447mg; Carbs 4.25g; Fibre 0.6g; Sugar 2.11g; Protein 85.12g

Canned Tuna Casserole

Prep time: 10 minutes | Cook time: 5 minutes | Serves: 4

100g canned tuna, drained
720ml water
700ml cream of mushroom soup

500g egg noodles
150g peas, frozen
Salt and ground black pepper to taste

100g cheddar cheese, grated
25g breadcrumbs, optional

1. In the cooking pot, combine the water and mushroom soup. 2. Add the egg noodles, tuna, peas, salt and pepper, and stir them well. 3. Install the pressure lid and turn the pressure release valve to the SEAL position. 4. Select PRESSURE COOK, set the cooking temperature to HI and adjust the cooking time to 4 minutes. 5. When cooked, let the unit naturally release pressure. 6. Sprinkle with cheese and breadcrumbs, close the lid and let it sit for 5 minutes. 7. Serve.
Per Serving: Calories 419; Fat 11.64g; Sodium 1254mg; Carbs 47.52g; Fibre 2.5g; Sugar 3.7g; Protein 31.28g

Tuna with Egg & Dried Onion

Prep time: 10 minutes | Cook time: 15 minutes | Serves: 4

2 cans tuna, drained
2 carrots, peeled and chopped
150g frozen peas
40g diced onions

2 eggs, beaten
1 can cream of celery soup
120ml water
180ml milk

2 tablespoon butter
Salt and ground black pepper to taste

1. In the cooking pot, combine all of the ingredients. 2. Install the pressure lid and turn the pressure release valve to the SEAL position. 3. Select PRESSURE COOK, set the cooking temperature to HI and adjust the cooking time to 15 minutes. 4. When cooked, let the unit naturally release pressure. 5. Serve.
Per Serving: Calories 264; Fat 13.71g; Sodium 693mg; Carbs 13.24g; Fibre 2.5g; Sugar 3.5g; Protein 22.63g

Tasty Prawns with Parsley

Prep time: 10 minutes | Cook time: 5 minutes | Serves: 4-6

900g prawns
2 tablespoon butter
1 tablespoon garlic, minced

1 tablespoon lemon juice
120ml white wine
120ml chicken stock

Salt and ground black pepper to taste
1 tablespoon parsley for garnish

1. Add the butter, garlic, and lemon juice to the cooking pot. 2. Pour in the stock and wine, stir well. 3. Add the prawns and season with salt and pepper, stir well again. 4. Install the pressure lid and turn the pressure release valve to the SEAL position. 5. Select PRESSURE COOK, set the cooking temperature to HI and adjust the cooking time to 3 minutes. 6. When cooked, let the unit naturally release pressure. 7. Top the dish with parsley and serve.
Per Serving: Calories 177; Fat 4.88g; Sodium 241mg; Carbs 2.32g; Fibre 0.2g; Sugar 1g; Protein 31.3g

Prawns and Asparagus

Prep time: 8 minutes | Cook time: 2 minutes | Serves: 2

455g prawns , frozen or fresh, peeled and deveined
240ml water

150g asparagus
1 teaspoon olive oil
½ tablespoon Cajun seasoning (or your

choice of seasoning)

1. Add the water to the cooking pot, place the reversible rack in the pot in the lower position and drop the lower rack through the reversible rack handles. 2. Arrange the asparagus onto the rack. 3. Install the pressure lid and turn the pressure release valve to the VENT position. 4. Select STEAM and adjust the cooking time to 2 minutes. 5. When cooked, let the unit naturally release pressure. 6. Serve.
Per Serving: Calories 237; Fat 3.51g; Sodium 429mg; Carbs 4.55g; Fibre 2.1g; Sugar 1.83g; Protein 47.55g

Onion Prawns Risotto

Prep time: 15 minutes | Cook time: 25 minutes | Serves: 4-6

455g peeled and cleaned prawns
4 tablespoon butter
2 cloves garlic, minced
1 yellow onion, chopped

270g Arborio rice
2 tablespoon dry white wine
1.1L chicken stock
Salt and ground black pepper to taste

75g parmesan cheese
10g fresh herbs

1. Melt 2 tablespoons of butter in the cooking pot at MD on SEAR/SAUTÉ mode; add garlic and onion and sauté them for 4 minutes; add the rice, stir and cook for 1 minute more; pour in the wine, stir them and cook for about 3 minutes or until much of the wine has evaporated. 2. Stop the process, and pour in 720ml of stock. Season them with salt and pepper. 3. Install the pressure lid and turn the pressure release valve to the SEAL position. 4. Select PRESSURE COOK, set the cooking temperature to HI and adjust the cooking time to 9 minutes. 5. When cooked, let the unit naturally release pressure. 6. Add the prawns with the remaining stock to the pot, and cook the food at MD on SEAR/SAUTÉ mode for 4 to 5 minutes more or until the prawns have become bright pink and solid; add cheese and 2 tablespoons of butter, stir well. 7. Top the dish with fresh herbs and serve.
Per Serving: Calories 348; Fat 19.52g; Sodium 1529mg; Carbs 23.8g; Fibre 6.9g; Sugar 1.98g; Protein 27.46g

Curry Prawns

Prep time: 10 minutes | Cook time: 5 minutes | Serves: 2-4

455g prawns , peeled and deveined
480ml water

200ml unsweetened coconut milk
1 tablespoon garlic, minced

1 teaspoon curry powder
Salt and ground black pepper to taste

1. In a large bowl, combine the prawns , coconut milk, garlic, and curry powder. Season them with salt and pepper. 2. Transfer the mixture to a suitable pan. 3. Add the water to the cooking pot, place the reversible rack in the pot in the lower position and drop the lower rack through the reversible rack handles. 4. Arrange the pan onto the rack. 5. Install the pressure lid and turn the pressure release valve to the SEAL position. 6. Select PRESSURE COOK, set the cooking temperature to HI and adjust the cooking time to 4 minutes. 7. When cooked, let the unit naturally release pressure. 8. Stir the curry and serve.
Per Serving: Calories 113; Fat 0.79g; Sodium 198mg; Carbs 3.45g; Fibre 1.1g; Sugar 1.52g; Protein 23.47g

Mussels Fra Diavolo

Prep time: 15 minutes | Cook time: 5 minutes | Serves: 2

150g linguine
1 tablespoon oil, plus more for the pasta
½ large onion, chopped
3 garlic cloves, minced
2 tablespoons red pepper flakes
To Serve
Lime wedges

120ml dry white wine
1 (350g) can fire-roasted crushed tomatoes
with their juices
100ml canned clam juice
Salt

Crusty bread

Freshly ground black pepper
455g fresh mussels, rinsed, scrubbed, and
debearded
10g fresh chopped basil

1. Cook the pasta according to package directions. Drain and toss with some oil. 2. Sort through the mussels and discard any that aren't fully closed or have broken shells. 3. Heat 1 tablespoon of oil in the cooking pot at MD on SEAR/SAUTÉ mode; add onion and sauté for 2 minutes until softened; add garlic and red pepper flakes and sauté them for 1 minute until fragrant. 4. Pour in the wine and deglaze the pot, scraping up the browned bits from the bottom. Cook them for 1 to 2 minutes, or until the wine is reduced by half. 5. Add the tomatoes and their juices and the clam juice and stir well. Season them with salt and pepper. Let the mixture simmer briefly, and then stir in the mussels. 6. Stop the process, and install the pressure lid and turn the pressure release valve to the SEAL position. 7. Select PRESSURE COOK, set the cooking temperature to HI and adjust the cooking time to 3 minutes. 8. When cooked, turn the pressure release valve to the VENT position to quick release the steam. 9. Stir in the chopped basil. Season the dish with more salt and pepper as desired. 10. Portion the pasta into bowls and immediately ladle the mussels and sauce on top. Serve the dish with lime wedges and crusty bread.
Per Serving: Calories 580; Fat 19.3g; Sodium 2121mg; Carbs 60.94g; Fibre 2.6g; Sugar 10.75g; Protein 40.82g

Sausage Seafood Gumbo

Prep time: 30 minutes | Cook time: 5 minutes | Serves: 2

3 tablespoons oil, divided
225g andouille sausage, cut into 1.5cm
slices
1 small onion, diced
1 celery stalk, diced
150g diced green pepper
3 garlic cloves, minced
2 tablespoons butter
To Serve
Cooked white rice

3 tablespoons plain flour
720ml chicken stock
2 tablespoons tomato paste
1 tablespoon Cajun seasoning, plus more
for seasoning (optional)
¼ teaspoon cayenne pepper, plus more for
seasoning (optional)
Salt

Chopped spring onions

Freshly ground black pepper
1 medium tomato, diced
225g raw medium prawns , tail-on, peeled
and deveined
115g crabmeat, picked over
Gumbo filé powder (optional)

1. Heat 2 tablespoons of oil in the cooking pot at MD on SEAR/SAUTÉ mode; add the sausage, onion, celery, and pepper and sauté them for 6 to 8 minutes until browned; add the garlic and cook for 1 minute. 2. Transfer the mixture to a plate and set aside. 3. Add the remaining 1 tablespoon of oil and the butter to the pot to melt. Sprinkle in the flour and whisk to combine. Cook them for 12 to 15 minutes, whisking constantly to avoid burning, until the roux is a medium to dark brown (the darker the roux, the more intense the flavour). 4. Stop the process, and stir in the sausage mixture, stock, tomato paste, Cajun seasoning, and cayenne pepper. Season them with salt and black pepper to taste, and add the tomato. 5. Install the pressure lid and turn the pressure release valve to the SEAL position. 6. Select PRESSURE COOK, set the cooking temperature to HI and adjust the cooking time to 4 minutes. 7. When cooked, turn the pressure release valve to the VENT position to quick release the steam. 8. Select SEAR/SAUTÉ again, season the food with seasonings, adding more cayenne pepper or Cajun seasoning if needed; stir in the prawns , sprinkle the crabmeat loosely on the top, and cook them at MD for 4 to 5 minutes or until the prawns are pink; add gumbo filé powder (optional). 9. Serve the dish with white rice and a sprinkle of spring onions.
Per Serving: Calories 1328; Fat 57.22g; Sodium 3553mg; Carbs 139.55g; Fibre 21g; Sugar 9.41g; Protein 71.82g

Onion Prawns Cajun

Prep time: 10 minutes | Cook time: 7 minutes | Serves: 2-4

455g frozen jumbo prawns , peeled and deveined
2 teaspoon olive oil
2 cloves garlic, minced
1 medium onion, chopped

2 stalks celery, diced
1 pepper, diced
1 tablespoon tomato paste
1 can (700g) crushed tomatoes
1 bay leaf

1 teaspoon thyme
1 teaspoon salt
½ teaspoon pepper
¼ teaspoon cayenne pepper

1. Heat the oil in the cooking pot at MD on SEAR/SAUTÉ mode; add garlic, onion, celery, and pepper, and sauté the veggies for 3 to 4 minutes; add the tomato paste and cook for 1 minute more, stirring occasionally. 2. Stop the process, and add the prawns , tomatoes, bay leaf, thyme, salt, pepper, and cayenne pepper; stir them well. 3. Install the pressure lid and turn the pressure release valve to the SEAL position. 4. Select PRESSURE COOK, set the cooking temperature to HI and adjust the cooking time to 2 minutes. 5. When cooked, let the unit naturally release pressure. 6. Serve with cooked rice.
Per Serving: Calories 195; Fat 5.7g; Sodium 1150mg; Carbs 27.02g; Fibre 6.5g; Sugar 9.98g; Protein 11.42g

Onion Prawns Paella

Prep time: 10 minutes | Cook time: 5 minutes | Serves: 2

2 tablespoons oil
½ onion, chopped
2 garlic cloves, minced
Salt
Freshly ground black pepper
To Serve
Chopped fresh coriander

1 teaspoon paprika
¼ teaspoon red pepper flakes
Pinch saffron threads
60ml white wine
100g basmati rice

Lime wedges

1 (350g) can diced tomatoes and chilies, with their juices
120ml chicken stock
225g peel-on large raw prawns , deveined

1. Heat the oil in the cooking pot at MD on SEAR/SAUTÉ mode; add the onion and sauté for 3 minutes until softened; add the garlic and cook for 1 minute; season them with salt and pepper, and then stir in the paprika, red pepper flakes, and saffron. 2. Stop the process, and pour in wine and deglaze the pot, scraping up the browned bits from the bottom; stir in the rice, and then add the tomatoes and chilies and their juices, and the stock. 3. Stir them and make sure all the rice is covered. 4. Install the pressure lid and turn the pressure release valve to the SEAL position. 5. Select PRESSURE COOK, set the cooking temperature to HI and adjust the cooking time to 5 minutes. 6. When cooked, let the unit naturally release pressure. 7. Select SEAR/SAUTÉ, stir the prawns into the rice, loosely cover the pot and cook the food for 3 to 5 minutes. 8. Serve the dish with chopped fresh coriander and lime wedges.
Per Serving: Calories 313; Fat 21.43g; Sodium 414mg; Carbs 34.14g; Fibre 12.4g; Sugar 10.43g; Protein 8.9g

Easy Prawns Scampi

Prep time: 10 minutes | Cook time: 10 minutes | Serves: 2

150g linguine
1 tablespoon oil
1 tablespoon butter
1 shallot, chopped
1 tablespoon minced garlic
To Serve
Chopped parsley

Pinch red pepper flakes, plus more for seasoning (optional)
60ml white wine
60ml chicken stock
1 tablespoon freshly squeezed lemon juice

Crusty bread

340g thawed frozen raw jumbo prawns , tails removed, peeled and deveined
Salt
Freshly ground black pepper

1. Cook the pasta according to package directions while you cook everything else in the pressure cooker. Drain the pasta but do not rinse, transfer to a serving bowl, cover, and set aside. 2. Heat the oil and butter in the cooking pot at MD on SEAR/SAUTÉ mode; add the shallot, garlic, and red pepper flakes and sauté them for 2 minutes; pour in the wine and deglaze, scraping up the browned bits from the bottom using a wooden spoon and stirring them into the liquid. 3. Let the liquid cook for 1 minute to reduce by half. 4. Stop the process, and add the stock, lemon juice, and prawns to the pot. 5. Install the pressure lid and turn the pressure release valve to the SEAL position. 6. Select PRESSURE COOK, set the cooking temperature to HI and adjust the cooking time to 1 minute. 7. When cooked, turn the pressure release valve to the VENT position to quick release the steam. 8. Season the food with salt, pepper, and additional red pepper flakes (if desired) and stir in the parsley. Pour into the serving bowl with the pasta and toss. Serve with slices of crusty bread.
Per Serving: Calories 525; Fat 20.06g; Sodium 506mg; Carbs 76.5g; Fibre 2.3g; Sugar 37.57g; Protein 12.68g

Fish in Orange Sauce

Prep time: 15 minutes | Cook time: 7 minutes | Serves: 4

4 pieces white fish fillets
4 spring onions, chopped
2 teaspoon ginger, grated

1 orange for juice and zest
1 teaspoon orange zest
240ml white wine or fish stock

2 tablespoon olive oil
Salt and ground black pepper to taste

1. Rub the fish fillets with the olive oil and season with salt and pepper. 2. In the cooking pot, combine the ginger, orange juice, orange zest, and wine. 3. Add the water to the cooking pot, place the reversible rack in the pot in the lower position and drop the lower rack through the reversible rack handles. 4. Arrange the fish fillets onto the rack. 5. Install the pressure lid and turn the pressure release valve to the SEAL position. 6. Select PRESSURE COOK, set the cooking temperature to HI and adjust the cooking time to 7 minutes. 7. When cooked, let the unit naturally release pressure. 8. Pour the sauce over the fish fillets and serve.
Per Serving: Calories 352; Fat 23.76g; Sodium 380mg; Carbs 7.41g; Fibre 0.6g; Sugar 4.98g; Protein 26.18g

Flavourful Cioppino

Prep time: 15 minutes | Cook time: 10 minutes | Serves: 2

2 tablespoons butter
1 tablespoon oil
1 shallot, thinly sliced
½ small fennel bulb, thinly sliced
2 garlic cloves, minced
½ teaspoon red pepper flakes, plus more for seasoning (optional)
To Serve
Chopped fresh parsley

½ teaspoon dried oregano
Pinch salt
1 (350g) can diced tomatoes with their juices
180ml canned clam juice
240ml white wine
Freshly ground black pepper

Lemon wedges

225g mussels, rinsed, scrubbed, and debearded
225g manila clams, scrubbed
225g flaky white fish, such as cod or flounder
225g medium prawns , tail-on, peeled and deveined

Toasted crusty bread slices

1. Melt the butter in the cooking pot at MD on SEAR/SAUTÉ mode; add shallot and fennel and sauté for 2 minutes until softened; add the garlic, ½ teaspoon of red pepper flakes, the oregano, and a pinch of salt and cook for 1 minute. 2. Stop the process, and stir in the tomatoes and their juices, the clam juice, and wine; season them with salt and pepper. 3. Install the pressure lid and turn the pressure release valve to the SEAL position. 4. Select PRESSURE COOK, set the cooking temperature to HI and adjust the cooking time to 10 minutes. 5. When cooked, let the unit naturally release pressure. 6. Select SEAR/SAUTÉ again, add the mussels and clams to the pot and cook them at MD for 5 to 6 minutes until the clams and mussels begin to open; add the fish and prawns and simmer them at LO for 3 to 4 minutes. 7. Discard any mussels or clams that do not open. Taste and season with salt and more red pepper flakes (if desired). 8. Divide the cioppino between two large bowls and serve with a sprinkling of chopped parsley, lemon wedges, and toasted crusty bread.
Per Serving: Calories 633; Fat 24.01g; Sodium 2519mg; Carbs 72.73g; Fibre 6.3g; Sugar 35.8g; Protein 36.63g

Bacon Clam Chowder

Prep time: 25 minutes | Cook time: 5 minutes | Serves: 2

4 uncooked bacon slices, chopped
2 tablespoons butter
1 small onion, diced
1 garlic clove, minced
60ml white wine
240ml clam juice

240ml chicken stock or water
1 large Russet potato, cubed
2 thyme sprigs or ¼ teaspoon dried thyme
½ teaspoon red pepper flakes (optional)
Salt
Freshly ground black or white pepper

1 tablespoon cornflour
675g fresh clams in the shell
240g heavy cream
120ml whole milk

1. Cook the bacon in the cooking pot at MD on SEAR/SAUTÉ mode for 5 minutes or until barely crispy. 2. Transfer the bacon to a paper towel–lined plate to drain. Do not wipe out the pot. 3. Melt the butter in the bacon grease in the pot; add the onion and garlic and sauté them for 3 to 4 minutes until softened. 4. Add the wine and deglaze the pot, scraping up the browned bits from the bottom. Let the liquid reduce by half. 5. Stop the process, add the clam juice, stock, potato, thyme, and red pepper flakes (optional) and season them with salt and pepper; stir them well. 6. Install the pressure lid and turn the pressure release valve to the SEAL position. 7. Select PRESSURE COOK, set the cooking temperature to HI and adjust the cooking time to 5 minutes. 8. When cooked, let the unit naturally release pressure. 9. Remove the thyme sprigs. Using a potato masher, carefully mash some or all of the potato cubes. 10. In a small bowl, whisk 2 tablespoons of the chowder with the cornflour until dissolved. 11. Select SEAR/SAUTÉ again, and stir the cornflour mixture back into the pot, along with the clams, cream, and milk; simmer the mixture at LO for 5 minutes. 12. Serve warm.
Per Serving: Calories 899; Fat 57.53g; Sodium 1472mg; Carbs 82g; Fibre 4.7g; Sugar 20.79g; Protein 16.97g

Lobster Tails with Lemon-Butter Sauce

Prep time: 5 minutes | Cook time: 3 minutes | Serves: 2

240ml Chicken Stock or water
1 teaspoon Old Bay seasoning
2 (about 455g) fresh Maine lobster tails

Juice of 1 lemon, divided
115g butter, melted
½ tablespoon minced garlic

½ lemon, cut into wedges

1. Add the stock and Old Bay to the cooking pot, place the reversible rack in the pot in the lower position and drop the lower rack through the reversible rack handles. 2. Arrange the lobster tail onto the rack with shell-side down. Drizzle half of the lemon juice over the lobster. 3. Install the pressure lid and turn the pressure release valve to the SEAL position. 4. Select PRESSURE COOK, set the cooking temperature to HI and adjust the cooking time to 3 minutes. 5. When cooked, turn the pressure release valve to the VENT position to quick release the steam. 6. Fill a large bowl with ice water. Using tongs, immediately transfer the lobster tails to the ice bath to avoid overcooking. Let chill for 1 to 2 minutes. 7. In a small bowl, whisk together the butter, the remaining lemon juice, and the garlic. 8. Transfer the lobster tails to a dish towel-covered cutting board. 9. Butterfly the lobster tail using kitchen shears or a large knife: with the meat side of the tail up, cut the underside of the tail down the centre. 10. Serve with the lemon wedges and the lemon-butter sauce for dipping.
Per Serving: Calories 534; Fat 47.28g; Sodium 1003mg; Carbs 3.45g; Fibre 0.2g; Sugar 0.96g; Protein 25.55g

Coconut Curry Seafood

Prep time: 10 minutes | Cook time: 5 minutes | Serves: 2

2 teaspoons oil
5 to 6 curry leaves or kaffir lime leaves, plus more for garnish
½ onion, sliced
1 green chili (preferably serrano or jalapeño), stemmed, seeded, and sliced
To Serve
Cooked jasmine rice

2 garlic cloves, minced
½ tablespoon grated peeled fresh ginger
2 tablespoons curry powder
240ml unsweetened coconut milk
105g cherry tomatoes
10g chopped fresh coriander

Lime wedges

225g fresh or thawed frozen tilapia fillets, cut into bite-size pieces
Salt
1 tablespoon freshly squeezed lime juice
115g raw medium prawns , peeled and deveined

Unsweetened shredded coconut

1. Heat the oil in the cooking pot at MD on SEAR/SAUTÉ mode; add the curry leaves and sauté for 1 minute, then add the onion, chili, garlic, and ginger and sauté them for 30 seconds until softened. 2. Stir in the curry powder and sauté for 30 seconds; add the coconut milk and mix well, deglazing the pot and scraping up any browned bits from the bottom. Simmer them for 30 to 60 seconds. 3. Stop the process, and add the tomatoes, coriander, and tilapia pieces. Stir gently to coat the fish. 4. Install the pressure lid and turn the pressure release valve to the SEAL position. 5. Select PRESSURE COOK, set the cooking temperature to HI and adjust the cooking time to 3 minutes. 6. When cooked, let the unit naturally release pressure. 7. Season with salt and add the lime juice. Stir in the prawns and loosely cover the pot with the lid, allowing the prawns to cook in the residual heat for 3 to 4 minutes, or until pink. 8. Serve in bowls with cooked jasmine rice, lime wedges, and shredded coconut, garnished with more curry leaves.
Per Serving: Calories 1052; Fat 15.82g; Sodium 592mg; Carbs 208.72g; Fibre 8.9g; Sugar 99.29g; Protein 21.13g

Spiced Prawns Scampi

Prep time: 10 minutes | Cook time: 5 minutes | Serves: 2-4

455g prawns, peeled and deveined
2 tablespoon olive oil
1 clove garlic, minced
80g tomato paste

250g canned tomatoes, chopped
80ml water
¼ teaspoon oregano, dried
1 tablespoon parsley, finely chopped

½ teaspoon salt
½ teaspoon ground black pepper to taste
100g parmesan, grated

1. Heat the oil in the cooking pot at MD on SEAR/SAUTÉ mode; add the garlic and sauté for 1 minute. 2. Stop the cooker, and add the prawns , tomato paste, tomatoes, water, oregano, parsley, salt and pepper; stir them well. 3. Install the pressure lid and turn the pressure release valve to the SEAL position. 4. Select PRESSURE COOK, set the cooking temperature to HI and adjust the cooking time to 3minutes. 5. When cooked, let the unit naturally release pressure. 6. Sprinkle with parmesan and serve.
Per Serving: Calories 263; Fat 8.63g; Sodium 752mg; Carbs 15.47g; Fibre 2.4g; Sugar 5.07g; Protein 32.49g

Mango Fish Tacos

Prep time: 15 minutes | Cook time: 8 minutes | Serves: 2

For Mango Salsa
165g mango, diced
35g red onion, diced

For Fish
1 teaspoon salt, divided
½ teaspoon ground cumin
½ teaspoon paprika

To Serve
Warmed flour or corn tortillas
Shredded red cabbage

½ avocado, chopped
1 jalapeño pepper, stemmed, seeded and

½ teaspoon garlic powder
¼ teaspoon cayenne pepper
300g flaky white fish (cod, snapper, or

Chopped fresh coriander
Lime wedges

diced
1 tablespoon lime juice

mahi-mahi), cut into fingers
Juice of ½ lime, divided

1. Combine the mango, onion, avocado, jalapeño, and lime juice in a small bowl; cover the bowl and refrigerate the mixture. 2. Mix ½ teaspoon of salt, the cumin, paprika, garlic powder, and cayenne pepper together in another small bowl. 3. Cut two oblong pieces of parchment paper, set them over the top of the pressure cooker, and fold both so there is about 2.5cm of room on either side of the cooker. Transfer to a work surface. 4. Place half of the fish on one side of a piece of the parchment paper. Drizzle some of the lime juice on the fish, and then rub on the seasoning mix. 5. Fold the parchment packet closed and wrap in a large piece of aluminum foil. Repeat the process with the remaining fish to create another packet. 6. Add 240ml of water to the cooking pot, place the reversible rack in the pot in the lower position and drop the lower rack through the reversible rack handles. 7. Arrange the packets onto the rack. 8. Install the pressure lid and turn the pressure release valve to the SEAL position. 9. Select PRESSURE COOK, set the cooking temperature to HI and adjust the cooking time to 8 minutes. 10. When cooked, turn the pressure release valve to the VENT position to quick release the steam. 11. Transfer the packets to a work surface, open them carefully, and remove the fish from the packets and put in a medium bowl. Flake the fish with a fork and toss with the remaining lime juice. 12. Serve wrapped in warmed flour or corn tortillas with the mango salsa, shredded cabbage, coriander, and lime wedges.

Per Serving: Calories 343; Fat 9.46g; Sodium 1708mg; Carbs 38.13g; Fibre 8.1g; Sugar 15.72g; Protein 30.66g

Mushroom Tuna Casserole

Prep time: 15 minutes | Cook time: 5 minutes | Serves: 2

2 teaspoons butter, plus more for greasing
1 shallot, chopped
1 celery stalk, chopped
50g sliced cremini mushrooms
1 garlic clove, minced
240ml Chicken Stock

360ml water
240g egg noodles
Salt
Freshly ground black pepper
2 tablespoons heavy cream
1 tablespoon Dijon mustard

1 tablespoon freshly squeezed lemon juice
1 (125g) can tuna, drained and broken up
50g shredded Cheddar cheese
55g panko bread crumbs
4 lemon wedges

1. Melt 2 teaspoons of butter in the cooking pot at MD on SEAR/SAUTÉ mode; add the shallot, celery, and mushrooms and sauté them for 3 minutes until softened; add the garlic and sauté for 1 minute. 2. Stop the process, add the stock, water, and noodles, and season them with salt and pepper. 3. Install the pressure lid and turn the pressure release valve to the SEAL position. 4. Select PRESSURE COOK, set the cooking temperature to HI and adjust the cooking time to 2 minutes. 5. When cooked, turn the pressure release valve to the VENT position to quick release the steam. 6. Carefully pour the contents of the cooker pot into a colander or fine-mesh strainer to drain the excess liquid, and then return the solids to the pot. 7. Stir in the cream, mustard, lemon juice, and tuna and season with salt and pepper. Top them with the shredded cheese and the panko. 8. Press FUNCTION and turn the dial to select BAKE/ROAST. 9. Press TEMP and turn the dial to adjust the cooking temperature to 160°C (325°F), press TIME and turn the dial to set the cooking time to 15 minutes, and then press START/STOP to begin cooking. 10. Serve the dish with the lemon wedges.

Per Serving: Calories 1129; Fat 31.7g; Sodium 2881mg; Carbs 45.2g; Fibre 2.7g; Sugar 5.26g; Protein 169.38g

Cod & Vegetables

Prep time: 5 minutes | Cook time: 5 minutes | Serves: 2

2 (150g) cod fillets
Salt
Freshly ground black pepper
2 tablespoons melted butter
To Serve
Cooked rice or couscous

2 tablespoons freshly squeezed lemon
juice, divided
1 garlic clove, minced
150g cherry tomatoes

Lemon wedges

1 courgette or yellow summer squash, cut
into thick slices
90g whole Brussels sprouts
2 thyme sprigs or ½ teaspoon dried thyme

1. Season the fish with salt and pepper. 2. In a small bowl, combine the butter, 1 tablespoon of the lemon juice, and the garlic. Set aside. 3. Add 120ml of water to the pressure cooker pot, place the reversible rack in the pot in the lower position and drop the lower rack through the reversible rack handles. 4. Arrange the tomatoes onto the rack, and then add the courgette and Brussels sprouts; season them with salt and pepper, then drizzle with the remaining 1 tablespoon of lemon juice. 5. Place the fish fillets on the vegetables, brush them with garlic-lemon butter, then flip the fish fillets and repeat on the other side. 6. Drizzle any remaining butter over the vegetables. Top with the thyme sprigs. 7. Install the pressure lid and turn the pressure release valve to the SEAL position. 8. Select PRESSURE COOK, set the cooking temperature to HI and adjust the cooking time to 4 minutes. 9. When cooked, turn the pressure release valve to the VENT position to quick release the steam. 10. Serve the vegetables topped with the fish, and pair them with cooked rice or couscous and lemon wedges.
Per Serving: Calories 514; Fat 27.39g; Sodium 620mg; Carbs 44.76g; Fibre 9.9g; Sugar 12.15g; Protein 25.46g

Poached Red Snapper

Prep time: 5 minutes | Cook time: 5 minutes | Serves: 2

2 (150g) snapper fillets
1 teaspoon salt
To Serve
Cooked rice or quinoa
Steamed vegetables

½ teaspoon freshly ground black pepper
380g fresh salsa

Salsa
Chopped fresh coriander

60ml pale lager beer or water
½ lime

Lime wedges

1. Season the fish with the salt and pepper. 2. Add the salsa and beer to the pot, place the reversible rack in the pot in the lower position and drop the lower rack through the reversible rack handles. 3. Arrange the fish onto the rack. Squeeze the juice from the lime over the fish and salsa. 4. Install the pressure lid and turn the pressure release valve to the SEAL position. 5. Select PRESSURE COOK, set the cooking temperature to HI and adjust the cooking time to 4 minutes. 6. When cooked, turn the pressure release valve to the VENT position to quick release the steam. 7. Serve the poached snapper over rice, quinoa, or steamed vegetables. Top the dish with more salsa and chopped coriander and serve with lime wedges.
Per Serving: Calories 422; Fat 5.48g; Sodium 2962mg; Carbs 41.49g; Fibre 7.2g; Sugar 13.06g; Protein 53.31g

Tiger Prawns with Sausage Slices

Prep time: 15 minutes | Cook time: 15 minutes | Serves: 2-4

240g tiger prawns, peeled and deveined
1 tablespoon olive oil
1 small red onion, roughly chopped
1 red pepper, chopped
2 chorizo sausage slices

135g risotto rice or paella rice
480g vegetable stock (or chicken stock)
110g green peas, frozen
165g sweet corn
1 tablespoon fresh parsley, finely chopped

1 teaspoon salt
A pinch of saffron threads
1 whole lemon, quartered

1. Heat the oil in the cooking pot at MD on SEAR/SAUTÉ mode; add the onion and chorizo slices, and sauté them for 3 minutes; add the tiger prawns and cook for 2 to 3 minutes more, stirring occasionally; add the rice and stock, and stir them well. 2. Stop the process, and add the peas, sweet corn, and parsley; season them with salt and saffron. 3. Install the pressure lid and turn the pressure release valve to the SEAL position. 4. Select PRESSURE COOK, set the cooking temperature to HI and adjust the cooking time to 7 minutes. 5. When cooked, let the unit naturally release pressure. 6. Place the lemon on top. Close the lid and let sit for 10 minutes. Serve.
Per Serving: Calories 231; Fat 11.47g; Sodium 1429mg; Carbs 32.82g; Fibre 8.1g; Sugar 5.87g; Protein 9.59g

Honey Salmon Salad

Prep time: 10 minutes | Cook time: 5 minutes | Serves: 2

60ml sesame oil
60ml soy sauce
60ml lime juice
2 tablespoons honey
2 tablespoons fish sauce
To Serve
Fresh salad greens
Shredded red cabbage
Shredded carrots

1 tablespoon sesame seeds
1 teaspoon grated peeled fresh ginger
1 teaspoon minced garlic
Grated zest of 1 lime
1 spring onion, chopped, plus more for

Sliced green pepper
Shelled edamame
Mandarin orange sections

serving
2 (100g-150g) skinless or skin-on salmon fillets
2 teaspoons cornflour

Slivered almonds

1. In a gallon-size zip-top bag, combine the sesame oil, soy sauce, lime juice, honey, fish sauce, sesame seeds, ginger, garlic, lime zest, scallion, and salmon. 2. Seal the bag and shake gently. Let the fish marinate in the refrigerator for 1 to 2 hours. 3. Remove the salmon from the marinade and transfer to a plate. 4. Pour the marinade in the cooking pot, and simmer at LO on SEAR/SAUTÉ mode. 5. Stop the process, add the salmon and spoon the marinade over the salmon. 6. Install the pressure lid and turn the pressure release valve to the SEAL position. 7. Select PRESSURE COOK, set the cooking temperature to HI and adjust the cooking time to 4 minutes. 8. When cooked, turn the pressure release valve to the VENT position to quick release the steam. 9. Gently transfer the fish to a clean plate. Remove the skin if necessary. Transfer 2 teaspoons of the warm teriyaki liquid from the pot to a small bowl. 10. Whisk in the cornflour, and then pour it back into the pot. 11. Select SEAR/SAUTÉ again and let the liquid simmer at LO for 8 to 10 minutes or until reduced to a glaze-like consistency, stirring frequently. 12. To serve, toss salad greens with shredded cabbage and carrots, sliced pepper, edamame, mandarin orange sections, and slivered almonds and divide between two plates. 13. Top each with a salmon fillet. 14. Brush or spoon the teriyaki sauce over the fish and salad.
Per Serving: Calories 1121; Fat 64.73g; Sodium 2973mg; Carbs 47.96g; Fibre 4.5g; Sugar 33.74g; Protein 91.85g

Fish Curry

Prep time: 20 minutes | Cook time: 10 minutes | Serves: 4

675g fish fillets, cut into 5cm pieces
2 tablespoon olive oil
4 cloves garlic, minced
2 medium onions, chopped
2 teaspoon fresh ginger, grated finely

½ teaspoon ground turmeric
1 teaspoon red chili powder
2 teaspoon ground cumin
2 teaspoon ground coriander
2 tablespoon curry powder

480ml unsweetened coconut milk
150g tomatoes, chopped
2 Serrano peppers, seeded and chopped
Salt to taste
1 tablespoon fresh lemon juice

1. Heat the oil in the cooking pot at MD on SEAR/SAUTÉ mode; add the garlic, onion, and ginger and sauté for 4 minutes; add the turmeric, chili powder, cumin, coriander, and curry, and cook them for 1 minute more. 2. Stop the process, and add the fish, tomatoes, and Serrano pepper; season them with salt and stir them well. 3. Install the pressure lid and turn the pressure release valve to the SEAL position. 4. Select PRESSURE COOK, set the cooking temperature to LO and adjust the cooking time to 5 minutes. 5. When cooked, let the unit naturally release pressure. 6. Drizzle the dish with the lemon juice and serve.
Per Serving: Calories 582; Fat 32.6g; Sodium 1024mg; Carbs 45.74g; Fibre .6g; Sugar 9.91g; Protein 30.76g

Coriander-Braised Pork

Prep time: 40 minutes | Cook time: 40 minutes/5 hours | Serves: 4-6

3 tablespoons extra-virgin olive oil, plus more to serve
1 medium yellow onion, halved and thinly sliced
3 tablespoons ground coriander

240ml dry red wine
1.3kg boneless pork shoulder, trimmed and cut into 2.5cm chunks
Salt and ground black pepper
6 bay leaves

1 tablespoon cornflour
3 tablespoons minced fresh oregano
1 tablespoon lemon juice
50g feta cheese, crumbled
10g finely chopped fresh flat-leaf parsley

1. Heat the oil in the cooking pot at HI on SEAR/SAUTÉ mode until simmering; add the onion and sauté for 7 minutes; add the coriander and sauté for 1 minute until fragrant; pour in the wine and cook for 2 to 3 minutes until most of the moisture has evaporated. 2. Stop the process, and add the pork, 1 teaspoon salt, ½ teaspoon pepper and the bay; stir to combine, then distribute in an even layer. 3. Install the pressure lid and turn the pressure release valve to the SEAL position. 4. Select PRESSURE COOK, set the cooking temperature to HI and adjust the cooking time to 25 minutes. 5. When cooked, let the unit naturally release pressure. 6. If you want to cook them slowly, with the cooker still on SEAR/SAUTÉ mode, bring the mixture to a boil, and then cook them at HI on SLOW COOK mode for 4 to 5 hours. 7. The pork is done when a skewer inserted into a piece meets no resistance. 8. Transfer the pork to a medium bowl. Skim off and discard the fat from the surface of the cooking liquid. 9. Remove and discard the bay leaves. 10. Select SEAR/SAUTÉ again, and bring the liquid to a boil at HI; cook them for 10 minutes until the liquid is reduced to about 240ml (or 1cm depth in the pot). 11. In a small bowl, whisk the cornflour and 2 tablespoons of water, and then stir into the pot. 12. Cook them for 1 minute until lightly thickened, stirring constantly. 13. Stop the cooler and stir in the pork, oregano and lemon juice. 14. Taste and season the dish with salt and pepper. 15. Transfer the dish to a serving dish and sprinkle with feta and parsley, then drizzle with additional oil.
Per Serving: Calories 341; Fat 9.93g; Sodium 282mg; Carbs 5.32g; Fibre 1.4g; Sugar 1.37g; Protein 53.25g

Glazed Baby Back Ribs

Prep time: 25 minutes | Cook time: 35 minutes/9 hours | Serves: 4-6

240ml hoisin sauce
170g honey
1 tablespoon Chinese five-spice powder
5 tablespoons gochujang, divided

2 tablespoons minced fresh ginger
1kg-1.3kg racks baby back pork ribs, each cut in half if pressure cooking or cut into 3 or 4-rib sections if slow cooking

2 tablespoons finely chopped fresh coriander
2 tablespoons sesame seeds, toasted
3 spring onions , thinly sliced

1. In a large bowl, whisk together the hoisin, honey, five-spice powder and 2 tablespoons gochujang. 2. Measure ¾ cup of the mixture into a small bowl and stir in the remaining 3 tablespoons gochujang and the ginger; set aside at room temperature if pressure cooking or cover and refrigerate if slow cooking. 3. Add the rib sections to the remaining hoisin mixture in the large bowl and turn to coat. 4. Add 240ml of water to the cooking pot, place the reversible rack in the pot in the lower position and drop the lower rack through the reversible rack handles. 5. Arrange the ribs upright in a circle onto the rack with the meaty sides facing the walls of the pot. 6. Install the pressure lid and turn the pressure release valve to the SEAL position. 7. Select PRESSURE COOK, set the cooking temperature to HI and adjust the cooking time to 25 minutes. 8. When cooked, let the unit naturally release pressure. 9. Let cool for 5 minutes. 9. If you want to cook them slowly, bring the water to a boil at HI on SEAR/SAUTÉ mode. Stop the process and cook them at HI on SLOW COOK mode for 8 to 9 hours; the ribs are done when a skewer inserted into the meat between the bones meets no resistance. Let cool for 5 minutes. 10. While the ribs cool, heat the grill with a rack about 15 cm from the element. 11. Line a rimmed baking sheet with foil. Carefully transfer the ribs meat side up to the prepared baking sheet. 12. Generously brush with half of the reserved hoisin mixture and grill until the glaze begins to bubble, 2 to 3 minutes. 13. Remove from the grill, brush with the remaining mixture and continue to grill until bubbling, another 2 to 3 minutes. Cool for 5 minutes, and then cut between the bones to separate into individual ribs. 14. Transfer the dish to a platter, and then sprinkle with the coriander, sesame seeds and spring onions .
Per Serving: Calories 310; Fat 5.78g; Sodium 737mg; Carbs 43.47g; Fibre 1.8g; Sugar 35.08g; Protein 22.07g

Mojo Pork

Prep time: 30 minutes | Cook time: 50 minutes/6 hours | Serves: 4

1 tablespoon ground cumin
1 tablespoon smoked paprika
1 teaspoon dried oregano
Salt and ground black pepper
900g boneless pork butt, trimmed and cut into 2.5cm chunks

1 tablespoon grapeseed or other neutral oil
1 large yellow onion, finely chopped
8 medium garlic cloves, finely chopped
2 chipotle chilies in adobo sauce, minced, plus 2 tablespoons adobo sauce
1 teaspoon grated orange zest, plus 300ml

orange juice, divided
1 teaspoon grated lime zest, plus 3 tablespoons lime juice
30g finely chopped fresh coriander

1. In a medium bowl, stir together the cumin, paprika, oregano, 1 teaspoon salt and ½ teaspoon pepper. 2. Add the pork and toss until evenly coated; set aside. Heat the oil in the cooking pot at HI on SEAR/SAUTÉ mode until simmering; add the onion and sauté for 3 minutes until softened; stir in the garlic and cook until fragrant, about 30 seconds, then stir in the chipotle chilies and adobo sauce. 3. Stop the process, and add the pork and 240ml of the orange juice; stir to combine, then distribute in an even layer. 4. Install the pressure lid and turn the pressure release valve to the SEAL position. 5. Select PRESSURE COOK, set the cooking temperature to HI and adjust the cooking time to 25 minutes. 6. When cooked, let the unit naturally release pressure. 7. If you want to cook them slowly, bring the mixture to a boil at HI on SEAR/SAUTÉ mode. Stop the process and cook them at HI on SLOW COOK mode for 5 to 6 hours. 8. Transfer the pork to a medium bowl. Let cool for about 5 minutes, then use two forks to shred the meat into bite-size pieces. 9. Skim off and discard the fat from the surface of the cooking liquid. 10. Select SEAR/SAUTÉ again, and bring the liquid at HI; cook them for 15 minutes until reduced to 180ml; stir in the remaining 60ml orange juice, the lime juice and the coriander. 11. Stop the cooker, add the pork and both zests, and then stir for 2 to 3 minutes until the pork is heated through. 12. Taste and season the dish with salt and pepper.
Per Serving: Calories 726; Fat 46.6g; Sodium 206mg; Carbs 15.37g; Fibre 2g; Sugar 7.56g; Protein 58.9g

Beef Stroganoff

Prep time: 25 minutes | Cook time: 20 minutes | Serves: 8

900g beef mince
1½ teaspoon salt
1 teaspoon pepper
1 tablespoon butter
225g sliced fresh mushrooms

2 medium onions, chopped
2 garlic cloves, minced
1 can condensed beef consommé, undiluted
40g plain flour

2 tablespoon tomato paste
360g sour cream
Hot cooked noodles

1. Add half of beef mince, salt and pepper to the cooking pot, and sauté them for 6 to 8 minutes until no longer pink, crumbling meat. 2. Remove meat; drain any liquid from pressure cooker. Repeat with remaining beef mince, salt and pepper. 3. Add butter, mushrooms and onions to the pot, and sauté them for 6 to 8 minutes until onions are tender and mushrooms have released their liquid and are beginning to brown; add garlic and sauté for 1 minute. 4. Stop the process and place the meat back in the pot. 5. Install the pressure lid and turn the pressure release valve to the SEAL position. 6. Select PRESSURE COOK, set the cooking temperature to HI and adjust the cooking time to 5 minutes. 7. When cooked, let the unit naturally release pressure. 8. In a small bowl, whisk together consommé, flour and tomato paste. 9. Select SEAR/SAUTÉ again, pour the flour mixture over the food in the pot and stir them to combine, and then sauté them at MD until thickened; stir in sour cream and cook the food until heated through. 10. Serve the dish with noodles.
Per Serving: Calories 435; Fat 20.79g; Sodium 625mg; Carbs 18.09g; Fibre 1.2g; Sugar 2.62g; Protein 42.27g

BBQ Beef Ribs

Prep time: 15 minutes | Cook time: 45 minutes | Serves: 8

2 tablespoons rapeseed oil
1.7kg bone-in beef short ribs, trimmed
1 large sweet onion, halved and sliced
120ml water

1 bottle (300g) chili sauce
235g plum preserves or preserves of your choice
2 tablespoons packed brown sugar

2 tablespoons red wine vinegar
2 tablespoons Worcestershire sauce
2 tablespoons Dijon mustard
¼ teaspoon ground cloves

1. Heat the oil in the cooking pot at MD on SEAR/SAUTÉ mode; brown the ribs in batches, adding additional oil as needed, and transfer the ribs to a plate. 2. Brown the onions at the same settings. 3. Stop the cooker, add the ribs back to the pot and then pour in water. 4. Install the pressure lid and turn the pressure release valve to the SEAL position. 5. Select PRESSURE COOK, set the cooking temperature to HI and adjust the cooking time to 40 minutes. 6. When cooked, let the unit naturally release pressure. 7. In a small saucepan, combine remaining ingredients; cook and stir over medium heat until heated through. 8. Remove ribs from pressure cooker; discard cooking juices. 9. Return ribs to pressure cooker. Pour sauce over top. 10. Cook them at LO on PRESSURE COOK for 5 minutes. 11. When cooked, let the unit naturally release pressure. 12. Serve ribs with sauce.
Per Serving: Calories 521; Fat 28.09g; Sodium 846mg; Carbs 20.92g; Fibre 3.3g; Sugar 14.38g; Protein 45.59g

Pork Chunks with Pickled Red Onions

Prep time: 35 minutes | Cook time: 5 minutes | Serves: 4-6

2 tablespoons grapeseed or other neutral oil
1 large yellow onion, halved and thinly sliced
10 medium garlic cloves, smashed and
For Pickled Red Onions
240ml white vinegar
2 teaspoons white sugar
Salt

peeled
1.3kg boneless pork shoulder, untrimmed, cut into 2.5cm chunks
2 tablespoons ground cumin
2 tablespoons ground coriander

2 medium red onions, halved and thinly sliced
1 jalapeño chili, stemmed, halved

2 teaspoons dried oregano
½ teaspoon dried thyme
1 teaspoon red pepper flakes
Salt and ground black pepper

lengthwise and seeded

1. Heat the oil in the cooking pot at HI on SEAR/SAUTÉ mode until simmering; add the onion and sauté for 3 minutes until softened; stir in the garlic and sauté for 30 seconds until fragrant. 2. Add the pork, cumin, coriander, oregano, thyme, pepper flakes and 1 teaspoon salt and 240ml water; stir to combine, then distribute in an even layer. 3. Stop the cooker, and install the pressure lid and turn the pressure release valve to the SEAL position. 4. Select PRESSURE COOK, set the cooking temperature to HI and adjust the cooking time to 25 minutes. 5. When cooked, let the unit naturally release pressure. 6. If you want to cook them slowly, with the cooker still on SEAR/SAUTÉ mode, bring the mixture to a boil, and then cook them at HI on SLOW COOK mode for 5 to 6 hours. 7. Transfer the meat to a large bowl and cool for 5 minutes. 8. Shred the meat into bite-size pieces. 9. Skim off the fat from the surface of the cooking liquid. 10. Select SEAR/SAUTÉ again, and bring the liquid to a boil; cook the food for 10 to 15 minutes until reduced to about 240ml. 11. Stop the process, add the pork and stir for 2 minutes more. 12. Taste and season the dish with salt and pepper. 13. To make the pickled red onions, stir together the vinegar, sugar and 2 teaspoons salt in a medium bowl until dissolved. Stir in the onions and jalapeño. 14. Cover the bowl and refrigerate for at least 1 hour or up to 24 hours.
Per Serving: Calories 691; Fat 45.2g; Sodium 166mg; Carbs 8.06g; Fibre 1.2g; Sugar 3.06g; Protein 58.19g

Bacon & Beef Flank Steak

Prep time: 25 minutes | Cook time: 20 minutes | Serves: 8

6 bacon strips, chopped
2 beef flank steak (455g each), cut in half
1 can (700g) crushed tomatoes
480ml beef stock
1 can (150g) tomato paste

5 garlic cloves, minced
1 tablespoon ground cumin
2 teaspoon dried thyme
¾ teaspoon salt
½ teaspoon pepper

1 medium onion, thinly sliced
1 medium sweet pepper, sliced
1 medium green pepper, sliced
10g minced fresh coriander
Hot cooked rice

1. Sauté the bacon at HI on SEAR/SAUTÉ mode until crispy; remove bacon and drain on paper towels. 2. Still in the cooking pot, brown the steak in batches. 3. In a large bowl, combine tomatoes, beef stock, tomato paste, garlic, seasonings, onions and peppers; pour the mixture over the meat. 4. Stop the cooker, and install the pressure lid and turn the pressure release valve to the SEAL position. 5. Select PRESSURE COOK, set the cooking temperature to HI and adjust the cooking time to 12 minutes. 6. When cooked, let the unit naturally release pressure. 7. Shred beef with two forks; return to pressure cooker. Stir in coriander. Remove with a slotted spoon; serve the dish with rice.
Per Serving: Calories 198; Fat 9.45g; Sodium 589mg; Carbs 19.95g; Fibre 7.2g; Sugar 7.58g; Protein 14.85g

Barbecue Pork Ribs

Prep time: 10 minutes | Cook time: 30 minutes | Serves: 6

1 rack pork ribs (approximately 1.5kg), cut into 2-rib sections

360g gluten-free barbecue sauce, divided
240ml water

1. In a medium bowl, toss ribs with 180g barbecue sauce. Refrigerate ribs covered at least 30 minutes or up to overnight. 2. Add the water to the cooking pot, place the reversible rack in the pot in the lower position and drop the lower rack through the reversible rack handles. 3. Arrange the ribs standing upright onto the rack with the meaty-side facing outward toward the pot walls. 4. Install the pressure lid and turn the pressure release valve to the SEAL position. 5. Select PRESSURE COOK, set the cooking temperature to HI and adjust the cooking time to 30 minutes. 6. When cooked, let the unit naturally release pressure. 7. Transfer ribs to a serving dish and serve warm with remaining barbecue sauce for dipping.
Per Serving: Calories 110; Fat 1.87g; Sodium 2783mg; Carbs 11.2g; Fibre 0.1g; Sugar 10.15g; Protein 11.09g

Sweet Onion Beef Carnitas

Prep time: 40 minutes | Cook time: 40 minutes | Serves: 16

2 tablespoons salt
2 tablespoons packed brown sugar
1 tablespoon ground cumin
1 tablespoon smoked paprika
1 tablespoon chili powder
1 teaspoon garlic powder
1 teaspoon ground mustard

1 teaspoon dried oregano
1 teaspoon cayenne pepper
1 (1.3kg) boneless beef chuck roast
3 tablespoons rapeseed oil
2 large sweet onion, thinly sliced
3 poblano pepper, seeded and thinly sliced
2 chipotle peppers in adobo sauce, finely

chopped
1 jar (400g) salsa
16 flour tortillas (20cm), warmed
300g shredded Monterey Jack cheese
Optional toppings: cubed avocado, sour
cream and minced fresh coriander

1. Mix the salt, brown sugar, cumin, paprika, chili powder, garlic powder, ground mustard, dried oregano and cayenne pepper in a bowl. 2. Cut roast in half; rub with 2 tbsp spice mixture. Cover remaining mixture and store in a cool dry place. 3. Heat the oil in the cooking pot at HI on SEAR/SAUTÉ mode; brown the roast on all sides. 4. Stop the process, and place the onions and peppers on meat, and then top them with salsa. 5. Install the pressure lid and turn the pressure release valve to the SEAL position. 6. Select PRESSURE COOK, set the cooking temperature to HI and adjust the cooking time to 40 minutes. 7. When cooked, let the unit naturally release pressure. 8. Remove roast; shred with two forks. Skim fat from cooking juices. Return meat to pressure cooker; heat through. 9. Place meat mixture on each tortilla. Sprinkle the dish with cheese and add toppings of your choice.
Per Serving: Calories 335; Fat 14.44g; Sodium 1655mg; Carbs 32.92g; Fibre 2.8g; Sugar 7.09g; Protein 19.32g

Thai Beef Chuck

Prep time: 30 minutes | Cook time: 40 minutes | Serves: 10

1 boneless beef chuck roast (1.3kg) halved
1 teaspoon salt
1 teaspoon pepper
2 tablespoons rapeseed oil
1 large sweet red pepper, sliced
1 can (340ml) coconut milk

180ml beef stock
125g creamy peanut butter
60g red curry paste
2 tablespoons soy sauce
2 tablespoons honey
2 teaspoons minced fresh gingerroot

225g fresh sugar snap peas, trimmed
10g minced fresh coriander
Hot cooked brown or white rice
Optional toppings: thinly sliced green
onions, chopped unsalted peanuts, hot
sauce and lime wedges

1. Sprinkle beef with salt and pepper. 2. Heat the oil in the cooking pot at MD on SEAR/SAUTÉ mode; add one roast half and brown it for 5 minutes on all sides. Do the same with the remaining beef. 3. Combine the remaining ingredients except for rice and toppings in a bowl. 4. Place the cooked beef roast halves back in the pot and add the red pepper; pour the honey mixture in the bowl over them. 5. Install the pressure lid and turn the pressure release valve to the SEAL position. 6. Select PRESSURE COOK, set the cooking temperature to HI and adjust the cooking time to 40 minutes. 7. After 35 minutes of cooking time, add the sugar snap peas to the pot. 8. When cooked, let the unit naturally release pressure. 9. Remove beef; cool slightly. Skim fat from cooking juices. Shred beef with two forks. Stir in coriander. 10. Serve the dish with rice and toppings of your choice. 11. Place cooled meat mixture in freezer containers. To use, partially thaw in refrigerator overnight. Cover and microwave the food on high in a microwave-safe dish until heated through, gently stirring and adding a little stock or water if necessary.
Per Serving: Calories 411; Fat 22.53g; Sodium 517mg; Carbs 13.08g; Fibre 3.8g; Sugar 7.53g; Protein 41.64g

French Sandwiches

Prep time: 20 minutes | Cook time: 60 minutes | Serves: 10

1 boneless beef chuck roast (about 1.3kg)
1 teaspoon dried oregano
1 teaspoon dried rosemary, crushed

½ teaspoon seasoned salt
¼ teaspoon pepper
720ml beef stock

1 bay leaf
1 garlic clove, peeled
French bread, sliced

1. Add stock, bay leaf and garlic to the cooking pot, place the reversible rack in the pot in the lower position and drop the lower rack through the reversible rack handles. 2. Arrange the roast onto the rack. 3. Install the pressure lid and turn the pressure release valve to the SEAL position. 4. Select PRESSURE COOK, set the cooking temperature to HI and adjust the cooking time to 75 minutes. 5. When cooked, let the unit naturally release pressure. 6. Remove beef; shred with two forks. Discard bay leaf and garlic from stock. Serve shredded beef on French bread with stock for dipping.
Per Serving: Calories 185; Fat 8.48g; Sodium 434mg; Carbs 8.96g; Fibre 0.8g; Sugar 1.39g; Protein 18.62g

Special Sausage-Stuffed Flank Steak

Prep time: 40 minutes | Cook time: 15 minutes | Serves: 4

180ml dry red wine or beef stock, divided
40g dried cherries, coarsely chopped
1 beef flank steak (675g)
½ teaspoon salt
½ teaspoon pepper, divided

3 tablespoon olive oil, divided
1 medium onion, finely chopped
4 garlic cloves, minced
50g seasoned bread crumbs
45g pitted Greek olives, coarsely chopped

25g grated Parmesan cheese
10g minced fresh basil
225g bulk hot Italian sausage
1 jar (600g) marinara sauce
Hot cooked noodles

1. Combine 60ml wine with cherries; let stand for 10 minutes. 2. Cut steak into four serving-size pieces; pound with a meat mallet to ½ cm. thickness. 3. Using ½ teaspoon salt and ¼ teaspoon pepper, season the steak on both sides. 4. Heat 1 tablespoon of oil in the cooking pot at MD on SEAR/SAUTÉ mode; add and sauté the onion until tender; add garlic and cook for 1 minute; transfer the food to a large owl, and then stir in bread crumbs, olives, cheese, basil, cherry mixture and remaining pepper. 5. Crumble sausage over bread crumb mixture; mix them well. 6. Divide the sausage mixture into four portions; spread evenly over each steak piece. Roll up steaks jelly-roll style, starting with a long side; tie with kitchen string. 7. Heat the remaining oil in the cooking pot at HI on SEAR/SAUTÉ mode; brown meat on all sides. 8. Pour in the marinara sauce and remaining wine. 9. Install the pressure lid and turn the pressure release valve to the SEAL position. 10. Select PRESSURE COOK, set the cooking temperature to HI and adjust the cooking time to 15 minutes. 11. When cooked, let the unit naturally release pressure. 12. Serve the dish with pasta.
Per Serving: Calories 523; Fat 28.09g; Sodium 1860mg; Carbs 43.45g; Fibre 12.25g; Sugar 6g; Protein 27.21g

Beef Short Ribs

Prep time: 30 minutes | Cook time: 50 minutes | Serves: 6

1.3kg bone-in beef short ribs
½ teaspoon salt
½ teaspoon pepper
1 tablespoon rapeseed oil
2 large onions, cut into 1cm wedges

6 garlic cloves, minced
1 tablespoon tomato paste
240ml beef stock
480ml dry red wine or beef stock
4 fresh thyme sprigs

1 bay leaf
4 medium carrots, cut into 2.5cm pieces
4 teaspoons cornflour
3 tablespoons cold water
Additional salt and pepper, optional

1. Sprinkle the ribs with salt and pepper. 2. Heat the oil in the cooking pot at HI on SEAR/SAUTÉ mode; brown the ribs on all sides and brown them in batches, then transfer them to a plate. 3. Add onions to the pot and sauté them for 8 to 9 minutes until tender; add the garlic and tomato paste, and sauté them for 1 minute; stir in beef stock, wine, thyme and bay leaf, and bring to a boil, and then cook for 8 to 10 minutes until liquid is reduced by half. 4. Stop the process, and add ribs back to cooker, partially but not fully submerging them. 5. Install the pressure lid and turn the pressure release valve to the SEAL position. 6. Select PRESSURE COOK, set the cooking temperature to HI and adjust the cooking time to 40 minutes. 7. When cooked, let the unit naturally release pressure. 8. Add the carrots to the pot and resume cooking the food at the same settings for 7 minutes. 9. Remove ribs and vegetables; keep warm. Skim fat from cooking liquid. Discard thyme and bay leaf. 10. Select SEAR/SAUTÉ again, and bring the cooking juices to a boil at HI. 11. In a small bowl, mix cornflour and water until smooth; stir into juices. 12. Return to a boil; cook and stir for 1 to 2 minutes until thickened. If desired, sprinkle with the additional salt and pepper. 13. Serve and enjoy.
Per Serving: Calories 529; Fat 31.77g; Sodium 718mg; Carbs 15.64g; Fibre 3.2g; Sugar 5.83g; Protein 46.79g

Mexican Flank Steak in Beef Stock

Prep time: 10 minutes | Cook time: 40 minutes | Serves: 8

60ml lime juice
1 tablespoon apple cider vinegar
2 tablespoons honey
1 teaspoon ground cumin

1 teaspoon salt
2 teaspoons sriracha
3 cloves garlic, peeled and minced
20g chopped fresh coriander

3 tablespoons olive oil, divided
900g flank steak, trimmed
360ml beef stock

1. In a small bowl, combine lime juice, apple cider vinegar, honey, cumin, salt, sriracha, garlic, coriander, and 2 tablespoons of olive oil. Spread mixture on all sides of steak. Refrigerate steak covered 30 minutes. 2. Heat the oil in the cooking pot at HI for 30 seconds on SEAR/SAUTÉ mode; add steak and sear for 5 minutes, making sure to brown each side. 3. Stop the process, and add the beef stock to the pot. 4. Install the pressure lid and turn the pressure release valve to the SEAL position. 5. Select PRESSURE COOK, set the cooking temperature to HI and adjust the cooking time to 35 minutes. 6. When cooked, let the unit naturally release pressure. 7. Transfer meat to a cutting board and let rest 5 minutes. Thinly slice beef against the grain and serve.
Per Serving: Calories 239; Fat 10.86g; Sodium 422mg; Carbs 9.48g; Fibre 0.2g; Sugar 4.53g; Protein 24.78g

Perfect Pepper Steak

Prep time: 15 minutes | Cook time: 60 minutes | Serves: 12

1 beef top round roast (1.3kg)
240ml water, divided
120ml reduced-sodium soy sauce
4 garlic cloves, minced

1 large onion, halved and sliced
1 large green pepper, cut into 1 cm strips
1 large sweet red pepper, cut into 1 cm. strips

40g cornflour
2 teaspoon sugar
2 teaspoon ground ginger
1.6kg hot cooked brown rice

1. In the cooking pot, combine roast, 120ml water, soy sauce and garlic. 2. Install the pressure lid and turn the pressure release valve to the SEAL position. 3. Select PRESSURE COOK, set the cooking temperature to HI and adjust the cooking time to 60 minutes. 4. When cooked, turn the pressure release valve to the VENT position to quick release the steam. 5. Add the onion and peppers, and then resume cooking them at the same settings for 2 minutes longer. 6. When cooked, turn the pressure release valve to the VENT position to quick release the steam. 7. Transfer beef to a cutting board. 8. In a small bowl, mix cornflour, sugar, ginger and remaining water until smooth. 9. Select SEAR/SAUTÉ mode, and bring the liquid to a boil at HI; gradually stir the sugar mixture into vegetable mixture. Cook and stir them for 1 to 2 minutes until sauce is thickened. 10. Cut the beef into slices. Stir gently into sauce; heat through. Serve with rice. 11. Freeze cooled beef mixture in freezer containers. 12. To use, partially thaw in refrigerator overnight. Heat through in a saucepan, stirring occasionally and adding a little water if necessary.
Per Serving: Calories 319; Fat 4.98g; Sodium 455mg; Carbs 36.96g; Fibre 3.1g; Sugar 2.23g; Protein 31.51g

Rubbed Pork Ribs

Prep time: 10 minutes | Cook time: 30 minutes | Serves: 6

1 teaspoon salt
1 teaspoon ground black pepper
1 teaspoon garlic powder
1 teaspoon onion powder

½ teaspoon cayenne pepper
2 teaspoons chili powder
1 tablespoon smoked paprika
2 tablespoons light brown sugar

1 rack pork ribs (approximately 1.5kg), cut into 2-rib sections
240ml water

1 In a small bowl, combine salt, pepper, garlic powder, onion powder, cayenne pepper, chili powder, smoked paprika, and brown sugar. 2. Massage mixture into rib sections. Refrigerate ribs covered at least 30 minutes or up to overnight. 3. Add the water to the cooking pot, place the reversible rack in the pot in the lower position and drop the lower rack through the reversible rack handles. 4. Arrange the ribs standing upright onto the rack with the meaty-side facing outward toward the pot walls. 5. Install the pressure lid and turn the pressure release valve to the SEAL position. 6. Select PRESSURE COOK, set the cooking temperature to HI and adjust the cooking time to 30 minutes. 7. When cooked, let the unit naturally release pressure. 8. Transfer ribs to a serving dish and serve warm.
Per Serving: Calories 60; Fat 2.18g; Sodium 438mg; Carbs 3.13g; Fibre 1g; Sugar 1.21g; Protein 7.29g

Pork Loin with Creamed Spinach & Tomatoes

Prep time: 10 minutes | Cook time: 17 minutes | Serves: 2

For Pork Loin
1 teaspoon salt
1 teaspoon ground black pepper
1 teaspoon Italian seasoning

2 tablespoons plain gluten-free flour
1 tablespoon grated Parmesan cheese
2 (150g) boneless pork loin chops

1 tablespoon rapeseed oil
240ml water

For Creamed Spinach and Tomatoes
75g cherry tomatoes
80g heavy cream

120g baby spinach
⅛ teaspoon salt

⅛ teaspoon ground black pepper

1. Combine salt, pepper, Italian seasoning, flour, and cheese in a small bowl. Coat pork chops in mixture. Set aside. 2. Heat the oil in the cooking pot at MD on SEAR/SAUTÉ mode for 30 seconds; add pork chops to pot and sear 2 minutes on each side. Remove pork from pot and set aside. 3. Add the water to the cooking pot, place the reversible rack in the pot in the lower position and drop the lower rack through the reversible rack handles. 4. Arrange the pork chops onto the rack. 5. Install the pressure lid and turn the pressure release valve to the SEAL position. 6. Select PRESSURE COOK, set the cooking temperature to HI and adjust the cooking time to 6 minutes. 7. When cooked, let the unit naturally release pressure. 8. Remove the racks with pork chops from the pot. 9. Pour out water in pot, add the tomatoes and sauté for 5 minutes at HI on SEAR/SAUTÉ mode; add heavy cream, spinach, salt, and pepper, and cook for an additional 2 minutes until spinach is wilted. 10. Transfer the mixture to two plates and place pork chops on top. Serve warm.
Per Serving: Calories 499; Fat 29.05g; Sodium 1779mg; Carbs 12.56g; Fibre 2.3g; Sugar 2.37g; Protein 45.88g

Beef in Beer

Prep time: 15 minutes | Cook time: 70 minutes | Serves: 6

1 fresh beef brisket (1.3kg)
2 teaspoons liquid smoke, optional
1 teaspoon celery salt
½ teaspoon pepper

¼ teaspoon salt
1 large onion, sliced
1 can (300ml) beer or nonalcoholic beer
2 teaspoons Worcestershire sauce

2 tablespoons cornflour
60ml cold water

1. Cut brisket in half; rub with liquid smoke, if desired, along with celery salt, pepper and salt. 2. Place brisket fatty side up in the cooking pot. Top the meat with onion. Combine beer and Worcestershire sauce and pour over the meat. 3. Install the pressure lid and turn the pressure release valve to the SEAL position. 4. Select PRESSURE COOK, set the cooking temperature to HI and adjust the cooking time to 70 minutes. 5. When cooked, let the unit naturally release pressure. 6. Remove brisket; cover with foil and keep warm. Strain cooking juices; return juices to the pot. 7. In a small bowl, mix cornflour and water until smooth. 8. Select SEAR/SAUTÉ, and bring the liquid to a boil at HI; gradually stir the cornflour into the cooking juices, stir them for 2 minutes until the sauce is thickened. 9. Serve and enjoy.
Per Serving: Calories 527; Fat 35.06g; Sodium 2958mg; Carbs 8.02g; Fibre 0.5g; Sugar 1.54g; Protein 35.06g

Homemade Boeuf Bourguignon

Prep time: 30 minutes | Cook time: 30 minutes | Serves: 12

1.3kg beef stew meat
420ml dry red wine
3 tablespoons olive oil
3 tablespoons dried minced onion
2 tablespoons dried parsley flakes
1 bay leaf

1 teaspoon dried thyme
¼ teaspoon pepper
8 bacon strips, chopped
455g whole fresh mushrooms, quartered
24 pearl onions, peeled
2 garlic cloves, minced

40g plain flour
1 teaspoon salt
Hot cooked whole wheat egg noodles,
optional

1. Place beef in a large resealable plastic bag; add wine, oil and seasonings. Seal bag and turn to coat. Refrigerate the meat overnight. 2. Sauté the bacon in the cooking pot at HI on SEAR/SAUTÉ mode until crispy. 3. Remove the meat with a slotted spoon; drain on paper towels. Discard drippings, reserving 1 tablespoon in pressure cooker. 4. Add mushrooms and onions to drippings; cook and sauté until tender. Add garlic and sauté for 1 minute longer. 5. Drain beef, reserving marinade. 6. Add beef to the pot. Sprinkle beef with flour and salt; toss to coat. Top them with bacon and mushroom mixture. Add the reserved marinade. 7. Install the pressure lid and turn the pressure release valve to the SEAL position. 8. Select PRESSURE COOK, set the cooking temperature to HI and adjust the cooking time to 20 minutes. 9. When cooked, let the unit naturally release pressure. 10. Select SEAR/SAUTÉ again, and bring the liquid to a boil at HI; cook the food for 15 to 20 minutes until sauce reaches desired thickness. 11. Remove bay leaf. If desired, serve the stew with hot noodles.
Per Serving: Calories 402; Fat 9.53g; Sodium 352mg; Carbs 52.79g; Fibre 8.4g; Sugar 10.34g; Protein 31.71g

Sirloin Tips

Prep time: 20 minutes | Cook time: 15 minutes | Serves: 4

3 teaspoons olive oil
1 beef top sirloin steak (455g), cubed
½ teaspoon salt
¼ teaspoon pepper

80ml dry red wine or beef stock
225g sliced baby Portobello mushrooms
1 small onion, halved and sliced
480ml beef stock

1 tablespoon Worcestershire sauce
3 to 4 tablespoon cornflour
60ml cold water
Hot cooked mashed potatoes

1. Sprinkle beef with salt and pepper. 2. Heat 2 teaspoons of oil in the cooking pot at HI on SEAR/SAUTÉ mode; brown the beef in batches, and then transfer the meat to a bowl. 3. Stop the cooker, and add the wine to cooker, stirring to loosen browned bits. Return beef to cooker; add mushrooms, onion, and stock and Worcestershire sauce. 4. Install the pressure lid and turn the pressure release valve to the SEAL position. 5. Select PRESSURE COOK, set the cooking temperature to HI and adjust the cooking time to 15 minutes. 6. When cooked, let the unit naturally release pressure. 7. In a small bowl, mix cornflour and water until smooth. 8. Select SEAR/SAUTÉ again, and bring the liquid to a boil at HI; gradually stir the cornflour mixture into the beef mixture, and then cook them for 1 to 2 minutes until thickened. 9. Serve the dish with mashed potatoes.
Per Serving: Calories 480; Fat 25.28g; Sodium 877mg; Carbs 27.15g; Fibre 3.5g; Sugar 3.83g; Protein 35.61g

Beef Burritos

Prep time: 20 minutes | Cook time: 40 minutes | Serves: 6

1.1kg boneless beef chuck roast, cut into 4 pieces
1 tablespoon chili powder
1½ teaspoons ground cumin
Dash salt
1 tablespoon rapeseed oil

1 small onion, finely chopped
1 jalapeno pepper, seeded and finely chopped
1 garlic clove, minced
1 can (360g) crushed tomatoes in puree
200g salsa verde

60ml beef stock
Tortillas
Optional toppings: shredded cheddar cheese, sour cream, guacamole, salsa and fresh coriander leaves

1. Season the roast with chili powder, cumin and salt. 2. Heat the oil in the cooking pot at HI on SEAR/SAUTÉ mode; brown roast on all sides. 3. Stop the cooker, and top the roast with onion, pepper and garlic; add tomatoes, salsa verde and beef stock. 4. Install the pressure lid and turn the pressure release valve to the SEAL position. 5. Select PRESSURE COOK, set the cooking temperature to HI and adjust the cooking time to 40 minutes. 6. When cooked, let the unit naturally release pressure. 7. Remove roast; shred with two forks. Skim fat from cooking juices. Return meat to pressure cooker; heat through. 8. Wrap beef in tortillas with adding toppings as desired. 9. Freeze cooled beef mixture in freezer containers. To use, thaw in refrigerator overnight. Heat through in a saucepan, stirring occasionally.
Per Serving: Calories 446; Fat 19.36g; Sodium 611mg; Carbs 16.86g; Fibre 3.2g; Sugar 6.31g; Protein 53.42g

Tomato Beef Osso Bucco

Prep time: 45 minutes | Cook time: 40 minutes | Serves: 6

65g plain flour
¾ teaspoon salt, divided
½ teaspoon pepper
6 beef shanks (350g each)
2 tablespoon butter
1 tablespoon olive oil
For Gremolata
10g minced fresh parsley
1 tablespoon grated lemon zest

120ml white wine or beef stock
1 can (350g) diced tomatoes, undrained
360ml beef stock
2 medium carrots, chopped
1 medium onion, chopped
1 celery rib, sliced

1 tablespoon grated orange zest
2 garlic cloves, minced

1 teaspoon dried thyme
1 teaspoon dried oregano
2 bay leaves
2 tablespoon cornflour
60ml cold water

1. In a large resealable plastic bag, combine flour, ½ teaspoon salt and pepper. Pat beef dry with paper towels. Add beef to bag, a couple pieces at a time; shake to coat. 2. In a large bowl, combine tomatoes, stock, vegetables, seasonings and remaining salt. 3. Heat 1 tablespoon butter and 1½ teaspoons of oil in the cooking pot at HI on SEAR/SAUTÉ mode; brown three beef shanks, and then remove from the cooker. 4. Add 60ml of wine, stirring to loosen browned bits; return the browned beef shanks to the pot and pour in half of tomato mixture. 5. Install the pressure lid and turn the pressure release valve to the SEAL position. 6. Select PRESSURE COOK, set the cooking temperature to HI and adjust the cooking time to 40 minutes. 7. When cooked, let the unit naturally release pressure. 8. Remove meat and vegetables from the cooker; keep warm. Make second batch with remaining ingredients, repeating previous procedure. 9. After removing all meat and vegetables, discard bay leaves. 10. Skim fat from cooking juices. 10. Select SEAR/SAUTÉ again, and bring the liquid to a boil at HI; at the same time, mix cornflour and water until smooth. 11. Stir the cornflour mixture into the cooking juices and bring to a boil; cook and stir them for 2 minutes until thickened. 12. In a small bowl, combine gremolata ingredients. Serve beef with gremolata and sauce.
Per Serving: Calories 312; Fat 10.97g; Sodium 603mg; Carbs 25.23g; Fibre 3g; Sugar 4.18g; Protein 27.56g

Onion Pork Ragout

Prep time: 15 minutes | Cook time: 27 minutes | Serves: 6

1 (900g) boneless pork shoulder, cut into 5cm cubes
2 teaspoons salt
1 teaspoon ground black pepper
1 tablespoon Italian seasoning

1 tablespoon olive oil
1 (375g) can crushed tomatoes, including juice
60ml dry red wine
1 small yellow onion, peeled and diced

1 medium carrot, peeled and diced
1 stalk celery, diced
3 cloves garlic, peeled and minced
350g chopped chard, ribs removed
4 tablespoons Parmesan cheese

1 Pat pork butt cubes with paper towels. Season them with salt, pepper, and Italian seasoning and set aside. 2. Heat the oil in the cooking pot at HI for 30 seconds on SEAR/SAUTÉ mode; add pork to pot and sear 5 minutes, stirring continuously to ensure all sides are seared. 3. Stop the process, and add tomatoes with juice and wine to pot. Scatter onion, carrot, celery, and garlic on top. 4. Install the pressure lid and turn the pressure release valve to the SEAL position. 5. Select PRESSURE COOK, set the cooking temperature to HI and adjust the cooking time to 20 minutes. 6. When cooked, let the unit naturally release pressure. 7. Using a fork, shred pork in pot with juices. Add chard and simmer for 2 minutes until chard is wilted. 8. Transfer pork ragout to six bowls, garnish with Parmesan cheese, and serve warm.
Per Serving: Calories 471; Fat 30.2g; Sodium 1149mg; Carbs 7.33g; Fibre 2.5g; Sugar 3.23g; Protein 40.12g

Hawaiian Pork in Beef Stock

Prep time: 10 minutes | Cook time: 70 minutes | Serves: 8

1 (1.8kg) boneless pork butt or shoulder, quartered
2 teaspoons salt
1 teaspoon ground black pepper
2 tablespoons olive oil

2 tablespoons liquid smoke
1 tablespoon smoked paprika
6 cloves garlic, peeled and quartered
1 (500g) can crushed pineapple, including juice

2 teaspoons lime zest
Juice from 1 medium lime
½ teaspoon salt
480ml beef stock

1. Season all sides of pork with salt and pepper. 2. Heat the oil in the cooking pot at HI for 30 seconds on SEAR/SAUTÉ mode; sear the meat for 5 minutes, making sure to get each side, then remove from pot and set aside; add liquid smoke, smoked paprika, garlic cloves, crushed pineapple with juice, lime zest, lime juice, and salt to pot, and stir them well. 3. Stop the process, and add stock and pork to the pot. 4. Install the pressure lid and turn the pressure release valve to the SEAL position. 5. Select PRESSURE COOK, set the cooking temperature to HI and adjust the cooking time to 65 minutes. 6. When cooked, let the unit naturally release pressure. 7. Split pork and incorporate juices. Serve warm.
Per Serving: Calories 800; Fat 46.18g; Sodium 1016mg; Carbs 34.79g; Fibre 1.5g; Sugar 31.74g; Protein 58.82g

Polenta Breaded Pork Chops

Prep time: 10 minutes | Cook time: 15 minutes | Serves: 2

1 large egg
30ml polenta
1 tablespoon Italian seasoning

1 teaspoon salt
2 (2.5cm) bone-in pork chops
2 tablespoons olive oil

240ml water

1. In a small bowl, whisk egg. In a second small bowl, combine polenta, Italian seasoning, and salt. 2. Dip each pork chop in whisked egg and then dredge in polenta mixture. Set aside. 3. Heat the oil in the cooking pot at HI for 30 seconds on SEAR/SAUTÉ mode; brown the pork chops for 5 minutes on both sides. Remove chops and set aside. 4. Add the water to the cooking pot, place the Cook & Crisp Basket on top of diffuser and press down firmly, and then place in the pork chops. 5. Install the pressure lid and turn the pressure release valve to the VENT position. 6. Select STEAM and set the cooking time to 3 minutes. 7. When cooked, let the unit naturally release pressure. 8. Preheat oven to grill to 260°C. 9. Transfer pork chops to a baking sheet lined with parchment paper. Grill the food for 2 minutes until tops are browned. Remove from heat and serve.
Per Serving: Calories 561; Fat 33.46g; Sodium 1567mg; Carbs 18.41g; Fibre 1.3g; Sugar 0.83g; Protein 43.15g

Pork Meatballs

Prep time: 15 minutes | Cook time: 30 minutes | Serves: 4

For Slaw
120g shredded carrots, scrubbed
110g julienned radishes
120g peeled and finely diced cucumber
For Spicy Aioli
120g mayonnaise
For Meatballs
455g pork mince
2 large eggs
1 teaspoon garlic powder

10g chopped fresh coriander
1 tablespoon honey
2 tablespoons rice vinegar

2 teaspoons sriracha

40g oats
2 tablespoons sesame oil, divided
480ml water

¼ teaspoon salt
2 teaspoons orange zest

2 teaspoons freshly squeezed orange juice

Sandwiches
4 gluten-free baguettes, sliced lengthwise

1. Combine slaw ingredients in a medium bowl. Cover and refrigerate until ready to use. 2. Combine aioli ingredients in a small bowl. Cover and refrigerate until ready to use. 3. In a medium bowl, combine pork, eggs, garlic powder, and oats. Form into twenty meatballs. Set aside. 4. Heat 1 tablespoon of oil in the cooking pot at HI for 30 seconds on SEAR/SAUTÉ mode; place ten meatballs around the edge of pot and sear them for 4 minutes. 5. Place meatballs in a glass dish and set aside. Add another tablespoon of oil and remaining meatballs and sear for 4 minutes. Add meatballs to glass dish. 6. Discard extra juice and oil from the cooking pot and add water. 7. Place the reversible rack in the pot in the lower position and drop the lower rack through the reversible rack handles. 8. Arrange the dish onto the rack. 9. Install the pressure lid and turn the pressure release valve to the SEAL position. 10. Select PRESSURE COOK, set the cooking temperature to HI and adjust the cooking time to 20 minutes. 11. When cooked, let the unit naturally release pressure. 12. Place five meatballs on each sliced baguette. Add slaw. Drizzle with aioli. Serve.
Per Serving: Calories 703; Fat 44g; Sodium 550mg; Carbs 23.29g; Fibre 4g; Sugar 7.81g; Protein 56.78g

Cuban Picadillo

Prep time: 10 minutes | Cook time: 18 minutes | Serves: 4

2 tablespoons olive oil
1 medium sweet onion, peeled and diced
1 red pepper, seeded and diced
2 small red potatoes, scrubbed and small-diced
455g beef mince
455g chorizo, ground or cut from casings
3 cloves garlic, peeled and minced

1 teaspoon salt
½ teaspoon ground black pepper
1 tablespoon apple cider vinegar
1 tablespoon cooking sherry
1 (360g) can diced fire-roasted tomatoes, including juice
1 (150g) can tomato paste
1 tablespoon capers

1 teaspoon caper juice (from the jar)
60g pimento-stuffed green olives, sliced
1 tablespoon green olive juice (from the jar)
65g raisins
1 teaspoon ground cumin
1 teaspoon ground coriander

1. Heat the oil in the cooking pot at HI for 30 seconds on SEAR/SAUTÉ mode; add onion, red pepper, and potatoes, and sauté them for 5 minutes until onions are translucent; add beef and chorizo, and sauté them for 7 minutes until meat is browned; add garlic and sauté them for 1 minute. 2. Stop the process, and add the remaining ingredients to the pot. 3. Install the pressure lid and turn the pressure release valve to the SEAL position. 4. Select PRESSURE COOK, set the cooking temperature to HI and adjust the cooking time to 5 minutes. 5. When cooked, turn the pressure release valve to the VENT position to quick release the steam. 6. Stir the dish and enjoy.
Per Serving: Calories 1052; Fat 63.96g; Sodium 2476mg; Carbs 54.67g; Fibre 8.8g; Sugar 16.36g; Protein 65.6g

Homemade Meatloaf

Prep time: 15 minutes | Cook time: 35 minutes | Serves: 4

For Glaze
120g ketchup
For Meatloaf
455g beef mince
455g pork mince
3 large eggs
80g oats
65g peeled and finely diced yellow onion

1 tablespoon dark brown sugar

35g seeded and finely diced red pepper
120g tomato sauce
2 teaspoons tamari
1 tablespoon Italian seasoning
½ teaspoon smoked paprika

2 teaspoons Dijon mustard

½ teaspoon garlic powder
1 teaspoon salt
½ teaspoon ground black pepper
240ml water

1. Combine the glaze ingredients in a small bowl and set aside. 2. In a large bowl, combine all meatloaf ingredients (except water). 3. Form the mixture into a ball, flattening the top, then place meatloaf into a glass dish. Brush top of meatloaf with ½ of glaze mixture. 4. Add the water to the cooking pot, place the reversible rack in the pot in the lower position and drop the lower rack through the reversible rack handles. 5. Arrange the dish onto the rack. 6. Install the pressure lid and turn the pressure release valve to the SEAL position. 7. Select PRESSURE COOK, set the cooking temperature to HI and adjust the cooking time to 35 minutes. 8. When cooked, let the unit naturally release pressure. 9. Remove meatloaf from pot and let cool at room temperature for 10 minutes. 10. Gently tilt glass dish over the sink and pour out any liquid. Brush on remaining glaze. Slice meatloaf and serve warm.
Per Serving: Calories 788; Fat 42.08g; Sodium 1876mg; Carbs 35.73g; Fibre 6.6g; Sugar 12.59g; Protein 70.77g

Easy Sloppy Joes

Prep time: 10 minutes | Cook time: 15 minutes | Serves: 4-6

455g beef mince
1 small onion, chopped
60g chopped celery

1 (200g) can tomato sauce
60g ketchup
2 tablespoons light brown sugar

2 teaspoons Worcestershire sauce
1 teaspoon garlic powder
6 hamburger buns

1. Add the beef mince, onion, and celery to the cooking pot; brown the beef at HI on SEAR/SAUTÉ mode for about 3 minutes, but don't worry about cooking it all the way. 2. Stop the process, and add the tomato sauce, ketchup, brown sugar, Worcestershire sauce, and garlic powder to the pot. 3. Install the pressure lid and turn the pressure release valve to the SEAL position. 4. Select PRESSURE COOK, set the cooking temperature to HI and adjust the cooking time to 5 minutes. 5. When cooked, let the unit naturally release pressure. 6. Select SEAR/SAUTÉ again and cook them at HI for 2 to 4 minutes to thicken the sauce. 7. Scoop the sloppy joes onto the buns and serve.
Per Serving: Calories 308; Fat 10.11g; Sodium 419mg; Carbs 28.26g; Fibre 2.1g; Sugar 7.6g; Protein 24.96g

Beef Barbecue

Prep time: 15 minutes | Cook time: 65 minutes | Serves: 8

240g ketchup
2 tablespoons honey
60ml apple cider vinegar
1 tablespoon light brown sugar
1 teaspoon garlic powder

1 teaspoon chili powder
2 tablespoons Dijon mustard
1 (1.3kg) boneless chuck roast, quartered
1 teaspoon salt
½ teaspoon ground black pepper

3 tablespoons vegetable oil
1 large yellow onion, peeled and sliced
960ml beef stock

1. In a small bowl, combine ketchup, honey, apple cider vinegar, brown sugar, garlic powder, chili powder, and Dijon mustard. Refrigerate mixture covered until ready to use. 2. Season roast on all sides with salt and pepper. 3. Heat the oil in the cooking pot at HI for 30 seconds on SEAR/SAUTÉ mode; sear the meat for 5 minutes, making sure to brown each side. 4. Stop the process, and add the onion and beef stock to the pot. 5. Install the pressure lid and turn the pressure release valve to the SEAL position. 6. Select PRESSURE COOK, set the cooking temperature to HI and adjust the cooking time to 60 minutes. 7. When cooked, let the unit naturally release pressure. 8. Strain all but 60ml of liquid from pot. Set strained liquid aside. 9. Shred meat. 10. Add ketchup mixture to pot. Continue to use the forks to shred meat and stir in ketchup mixture to moisten the meat. 11. If more liquid is needed, use set-aside strained liquid. 12. Transfer meat to eight bowls, gluten-free buns, or lettuce wraps, and serve warm.
Per Serving: Calories 307; Fat 16.74g; Sodium 986mg; Carbs 18.96g; Fibre 16.74g; Sugar 14.04g; Protein 22.56g

Chi-Town Beef and Peppers

Prep time: 15 minutes | Cook time: 65 minutes | Serves: 8

60ml olive oil
1 tablespoon Italian seasoning
1 teaspoon garlic powder
1 teaspoon smoked paprika
½ teaspoon red pepper flakes

1 teaspoon salt
½ teaspoon ground black pepper
1 green pepper, seeded and sliced
1 red pepper, seeded and sliced
1 yellow pepper, seeded and sliced

1 large yellow onion, peeled and sliced
1 (1.3kg) boneless chuck roast, quartered
960ml beef stock

1. In a large bowl, combine oil, Italian seasoning, garlic powder, smoked paprika, red pepper flakes, salt, and black pepper. 2. Add sliced peppers, onion, and quartered roast and toss. Refrigerate roast covered at least 30 minutes or up to overnight. 3. Add the meat, veggies, and marinade to the pot, and sear the meat for 5 minutes at HI on SEAR/SAUTÉ mode, making sure to brown each side. 4. Stop the process, and add the beef stock to the pot. 5. Install the pressure lid and turn the pressure release valve to the SEAL position. 6. Select PRESSURE COOK, set the cooking temperature to HI and adjust the cooking time to 60 minutes. 7. When cooked, let the unit naturally release pressure. 8. Strain all but 60ml of liquid from pot. Set strained liquid aside. 9. Transfer the meat to a cutting board. Let meat rest 5 minutes, then thinly slice and add back to pot with veggies and liquid to moisten meat. 10. Using a slotted spoon, transfer meat and veggies to eight bowls, gluten-free buns, or lettuce wraps. Garnish with giardiniera and serve.
Per Serving: Calories 290; Fat 18.32g; Sodium 743mg; Carbs 10.05g; Fibre 2.2g; Sugar 3.82g; Protein 22.83g

Beef Biryani

Prep time: 10 minutes | Cook time: 25 minutes | Serves: 6

1 tablespoon ghee or unsalted butter
1 medium yellow onion, peeled and sliced
455g top round, cut into 1cm strips
50g golden raisins
1 tablespoon minced fresh ginger
2 cloves garlic, peeled and minced

½ teaspoon ground cloves
½ teaspoon ground cardamom
½ teaspoon ground coriander
½ teaspoon ground black pepper
½ teaspoon cinnamon
½ teaspoon ground cumin

1 teaspoon salt
240g plain full-fat yogurt
1 (700g) can whole stewed tomatoes, including juice
400g cooked basmati rice
10g chopped fresh mint leaves

1. Heat the ghee in the cooking pot at HI for 30 seconds on SEAR/SAUTÉ mode; add onion and sauté for 5 minutes until onions are browned and starting to caramelize. 2. Stop the process, and add all remaining ingredients except rice and mint to pot. 3. Install the pressure lid and turn the pressure release valve to the SEAL position. 4. Select PRESSURE COOK, set the cooking temperature to HI and adjust the cooking time to 10 minutes. 5. When cooked, let the unit naturally release pressure. 6. Simmer mixture uncovered for 10 minutes until most of liquid has evaporated. 7. Transfer into six bowls over cooked basmati rice. Garnish with mint leaves and serve warm.
Per Serving: Calories 335; Fat 13.52g; Sodium 640mg; Carbs 34.32g; Fibre 11.6g; Sugar 11.17g; Protein 31.59g

Beef Burgundy

Prep time: 15 minutes | Cook time: 27 minutes | Serves: 4

2 tablespoons gluten-free plain flour
1 teaspoon salt
1 teaspoon ground black pepper
900g boneless beef-round steak, cut into
2.5cm pieces

4 tablespoons olive oil, divided
3 shallots, peeled and diced
3 cloves garlic, peeled and minced
240ml dry red wine
200g sliced white mushrooms

2 medium carrots, peeled and thinly sliced
2 tablespoons fresh thyme leaves
240ml beef stock
2 tablespoons tomato paste
10g chopped fresh parsley

1. In a small bowl, combine flour, salt, and pepper. 2. Dredge steak pieces in mixture until well coated. 3. Heat 2 tablespoons of oil in the cooking pot at HI for 30 seconds on SEAR/SAUTÉ mode; add half of steak to pot and sear for 4 minutes, browning all sides of steak, and then transfer to a plate. 4. Heat the remaining oil and sear remaining steak for 4 minutes. Transfer steak to the plate. 5. Add shallots and garlic to pot and sauté for 2 minutes. 6. Deglaze pot by adding red wine, scraping any bits from the bottom or sides of pot, and cook them for 2 minutes to allow alcohol to cook off. 7. Stop the process, and add mushrooms, carrots, thyme, beef stock, and tomato paste to pot. 8. Install the pressure lid and turn the pressure release valve to the SEAL position. 9. Select PRESSURE COOK, set the cooking temperature to HI and adjust the cooking time to 15 minutes. 10. When cooked, let the unit naturally release pressure. 11. Transfer mixture to a serving dish and garnish with parsley. Serve warm.
Per Serving: Calories 562; Fat 24.89g; Sodium 922mg; Carbs 9.13g; Fibre 1.6g; Sugar 2.38g; Protein 69.53g

Beef & Pork Meatballs

Prep time: 15 minutes | Cook time: 30 minutes | Serves: 4

225g beef mince
225g pork mince
2 large eggs
1 tablespoon Italian seasoning

25g grated Parmesan cheese
60g ricotta cheese
50g gluten-free bread crumbs
3 tablespoons olive oil, divided

480g marinara sauce
480ml water

1. In a medium bowl, combine beef, pork, eggs, Italian seasoning, Parmesan cheese, ricotta cheese, and bread crumbs. Form mixture into twenty meatballs. Set aside. 2. Heat 2 tablespoons of oil in the cooking pot at HI for 30 seconds on SEAR/SAUTÉ mode; place ten meatballs around the edge of pot. Sear meatballs 5 minutes, making sure to get each side. Set aside. Add 1 tablespoon oil to pot and sear remaining meatballs 5 minutes. 3. Transfer seared meatballs to a glass dish. Top them with sauce. 4. Discard extra juice and oil from the cooking pot and add water. 5. Place the reversible rack in the pot in the lower position and drop the lower rack through the reversible rack handles. 6. Arrange the dish onto the rack. 7. Install the pressure lid and turn the pressure release valve to the SEAL position. 8. Select PRESSURE COOK, set the cooking temperature to HI and adjust the cooking time to 20 minutes. 9. When cooked, let the unit naturally release pressure. 10. Transfer meatballs to a serving dish and serve warm.
Per Serving: Calories 539; Fat 37.44g; Sodium 1305mg; Carbs 13.79g; Fibre 2.7g; Sugar 5.7g; Protein 36.24g

Rice Beef Meatballs

Prep time: 15 minutes | Cook time: 25 minutes | Serves: 4

455g beef mince
100g white rice
1 large egg
2 tablespoons peeled and finely diced
yellow onion

1 teaspoon salt
½ teaspoon ground black pepper
½ teaspoon garlic powder
3 tablespoons olive oil, divided
1 (250ml) can condensed cream of tomato

soup
60ml water
1 tablespoon light brown sugar
2 teaspoons Worcestershire sauce
20g chopped fresh parsley

1. In a medium bowl, combine beef, rice, egg, onion, salt, pepper, and garlic powder. Form mixture into twenty meatballs. Set aside. 2. Heat 2 tablespoons of oil in the cooking pot at HI for 30 seconds on SEAR/SAUTÉ mode; place ten meatballs around the edge of pot and sear them for 4 minutes, making sure to get each side. Set aside. Add 1 tablespoon oil to pot and sear the remaining meatballs for 4 minutes. Add first batch of meatballs to pot. 3. In a small bowl, whisk together tomato soup, water, brown sugar, and Worcestershire sauce. Pour mixture over meatballs. 4. Install the pressure lid and turn the pressure release valve to the SEAL position. 5. Select PRESSURE COOK, set the cooking temperature to HI and adjust the cooking time to 15 minutes. 6. When cooked, let the unit naturally release pressure. 7. Transfer meatballs and sauce to a serving dish and garnish with fresh parsley. Serve warm.
Per Serving: Calories 490; Fat 24.94g; Sodium 953mg; Carbs 30.59g; Fibre 1.9g; Sugar 4.7g; Protein 33.74g

Simple Beef and Broccoli

Prep time: 10 minutes | Cook time: 5 minutes | Serves: 2

For Sauce
2 cloves garlic, peeled and minced
80ml tamari
60ml rice wine vinegar

2 tablespoons honey
1 tablespoon sesame oil
¼ teaspoon ground ginger

¼ teaspoon salt
⅛ teaspoon cayenne pepper

For Beef and Broccoli
1 medium head broccoli, chopped
1 (455g) boneless sirloin, trimmed and

sliced into 8 cm strips
240ml water

1. In a medium bowl, combine sauce ingredients. Set aside 2 tablespoons of sauce. Add beef to the bowl and toss. Refrigerate beef for 30 minutes. 2. Sauté the meat in the pot at HI on SEAR/SAUTÉ mode for 2 minutes; add broccoli and sauté for 1 minute. 3. Transfer beef and broccoli to a large bowl. 4. Add the water to the cooking pot, place the reversible rack in the pot in the lower position and drop the lower rack through the reversible rack handles. 5. Arrange the molds onto the rack. 6. Install the pressure lid and turn the pressure release valve to the SEAL position. 7. Select PRESSURE COOK, set the cooking temperature to HI and adjust the cooking time to 1 minute. 8. When cooked, let the unit naturally release pressure. 9. Transfer beef and broccoli to a serving dish and toss with remaining sauce. Serve warm.
Per Serving: Calories 418; Fat 12.86g; Sodium 3137mg; Carbs 22.03g; Fibre 1.1g; Sugar 18.3g; Protein 51.73g

Beef Pork Meatballs with Sauce

Prep time: 15 minutes | Cook time: 30 minutes | Serves: 4

For Sauce
60ml tamari
85g honey

30ml rice vinegar
1 teaspoon sriracha

2.5cm knob ginger, peeled and sliced
2 teaspoons sesame oil

For Meatballs
225g beef mince
225g pork mince
1 large egg

1 medium shallot, peeled and finely diced
1 tablespoon Chinese five-spice powder
3 tablespoons sesame oil, divided

480ml water

1. In a small bowl, combine sauce ingredients. Set aside. 2. In a medium bowl, combine beef, pork, egg, shallot, and Chinese five-spice powder. Form mixture into twenty meatballs. Set aside. 3. Heat 2 tablespoons of oil in the cooking pot at HI for 30 seconds on SEAR/SAUTÉ mode; place ten meatballs around the edge of pot. Sear meatballs for 4 minutes, making sure to get each side. Set aside. Add 1 tablespoon oil to pot and sear remaining meatballs for 4 minutes. 4. Transfer seared meatballs to a glass dish. Top them with sauce. 5. Discard extra juice and oil from the cooking pot. 6. Add the water to the cooking pot, place the reversible rack in the pot in the lower position and drop the lower rack through the reversible rack handles. 7. Arrange the dish onto the rack. 8. Install the pressure lid and turn the pressure release valve to the SEAL position. 9. Select PRESSURE COOK, set the cooking temperature to HI and adjust the cooking time to 20 minutes. 10. When cooked, let the unit naturally release pressure. 11. Transfer meatballs to a serving dish and serve warm.
Per Serving: Calories 517; Fat 34.57g; Sodium 1101mg; Carbs 19.54g; Fibre 0.3g; Sugar 18.06g; Protein 31.7g

Cucumber Lamb Keftedes

Prep time: 15 minutes | Cook time: 18 minutes | Serves: 4

455g lamb mince
2 large eggs
1 tablespoon peeled and finely diced cucumber
1 large carrot, scrubbed and grated

1 tablespoon chopped fresh mint leaves
1 tablespoon chopped fresh dill
1 teaspoon garlic powder
⅛ teaspoon ground cinnamon
1 tablespoon lemon zest

40g oats
3 tablespoons olive oil, divided
480ml water

1. In a medium bowl, combine lamb, eggs, cucumber, carrot, mint, dill, garlic powder, cinnamon, lemon zest, and oats. Form mixture into twenty meatballs. Set aside. 2. Heat 2 tablespoons of oil in the cooking pot at HI for 30 seconds on SEAR/SAUTÉ mode; place ten meatballs around the edge of pot. Sear meatballs for 4 minutes, making sure to get each side. Set aside. Add 1 tablespoon oil to pot and sear remaining meatballs for 4 minutes. 3. Transfer seared meatballs to a glass dish. 4. Discard extra juice and oil from the cooking pot. 5. Add the water to the cooking pot, place the reversible rack in the pot in the lower position and drop the lower rack through the reversible rack handles. 6. Arrange the dish onto the rack. Install the pressure lid and turn the pressure release valve to the SEAL position. 7. Select PRESSURE COOK, set the cooking temperature to HI and adjust the cooking time to 10 minutes. 8. When cooked, let the unit naturally release pressure. 9. Transfer meatballs to a serving dish and serve warm.
Per Serving: Calories 392; Fat 27.67g; Sodium 87mg; Carbs 14.38g; Fibre 3.2g; Sugar 2.46g; Protein 27.51g

Cheese Chili Mac

Prep time: 15 minutes | Cook time: 10 minutes | Serves: 4-6

For the Chili
455g beef mince
1 small onion, chopped
1 (375g) can kidney beans, drained and
rinsed
1 (375g) can tomato sauce
1 tablespoon chili powder
1 teaspoon ground cumin

For the Mac
720ml water
300g elbow macaroni
1 tablespoon butter
300g shredded Cheddar cheese
120ml whole milk

1. Add the beef mince and onions to the cooking pot, and sauté them at HI on SEAR/SAUTÉ mode for about 5 minutes to brown the meat and soften the onions. 2. Stop the process, and stir the meat and onions so that nothing is sticking to the bottom of the pot. Add the kidney beans, tomato sauce, chili powder, and cumin. 3. Add the water, macaroni, and butter to the chili in the pot, making sure the macaroni is submerged in the liquid. 4. Install the pressure lid and turn the pressure release valve to the SEAL position. 5. Select PRESSURE COOK, set the cooking temperature to HI and adjust the cooking time to 5 minutes. 6. When cooked, let the unit naturally release pressure. 7. Add the Cheddar cheese while the noodles are still piping hot. 8. Stir in the milk and serve.
Per Serving: Calories 732; Fat 36.98g; Sodium 628mg; Carbs 52.45g; Fibre 4g; Sugar 6.82g; Protein 46.32g

Beef and Broccoli Florets

Prep time: 10 minutes | Cook time: 15 minutes | Serves: 4-6

180ml fresh tangerine juice
60ml soy sauce
3 tablespoons light brown sugar
2 tablespoons sesame oil
3 garlic cloves, minced
1 teaspoon ground ginger
455g stewing beef, cut into 1 cm-wide strips
1 tablespoon cornflour
1 (300g) bag microwaveable broccoli florets

1. In the cooking pot, combine the tangerine juice, soy sauce, brown sugar, sesame oil, garlic, and ginger. Whisk the ingredients together until well combined. Add the beef to the pot. 2. Install the pressure lid and turn the pressure release valve to the SEAL position. 3. Select PRESSURE COOK, set the cooking temperature to HI and adjust the cooking time to 8 minutes. 4. When cooked, let the unit naturally release pressure. 5. Whisk the cornflour into the pot, and select SEAR/SAUTÉ again; whisk the food at HI for 5 minutes to thicken the sauce. 6. Steam the broccoli in the microwave and add it to the beef and sauce. Serve.
Per Serving: Calories 204; Fat 9.83g; Sodium 242mg; Carbs 10.94g; Fibre 1.9g; Sugar 6.8g; Protein 19.39g

Steak Gyros

Prep time: 10 minutes | Cook time: 10 minutes | Serves: 4-6

For the Tzatziki Sauce
240g plain yogurt, store-bought or homemade
1 small English cucumber, chopped
2 garlic cloves, minced
2 teaspoons dried or fresh dill
½ teaspoon freshly squeezed lemon juice
Dash sea salt

For the Steak
1 tablespoon olive oil
455g skirt or flank steak, cut into 1 cm-wide strips
1 red onion, chopped
120ml beef stock, store-bought or homemade
4 garlic cloves, minced
1 teaspoon dried marjoram
1 teaspoon dried oregano
1 teaspoon Greek seasoning

For the Gyros
4 to 6 pita breads or naan, warmed
1 red onion, chopped
1 tomato, sliced
75g crumbled feta cheese
90g sliced kalamata olives

1. In a medium bowl, mix the yogurt, cucumber, garlic, dill, lemon juice, and salt until well combined. Cover and marinate in the refrigerator for 30 minutes. 2. Add the oil, steak, and onions to the pot, and sauté them at HI on SEAR/SAUTÉ mode for 2 minutes or until the onion is translucent. 3. Stop the process, and add the beef stock, garlic, marjoram, oregano, and Greek seasoning. 4. Install the pressure lid and turn the pressure release valve to the SEAL position. 5. Select PRESSURE COOK, set the cooking temperature to HI and adjust the cooking time to 8 minutes. 6. When cooked, let the unit naturally release pressure. 7. Remove the lid and transfer the meat to a bowl. 8. Spoon the tzatziki sauce into warmed pita bread. 9. Top with the steak, onion, tomato slices, feta, and olives and serve.
Per Serving: Calories 426; Fat 16.18g; Sodium 689mg; Carbs 41.96g; Fibre 5g; Sugar 7.01g; Protein 28.02g

Onion Pot Roast

Prep time: 10 minutes | Cook time: 45 minutes | Serves: 4-6

1 tablespoon olive oil
3 onions, sliced
900g beef roast, such as rump or chuck
Sea salt

Freshly ground black pepper
240ml water
60ml soy sauce
2 tablespoons Worcestershire sauce

1 teaspoon Dijon mustard
455g Yukon Gold potatoes, peeled and
quartered
4 carrots, cut into 5cm chunks

1. Add the olive oil and onions to the pot, and sauté them at HI on SEAR/SAUTÉ mode for 2 minutes or until the onions are translucent. 2. Season the roast with salt and pepper. Add it to the pot and sear on all sides. 3. Stop the process, and add the water, soy sauce, Worcestershire sauce, and mustard to the pot. 4. Install the pressure lid and turn the pressure release valve to the SEAL position. 5. Select PRESSURE COOK, set the cooking temperature to HI and adjust the cooking time to 30 minutes. 6. When cooked, let the unit naturally release pressure. 7. Set a collapsible vegetable steamer over the roast. Place the potatoes and carrots on the steamer. 8. Secure the lid and cook at HI on PRESSURE COOK for 10 minutes, then quick release the pressure and remove the lid. 9. Check to make sure that the internal temperature of the beef is 160°F. 10. Slice the roast and serve with the pot juices and onions drizzled over, with the vegetables on the side.
Per Serving: Calories 403; Fat 17.12g; Sodium 395mg; Carbs 19.95g; Fibre 2.9g; Sugar 4.46g; Protein 42.89g

Sesame Beef with Snap Peas

Prep time: 10 minutes | Cook time: 16 minutes | Serves: 4-6

180ml water
60ml soy sauce
3 garlic cloves, minced
3 tablespoons light brown sugar
2 tablespoons sesame oil

1 teaspoon ground ginger
455g stewing beef, cut into 1 cm-wide
strips
1 tablespoon cornflour
200g sugar snap peas

25g chopped spring onions , green part
only
1 tablespoon sesame seeds

1. In the cooking pot, combine the water, soy sauce, garlic, brown sugar, sesame oil, and ginger. Whisk the ingredients together until well combined. Add the meat. 2. Install the pressure lid and turn the pressure release valve to the SEAL position. 3. Select PRESSURE COOK, set the cooking temperature to HI and adjust the cooking time to 8 minutes. 4. When cooked, let the unit naturally release pressure. 5. Select SEAR/SAUTÉ again and whisk the cornflour into the pot; whisk the food at HI for 5 minutes to thicken the sauce. 6. Add the sugar snap peas and toss with the meat for about 3 minutes with the heat still on. 7. Serve topped with the scallion greens and sesame seeds.
Per Serving: Calories 204; Fat 10.4g; Sodium 226mg; Carbs 9.38g; Fibre 1.5g; Sugar 5.16g; Protein 18.8g

Beef Sundaes with Horseradish

Prep time: 10 minutes | Cook time: 35 minutes | Serves: 4-6

For the Beef
1 tablespoon vegetable oil
900g beef rump roast, cut into 8 cm
chunks
For the Mashed Potatoes
900g Yukon Gold potatoes, peeled and
halved
For the Sundaes
50g shredded Cheddar cheese
120g sour cream

1 onion, chopped
2 garlic cloves, minced
480ml beef stock, store-bought or

2 tablespoons butter
Sea salt

25g chopped spring onions , green part
only

homemade, or water
80g horseradish sauce
1 bay leaf

Freshly ground black pepper

4 to 6 cherry tomatoes

1. Add the oil, beef, onions, and garlic to the pot, and sauté them at HI on SEAR/SAUTÉ mode for 5 minutes to brown the meat and soften the onions. 2. Stop the process, and add the beef stock, horseradish sauce, and bay leaf. 3. Place the reversible rack in the pot in the lower position and drop the lower rack through the reversible rack handles. 4. Arrange the potatoes onto the rack. 5. Install the pressure lid and turn the pressure release valve to the SEAL position. 6. Select PRESSURE COOK, set the cooking temperature to HI and adjust the cooking time to 30 minutes. 7. When cooked, let the unit naturally release pressure. 8. Transfer the potatoes to a large bowl, add the butter, smash with a fork, and season with salt and pepper. 9. Discard the bay leaf. Shred the beef directly in the pot and stir it into the juices. 10. Scoop the mashed potatoes into individual bowls. Top with the beef, Cheddar cheese, sour cream, and spring onions . Set a cherry tomato on top and serve.
Per Serving: Calories 594; Fat 30.74g; Sodium 528mg; Carbs 32.98g; Fibre 4.4g; Sugar 3.75g; Protein 48.24g

Thai Beef and Potato

Prep time: 10 minutes | Cook time: 10 minutes | Serves: 4-6

1 tablespoon vegetable oil
455g stewing beef, cut into 2.5cm chunks
3 or 4 Yukon Gold potatoes, cut into 5cm chunks

2 (375ml) cans full-fat coconut milk
60g Thai red curry paste
2 tablespoons sugar
1 teaspoon ground turmeric

260g frozen pineapple chunks, thawed
Sticky Rice, for serving
25g chopped spring onions
30g chopped peanuts

1. In the cooking pot, combine the vegetable oil, meat, potatoes, coconut milk, curry paste, sugar, and turmeric. 2. Install the pressure lid and turn the pressure release valve to the SEAL position. 3. Select PRESSURE COOK, set the cooking temperature to HI and adjust the cooking time to 8 minutes. 4. When cooked, let the unit naturally release pressure. 5. Remove the lid and stir in the pineapple. 6. Serve over the rice, topped with the spring onions and chopped peanuts.
Per Serving: Calories 728; Fat 45.99g; Sodium 165mg; Carbs 60.15g; Fibre 10.9g; Sugar 19.28g; Protein 27.73g

Short Ribs with Muffuletta

Prep time: 10 minutes | Cook time: 40 minutes | Serves: 4-6

1.8kg beef short ribs
Sea salt
Freshly ground black pepper

2 tablespoons butter
1 small onion, chopped
2 garlic cloves, minced

240ml water
20g muffuletta (Italian olive salad)

1. Season the ribs with salt and pepper. 2. Add the butter, onion, and garlic to the pot, and sauté them at HI on SEAR/SAUTÉ mode for 2 minutes or until the onions are translucent; add the ribs and sear them on each side for about 5 minutes in total. 3. Stop the cooker, and add the water and muffuletta. 4. Install the pressure lid and turn the pressure release valve to the SEAL position. 5. Select PRESSURE COOK, set the cooking temperature to HI and adjust the cooking time to 30 minutes. 6. When cooked, let the unit naturally release pressure. 7. Remove the lid and transfer the ribs to a serving dish. Top them with the muffuletta sauce and serve.
Per Serving: Calories 686; Fat 49.04g; Sodium 339mg; Carbs 1.43g; Fibre 0.2g; Sugar 0.51g; Protein 61.14g

Lamb Shepherd's Pie

Prep time: 10 minutes | Cook time: 30 minutes | Serves: 4-6

For the Filling
1 tablespoon olive oil
1 small onion, chopped
3 garlic cloves, minced
2 teaspoons herbes de Provence
455g lamb mince
For the Topping
900g Yukon Gold potatoes, peeled and cut into 5cm chunks

2 carrots, chopped
160g frozen corn kernels (no need to thaw)
100g frozen peas (no need to thaw)
480ml beef stock, store-bought or

2 tablespoons butter
Sea salt

homemade
2 tablespoons tomato paste
2 tablespoons Worcestershire sauce
1 tablespoon cornflour

Freshly ground black pepper

1. Add the olive oil, onion, garlic, and herbes de Provence, and sauté them at HI on SEAR/SAUTÉ mode for about 2 minutes or until the onion is translucent. 2. Add the lamb mince and sauté for about 5 minutes or until browned. 3. Stop the process, and add the carrots, corn, peas, beef stock, tomato paste, and Worcestershire sauce to the pot. 4. Place the reversible rack in the pot in the lower position and drop the lower rack through the reversible rack handles. 5. Arrange the potatoes onto the rack. 6. Install the pressure lid and turn the pressure release valve to the SEAL position. 7. Select PRESSURE COOK, set the cooking temperature to HI and adjust the cooking time to 15 minutes. 8. When cooked, let the unit naturally release pressure. 9. Transfer the potatoes to a large bowl, add the butter, smash with a fork, and season with salt and pepper. 10. Select SEAR/SAUTÉ again, and whisk the cornflour into the meat and vegetables, and sauté them for 5 minutes to thicken the sauce. 11. Spoon the potatoes on top of the lamb and serve.
Per Serving: Calories 425; Fat 19.41g; Sodium 389mg; Carbs 42.75g; Fibre 6.2g; Sugar 5.48g; Protein 21.58g

Chimichurri Beef Strips

Prep time: 5 minutes | Cook time: 15 minutes | Serves: 4-6

1 tablespoon olive oil
675g stewing beef, cut into 1cm-wide
strips
½ onion, chopped
120ml water
125g chimichurri

1. Add the oil, beef, and onion to the cooking pot, and sauté them at HI on SEAR/SAUTÉ mode for about 2 minutes to brown the beef and soften the onion. 2. Stop the cooker, and add the water and chimichurri. 3. Install the pressure lid and turn the pressure release valve to the SEAL position. 4. Select PRESSURE COOK, set the cooking temperature to HI and adjust the cooking time to 10 minutes. 5. When cooked, let the unit naturally release pressure. 6. Remove the lid and transfer the beef and sauce to a serving dish and serve.
Per Serving: Calories 164; Fat 6.78g; Sodium 93mg; Carbs 1.09g; Fibre 0.2g; Sugar 0.39g; Protein 24.94g

Salsa Beef Tacos

Prep time: 10 minutes | Cook time: 75 minutes | Serves: 6-10

For the Beef
1 tablespoon olive oil
5 garlic cloves, minced
1 onion, sliced
For the Tacos
6 to 10 (20cm) soft flour tortillas
25g shredded Cheddar cheese

1.3kg chuck roast
Sea salt
Freshly ground black pepper

120ml sour cream
30g shredded lettuce

610g salsa verde
240ml beef stock, store-bought or homemade or water

1 medium tomato, sliced

1. Add the oil, garlic, and onion and sauté them at HI on SEAR/SAUTÉ mode for about 2 minutes or until the onion is translucent. 2. Season the roast with salt and pepper, add it to the pot, and sear on all sides. 3. Stop the process, and add the salsa and beef stock. 4. Install the pressure lid and turn the pressure release valve to the SEAL position. 5. Select PRESSURE COOK, set the cooking temperature to HI and adjust the cooking time to 70 minutes. 6. When cooked, let the unit naturally release pressure. 7. Remove the lid and use two forks to shred the beef right in the pot. Let the shredded meat marinate in the sauce. 8. Set out the shredded beef, tortillas, Cheddar cheese, sour cream, lettuce, and tomato and let people build their own tacos.
Per Serving: Calories 318; Fat 11.91g; Sodium 1829mg; Carbs 21.24g; Fibre 2.1g; Sugar 3.86g; Protein 29.93g

Rosemary Lamb Chops

Prep time: 10 minutes | Cook time: 10 minutes | Serves: 6

2 tablespoons olive oil
3 shallots or 1 small onion, chopped
2 garlic cloves, minced
3 tablespoons freshly squeezed lemon
juice
1 teaspoon dried oregano
1 teaspoon Greek seasoning
6 lamb loin chops (5cm thick)
Sea salt
Freshly ground black pepper
240ml water

1. Add the olive oil, shallots, garlic, lemon juice, oregano, and Greek seasoning. Season the lamb with salt and pepper, add to the pot, and sear at HI on SEAR/SAUTÉ mode for 1 minute on each side. 2. Stop the cooker and add the water to the pot. 3. Install the pressure lid and turn the pressure release valve to the SEAL position. 4. Select PRESSURE COOK, set the cooking temperature to HI and adjust the cooking time to 8 minutes. 5. When cooked, let the unit naturally release pressure. 6. Remove the lid and transfer the lamb to serving plates. Spoon the pan juices over the lamb and serve.
Per Serving: Calories 121 Fat 7.47g; Sodium 96mg; Carbs 4.77g; Fibre 0.9g; Sugar 1.75g; Protein 8.94g

Chapter 7 Desserts

Arborio Rice Pudding

Prep time: 10 minutes | Cook time: 15 minutes | Serves: 8

195g Arborio rice
360ml water
1 teaspoon instant espresso powder
1 teaspoon vanilla extract

1 tablespoon unsalted butter
70g raisins
⅛ teaspoon ground cinnamon
⅛ teaspoon salt

75g light brown sugar
120ml whole milk
2 large eggs

1. Add rice, water, espresso powder, vanilla, and butter to the cooking pot. 2. Install the pressure lid and turn the pressure release valve to the SEAL position. 3. Select PRESSURE COOK, set the cooking temperature to HI and adjust the cooking time to 5 minutes. 4. When cooked, let the unit naturally release pressure. 5. Stir in raisins, cinnamon, salt, and brown sugar. 6. In a medium bowl, whisk together milk and eggs. Add 1 tablespoon of rice mixture to eggs, stirring quickly to temper. Quickly stir mixture in medium bowl back into pot, ensuring eggs don't scramble. 7. Let mixture simmer unlidded 5 minutes. 8. Transfer the food to eight bowls and serve warm.
Per Serving: Calories 89; Fat 5.85g; Sodium 53mg; Carbs 10.17g; Fibre 3.1g; Sugar 2.38g; Protein 3.27g

Flavourful Chai Latte

Prep time: 5 minutes | Cook time: 15 minutes | Serves: 4

720ml water
4 black tea bags
3 cardamom pods
4 whole cloves

1 cinnamon stick
4 whole allspice
¼ teaspoon ground nutmeg
¼ teaspoon ground ginger

240ml whole milk
50g granulated sugar

1. Add water, tea bags, cardamom, cloves, cinnamon stick, allspice, nutmeg, and ginger to the cooking pot. 2. Install the pressure lid and turn the pressure release valve to the VENT position. 3. Select STEAM and set the cooking time to 10 minutes. 4. When cooked, let the unit naturally release pressure. 5. Add milk and sugar to pot and let steep for an additional 5 minutes. 6. Strain. Press any additional liquid and flavour out of the tea bags. 7. Serve warm, chilled, or on ice.
Per Serving: Calories 101; Fat 2.48g; Sodium 36mg; Carbs 20.22g; Fibre 2.4g; Sugar 14g; Protein 2.28g

Mochaccino Cheesecakes

Prep time: 5 minutes | Cook time: 20 minutes | Serves: 6

For Crust
40g oats
8 whole raw almonds
For Cheesecake Filling
150g cream cheese, cubed and room
temperature
1 tablespoon sour cream, room

25g unsweetened cocoa
2 tablespoons granulated sugar

temperature
¼ teaspoon vanilla extract
2 teaspoons instant espresso powder

3 tablespoons unsalted butter, melted
⅛ teaspoon salt

50g granulated sugar
1 large egg, room temperature
240ml water

1. Lightly grease six silicone cupcake liners with either oil or cooking spray. 2. In a small food processor, pulse oats, almonds, unsweetened cocoa, sugar, butter, and salt. Transfer crumb mixture to liners and press down along the bottom and one-third of the way up the sides of the pan. 3. Add cream cheese, sour cream, vanilla, espresso powder, and sugar to a food processor. Pulse them until smooth. 4. Slowly add egg and pulse them for 10 seconds. 5. Scrape the bowl and pulse until batter is smooth. Transfer batter into silicone cupcake liners. 6. Add the water to the cooking pot, place the reversible rack in the pot in the lower position and drop the lower rack through the reversible rack handles. 7. Arrange the cupcake liners onto the rack. 8. Install the pressure lid and turn the pressure release valve to the SEAL position. 9. Select PRESSURE COOK, set the cooking temperature to HI and adjust the cooking time to 25 minutes. 10. When cooked, let the unit naturally release pressure. 11. Let cheesecakes cool at room temperature 10 minutes. 12. Cheesecakes will be a little jiggly in the centre. Refrigerate at least 1 hour to allow them to set.
Per Serving: Calories 194; Fat 14.75g; Sodium 183mg; Carbs 15.7g; Fibre 2.5g; Sugar 7.97g; Protein 5.11g

Chocolate Hot Cocoa

Prep time: 5 minutes | Cook time: 10 minutes | Serves: 4

1.4L whole milk
25g unsweetened cocoa powder

45g chocolate mint chips
50g granulated sugar

⅛ teaspoon salt
2 teaspoons vanilla extract

1. Add all ingredients to the cooking pot. 2. Install the pressure lid and turn the pressure release valve to the VENT position. 3. Select STEAM and set the cooking time to 8 minutes. 4. When cooked, let the unit naturally release pressure. 5. Whisk ingredients to ensure smoothness. 6. Ladle cocoa into four mugs and serve warm.
Per Serving: Calories 424; Fat 12.17g; Sodium 254mg; Carbs 69.09g; Fibre 2.1g; Sugar 62.77g; Protein 12.24g

Blackberry Crisp with Almond Topping

Prep time: 15 minutes | Cook time: 10 minutes | Serves: 4

For Blackberry Filling
290g fresh blackberries
60ml water
1 tablespoon freshly squeezed orange juice
For Topping
4 tablespoons unsalted butter, melted
80g oats

50g granulated sugar
1 teaspoon cornflour
1 teaspoon cinnamon

15g gluten-free flour
30g chopped almonds

¼ teaspoon ground nutmeg
⅛ teaspoon salt

55g packed light brown sugar
¼ teaspoon salt

1. Add filling ingredients to the cooking pot. Stir to evenly distribute ingredients. 2. Mix topping ingredients together in a small bowl. Spoon drops of topping over filling in pot. 3. Install the pressure lid and turn the pressure release valve to the SEAL position. 4. Select PRESSURE COOK, set the cooking temperature to HI and adjust the cooking time to 8 minutes. 5. When cooked, let the unit naturally release pressure. 6. Spoon crisp into four bowls and enjoy.
Per Serving: Calories 299; Fat 10.01g; Sodium 237mg; Carbs 57.07g; Fibre 8.5g; Sugar 32.3g; Protein 6.87g

Friendly Steel-Cut Oatcake

Prep time: 10 minutes | Cook time: 25 minutes | Serves: 4-6

1½ teaspoons butter
480ml whole milk
85g honey

Pinch salt
2 teaspoons chai concentrate (or ½
teaspoon vanilla extract and a dash of

pumpkin pie spice)
80g oats
50g raisins or diced dried fruit medley

1. Coat the inside of a suitable baking dish with the butter. 2. In a mixing bowl, whisk together the milk, honey, salt, and chai concentrate until very well combined. Add in the oats and raisins or dried fruit medley, and whisk until just combined. 3. Pour the oat mixture into the prepared baking dish and cover with foil. 4. Add the water to the cooking pot, place the reversible rack in the pot in the lower position and drop the lower rack through the reversible rack handles. 5. Arrange the dish onto the rack. 6. Install the pressure lid and turn the pressure release valve to the SEAL position. 7. Select PRESSURE COOK, set the cooking temperature to HI and adjust the cooking time to 25 minutes. 8. When cooked, let the unit naturally release pressure. 9. Remove the baking dish and let sit for 5 minutes before removing the foil. Invert the cake onto a plate and cut into wedges before serving.
Per Serving: Calories 164; Fat 4.59g; Sodium 71mg; Carbs 32.67g; Fibre 2.4g; Sugar 22.38g; Protein 5.22g

Red Wine-Poached Pears

Prep time: 5 minutes | Cook time: 10 minutes | Serves: 4-8

1 (750-milliliter) bottle red wine
105g brown sugar
3 whole cloves

1 lemon, zested and cut in half
4 whole pears, peeled
Vanilla ice cream, for serving (optional)

Toasted coconut, for serving (optional)
Mint leaves, for garnish (optional)

1. In the cooking pot, add the wine, brown sugar, cloves, lemon halves, and lemon zest. Stir until the sugar is dissolved. 2. Place the pears in the poaching liquid, and spoon some of the liquid over the tops of the pears. 3. Install the pressure lid and turn the pressure release valve to the SEAL position. 4. Select PRESSURE COOK, set the cooking temperature to HI and adjust the cooking time to 8 minutes. 5. When cooked, let the unit naturally release pressure.
6. Transfer the pears to serving dishes. If using, serve with vanilla ice cream and toasted coconut or mint leaves.
Per Serving: Calories 111; Fat 0.47g; Sodium 56mg; Carbs 26.74g; Fibre 2.5g; Sugar 21.94g; Protein 1.77g

Pineapple Tapioca Pudding

Prep time: 5 minutes | Cook time: 15 minutes | Serves: 4-6

1 (500g) can crushed pineapple
300ml coconut milk
60g tapioca pearls, rinsed

50g sugar
Pinch salt
25g sweetened toasted coconut flakes

(optional)

1. In a baking dish, mix the crushed pineapple, coconut milk, tapioca pearls, 120 ml water, sugar, and salt. Mix them well, and cover with foil. 2. Add the water to the cooking pot, place the reversible rack in the pot in the lower position and drop the lower rack through the reversible rack handles. 3. Arrange the dish onto the rack. 4. Install the pressure lid and turn the pressure release valve to the SEAL position. 5. Select PRESSURE COOK, set the cooking temperature to HI and adjust the cooking time to 15 minutes. 6. When cooked, let the unit naturally release pressure. 7. Top the dish with the coconut flakes (optional) and serve.
Per Serving: Calories 330; Fat 12.02g; Sodium 36mg; Carbs 56.21g; Fibre 1.8g; Sugar 47.23g; Protein 2.39g

Chocolate Chickpea Pudding

Prep time: 10 minutes | Cook time: 25 minutes | Serves: 8-10

1 (475g) can chickpeas, drained and rinsed
1 large egg

125g creamy peanut butter
115g honey

40g semisweet chocolate chips
45g pitted, diced dates (optional)

1. Cut a piece of parchment paper to fit a 18cm baking dish, large enough to extend about 5 cm over the edges of the dish. Place the parchment in the dish and set aside. 2. In a food processor, combine the chickpeas, egg, peanut butter, and honey. Blend them until smooth. 3. Pour the mixture into the prepared pan and sprinkle with the chocolate chips and the dates (optional), and cover the pan with aluminum foil. 4. Add the water to the cooking pot, place the reversible rack in the pot in the lower position and drop the lower rack through the reversible rack handles. 5. Arrange the pan onto the rack. Install the pressure lid and turn the pressure release valve to the SEAL position. 6. Select PRESSURE COOK, set the cooking temperature to HI and adjust the cooking time to 25 minutes. 7. When cooked, let the unit naturally release pressure. 8. Carefully lift the pan from the cooker and remove the foil. Lift the pudding out using the parchment, and place it on a serving plate. 9. Let the pudding cool for a few minutes; it will thicken as it sits. 10. Serve warm or cold.
Per Serving: Calories 173; Fat 9.31g; Sodium 101mg; Carbs 20.03g; Fibre 2.7g; Sugar 12.97g; Protein 5.41g

Mexican Cinnamon Hot Chocolate

Prep time: 5 minutes | Cook time: 5 minutes | Serves: 4-6

100g bittersweet chocolate
960ml whole milk

120ml sweetened condensed milk
½ teaspoon ground cinnamon

Pinch cayenne pepper
Pinch nutmeg (optional)

1. In the cooking pot, combine the chocolate, whole milk, condensed milk, 120ml water, cinnamon, cayenne, and nutmeg (optional). 2. Install the pressure lid and turn the pressure release valve to the SEAL position. 3. Select PRESSURE COOK, set the cooking temperature to HI and adjust the cooking time to 2 minutes. 4. When cooked, let the unit naturally release pressure. 5. Using a wire mesh strainer set over a bowl, strain the hot chocolate to remove any solids, and then return the strained liquid to the pressure-cooker pot. 6. Using an immersion blender or whisk, blend to create froth. 7. Serve.
Per Serving: Calories 213; Fat 5.93g; Sodium 94mg; Carbs 34.62g; Fibre 0.7g; Sugar 31.33g; Protein 5.92g

Mulled Orange Wine

Prep time: 5 minutes | Cook time: 5 minutes | Serves: 5-6

1 (750-milliliter) bottle red wine
85g honey

1 orange, sliced
1 cinnamon stick

1 whole star anise

1. In the cooking pot, combine the wine, honey, orange, cinnamon stick, and star anise. 2. Install the pressure lid and turn the pressure release valve to the SEAL position. 3. Select PRESSURE COOK, set the cooking temperature to HI and adjust the cooking time to 2 minutes. 4. When cooked, let the unit naturally release pressure. 5. Switch the pressure cooker to the Keep Warm setting, and enjoy the wine throughout the evening.
Per Serving: Calories 75; Fat 0.15g; Sodium 18mg; Carbs 19.53g; Fibre 2g; Sugar 14.19g; Protein 1.66g

Crème Brûlée

Prep time: 5 minutes | Cook time: 5 minutes | Serves: 6

8 egg yolks
70g sugar, plus more for torching

1 tablespoon matcha powder
1 teaspoon vanilla extract

480ml heavy cream

1. In a medium bowl, beat together the egg yolks, sugar, matcha, and vanilla until well combined. Fold in the heavy cream until just mixed together, about 1 minute. 2. Fill six small ramekins with filling. Cover each with foil. 3. Add 240ml of water to the cooking pot, place the reversible rack in the pot in the lower position and drop the lower rack through the reversible rack handles. 4. Arrange the ramekins onto the rack. 5. Install the pressure lid and turn the pressure release valve to the SEAL position. 6. Select PRESSURE COOK, set the cooking temperature to HI and adjust the cooking time to 20 minutes. 7. When cooked, let the unit naturally release pressure. 8. Carefully remove the ramekins and chill for 1 to 2 hours. 9. When ready to serve, sprinkle additional sugar evenly over the tops and torch until light brown or set the oven to grill and place the ramekins on the oven rack positioned on the second highest tier. 10. Serve.
Per Serving: Calories 238; Fat 20.83g; Sodium 27mg; Carbs 8.42g; Fibre 0.2g; Sugar 6.79g; Protein 4.54g

Fruit Cheesecake with Chocolate Crust

Prep time: 10 minutes | Cook time: 25 minutes | Serves: 6-8

10 Oreo cookies, filling removed and reserved
Cooking spray

200g cream cheese
1 large egg
2 tablespoons raspberry or pomegranate

spread
Fresh raspberries or pomegranate seeds, for garnish

1. In the bowl of a food processor, add the cookies and blend to a sand-like consistency. 2. Spray a suitable spring-form pan with cooking spray, and press the cookie crumbs into the bottom of the pan to form a crust. 3. In a medium bowl, combine the reserved cookie filling, cream cheese, and egg. Mix them until well combined. 4. Pour the mixture into the prepared pan and spread evenly. 5. Add the fruit spread in dollops and, using a knife or chopstick, swirl to make a design. Cover the pan with aluminum foil. 6. Add the water to the cooking pot, place the reversible rack in the pot in the lower position and drop the lower rack through the reversible rack handles. 7. Arrange the pan onto the rack. 8. Install the pressure lid and turn the pressure release valve to the SEAL position. 9. Select PRESSURE COOK, set the cooking temperature to HI and adjust the cooking time to 25 minutes. 10. When cooked, let the unit naturally release pressure. 11. Remove the pan from the cooker and let the cheesecake cool at room temperature for 15 minutes. 12. Transfer the dish to the refrigerator and chill for 3 to 4 hours. 13. Garnish the dish with fresh raspberries or pomegranate seeds. 14. Enjoy.
Per Serving: Calories 203; Fat 13.08g; Sodium 176mg; Carbs 19.13g; Fibre 1.9g; Sugar 11.93g; Protein 3.79g

Chocolate Cake

Prep time: 15 minutes | Cook time: 20 minutes | Serves: 6-8

Cooking spray
170g dark chocolate chips or chopped dark chocolate

4 tablespoons unsalted butter
3 large eggs, separated
4 tablespoons sugar, divided

Pinch cayenne pepper
Walnuts, chopped (optional)

1. Spray a suitable spring-form pan with cooking spray. Cut a parchment paper round to fit in the pan and place it inside the pan. Set aside. 2. Place the egg yolks in a small bowl and the whites in a large bowl. Add 2 tablespoons of sugar to the yolks and beat for 3 minutes until pale in color. Set aside. 3. Beat the egg whites with the remaining 2 tablespoons of sugar for 5 minutes until stiff peaks form. 4. In a medium bowl, combine the chocolate chips and butter. 5. Add 240ml of water to the pot and place the bowl in it. 6. Cook the food at HI on SEAR/SAUTÉ mode for 5 minutes until the chocolate and butter are melted, stirring regularly. 7. Add the egg yolks to the melted chocolate and whisk to combine. Mix in the cayenne and walnuts (optional). Carefully fold in the egg whites until incorporated. 8. Pour the mixture into the prepared pan and cover with aluminum foil. Place the reversible rack in the pot in the lower position and drop the lower rack through the reversible rack handles. 9. Arrange the pan onto the rack. 10. Install the pressure lid and turn the pressure release valve to the SEAL position. 11. Select PRESSURE COOK, set the cooking temperature to HI and adjust the cooking time to 15 minutes. 12. When cooked, let the unit naturally release pressure. 13. Carefully remove the cake and foil, and cool at room temperature for 10 minutes. 14. Remove the parchment paper and enjoy.
Per Serving: Calories 115; Fat 7.63g; Sodium 60mg; Carbs 8.79g; Fibre 0.2g; Sugar 6.22g; Protein 2.92g

Oat Strawberry Crisp

Prep time: 15 minutes | Cook time: 10 minutes | Serves: 2

Nonstick cooking spray
170g strawberries, hulled and quartered
75g packed light brown sugar, divided

30g plain flour
20g rolled oats
¼ teaspoon salt

3 tablespoons butter, melted
Vanilla ice cream, for serving (optional)

1. Spray a suitable pan with cooking spray. 2. In a small bowl, toss the strawberries with 2 tablespoons of brown sugar and let them sit for 5 minutes. Pour the strawberries into the prepared pan. 3. In a medium bowl, combine the flour, oats, remaining brown sugar, and salt. 4. Add the melted butter and stir until the mixture is crumbly. Scatter the topping over the strawberries. 5. Cover the pan tightly with aluminum foil. 6. Add 240ml of water to the cooking pot, place the reversible rack in the pot in the lower position and drop the lower rack through the reversible rack handles. 7. Arrange the pan onto the rack. 8. Install the pressure lid and turn the pressure release valve to the SEAL position. 9. Select PRESSURE COOK, set the cooking temperature to HI and adjust the cooking time to 10 minutes. 10. When cooked, let the unit naturally release pressure. 11. Once the float valve drops, open the lid and carefully remove the pan. Serve warm, topped with vanilla ice cream (optional).
Per Serving: Calories 281; Fat 20g; Sodium 450mg; Carbs 28g; Fibre 4g; Sugar 5g; Protein 5g

Digestive Biscuit Cheesecake

Prep time: 15 minutes | Cook time: 15 minutes | Serves: 2

Nonstick cooking spray
35g crushed digestive biscuits

3 tablespoons butter, melted
100g sugar, divided

1 (200g) package cream cheese, softened
2 large eggs

1. Place a trivet in the bottom of the cooking pot, then pour in 240ml water. Spray a 15cm spring-form pan with cooking spray. 2. In a small bowl, combine the crushed biscuits, butter, and 2 tablespoons of sugar. Press the mixture evenly into the bottom of the prepared pan. 3. In a medium bowl, beat together the cream cheese and remaining 6 tablespoons of sugar. Add the eggs, one at a time, and beat until well mixed. Pour the mixture over the biscuit crust. Place the pan on top of the trivet. 4. Lock the lid in place. Select Pressure Cook and adjust the pressure to High and the time to 25 minutes. After cooking, press Cancel to turn off the cooking pot and let the pressure release naturally for 10 minutes, then quick release any remaining pressure. 5. Once the float valve drops, open the lid and carefully remove the pan. Allow to cool, then refrigerate for at least 4 hours. Serve chilled.
Per Serving: Calories 935; Fat 64.42g; Sodium 768mg; Carbs 77.43g; Fibre 1.3g; Sugar 60.51g; Protein 15.22g

Lemon Graham Cheesecake

Prep time: 10 minutes | Cook time: 35 minutes | Serves: 6-10

For the Crust
Nonstick cooking spray
For the Cheesecake
400g full-fat cream cheese, at room temperature
120g sour cream, at room temperature
150g sugar

8 digestive biscuits, crushed

½ teaspoon sea salt
1 tablespoon cornflour
Grated zest of 2 lemons
1 tablespoon freshly squeezed lemon juice

3 tablespoons butter, melted

3 large eggs
240ml water

1. Line the bottom of a suitable spring-form pan with a round of parchment paper or mist the pan with cooking spray. 2. In a medium bowl, mix the biscuit crumbs and melted butter together and press the mixture evenly into the bottom of the spring-form pan. 3. In a medium bowl, with a hand mixer or by hand, beat together the cream cheese, sour cream, sugar, salt, cornflour, lemon zest, and lemon juice. 4. Beat in the eggs just until incorporated. Do not over-mix. 5. Spoon the cream cheese mixture into the spring-form pan and cover the pan with foil. 6. Add the water to the cooking pot, place the reversible rack in the pot in the lower position and drop the lower rack through the reversible rack handles. 7. Arrange the pan onto the rack. 8. Install the pressure lid and turn the pressure release valve to the SEAL position. 9. Select PRESSURE COOK, set the cooking temperature to HI and adjust the cooking time to 35 minutes. 10. When cooked, let the unit naturally release pressure. 11. Refrigerate the cheesecake for 6 to 8 hours to chill and set up. 12. Uncover and remove the sides of the pan. Cut the cheesecake into slices and serve. 13. Refrigerate the leftover in a sealed container for up to 3 days.
Per Serving: Calories 202; Fat 13.66g; Sodium 338mg; Carbs 15.24g; Fibre 0.1g; Sugar 10.52g; Protein 5.02g

Vanilla Crème Brûlée

Prep time: 15 minutes | Cook time: 15 minutes | Serves: 2

50g sugar
2 large egg yolks

180g heavy cream
1 teaspoon pure vanilla extract

1. In a medium bowl, combine the sugar and egg yolks. Add the cream and vanilla, and whisk until combined. 2. Pour the mixture into two 150g ramekins. Cover the ramekins tightly with aluminum foil. 3. Add 240ml of water to the cooking pot, place the reversible rack in the pot in the lower position and drop the lower rack through the reversible rack handles. 4. Arrange the pan onto the rack. 5. Install the pressure lid and turn the pressure release valve to the SEAL position. 6. Select PRESSURE COOK, set the cooking temperature to HI and adjust the cooking time to 10 minutes. 7. When cooked, let the unit naturally release pressure. 8. Remove the foil and allow the custards to cool, then refrigerate for at least 4 hours. 9. Serve chilled.
Per Serving: Calories 465; Fat 38.4g; Sodium 42mg; Carbs 30.34g; Fibre 0g; Sugar 28.1g; Protein 4.39.g

Vanilla Caramel Popcorn

Prep time: 15 minutes | Cook time: 15 minutes | Serves: 2

2 tablespoons coconut oil
45 g popcorn kernels
1 teaspoon salt

4 tablespoons butter
105g packed light brown sugar
2 tablespoons heavy cream

1 teaspoon vanilla extract

1. Heat the coconut oil in the cooking pot at MD on SEAR/SAUTÉ mode; add a few popcorn kernels to test. If the kernels pop, it is hot enough to add remaining kernels; if not, wait another minute or two. Stir well to coat the kernels evenly with the oil, and then cover with the lid. 2. Once the kernels start to pop, cook for 2 to 3 minutes, then press Cancel to turn off the cooking pot. Keep the lid on until the popping stops. 3. Transfer the popped popcorn to a bowl, toss with the salt, and set aside. 4. Select SEAR/SAUTÉ again and melt the butter at MD; add the brown sugar and stir to combine, and then add the cream and vanilla; stir them for 4 to 5 minutes until the sugar has dissolved and the mixture is a caramel consistency. 5. Stop the process and return the popcorn to the pot. Toss gently until the popcorn is evenly coated with caramel. 6. Transfer the caramel popcorn to a parchment-lined baking sheet to cool, and then serve.
Per Serving: Calories 753; Fat 44.52g; Sodium 1386mg; Carbs 85.63g; Fibre 5.8g; Sugar 54.1g; Protein 5.22g

Easy Dulce de Leche

Prep time: 5 minutes | Cook time: 40 minutes | Serves: 4

1 (350ml) can sweetened condensed milk

1. Remove the paper label from the can of condensed milk and discard it. Open the can and discard the top. Cover the can with aluminum foil. 2. Add the water to the cooking pot, place the reversible rack in the pot in the lower position and drop the lower rack through the reversible rack handles. 3. Arrange the can of condensed milk onto the rack. 4. Install the pressure lid and turn the pressure release valve to the SEAL position. 5. Select PRESSURE COOK, set the cooking temperature to HI and adjust the cooking time to 40 minutes. 6. When cooked, let the unit naturally release pressure. 7. Carefully remove the can and let it rest on a heatproof surface. Remove the foil and let it cool. 8. Use the dulce de leche immediately, or transfer to an airtight container and store, refrigerated, for up to 3 weeks.
Per Serving: Calories 61; Fat 3.25g; Sodium 43mg; Carbs 4.74g; Fibre 0g; Sugar 5.01g; Protein 3.13g

White Rice Pudding

Prep time: 5 minutes | Cook time: 20 minutes | Serves: 2

100g white rice
240ml milk
180ml water

½ teaspoon pure vanilla extract
½ teaspoon ground cinnamon
⅛ teaspoon salt

60ml sweetened condensed milk

1. Combine the rice, milk, water, vanilla, cinnamon, and salt in the cooking pot. 2. Install the pressure lid and turn the pressure release valve to the SEAL position. 3. Select PRESSURE COOK, set the cooking temperature to HI and adjust the cooking time to 20 minutes. 4. When cooked, let the unit naturally release pressure. 5. Stir the sweetened condensed milk into the rice pudding until combined. Serve warm.
Per Serving: Calories 337; Fat 8.14g; Sodium 268mg; Carbs 65g; Fibre 1.2g; Sugar 27.2g; Protein 9.26g

Lemon Apples

Prep time: 15 minutes | Cook time: 5 minutes | Serves: 2

2 Honeycrisp apples, peeled, cored, and sliced 1 cm thick
1½ teaspoons lemon juice

105g packed dark brown sugar
1½ teaspoons ground cinnamon
120ml water

1 tablespoon cornflour

1. In a medium bowl, toss the apple slices with the lemon juice. 2. Transfer the apple slices to the cooking pot and cover with the brown sugar and cinnamon. Toss to coat the apples. 3. In a small bowl, whisk together the water and cornflour and add the mixture to the apple slices. Stir them to combine. 4. Install the pressure lid and turn the pressure release valve to the SEAL position. 5. Select PRESSURE COOK, set the cooking temperature to HI and adjust the cooking time to 5 minutes. 6. When cooked, let the unit naturally release pressure. 7. Stir the apple slices gently and serve warm.
Per Serving: Calories 335; Fat 1.2g; Sodium 12mg; Carbs 87g; Fibre 5.1g; Sugar 75.1g; Protein 0g

Chocolate Brownies

Prep time: 5 minutes | Cook time: 10 minutes | Serves: 4

Nonstick cooking spray
65g plain flour
6 tablespoons unsweetened cocoa powder
50g sugar

½ teaspoon sea salt
4 tablespoons butter, melted
60ml whole milk
1 large egg

45g chocolate chips
240ml water

1. Mist each of 4 ramekins with cooking spray and set aside. 2. In a medium bowl, combine the flour, cocoa, sugar, and salt. Add the melted butter, milk, egg, and chocolate chips and mix well. 3. Divide the brownie batter among the ramekins. Cover each ramekin with foil. 4. Add the water to the cooking pot, place the reversible rack in the pot in the lower position and drop the lower rack through the reversible rack handles. 5. Arrange the ramekins onto the rack. 6. Install the pressure lid and turn the pressure release valve to the SEAL position. 7. Select PRESSURE COOK, set the cooking temperature to HI and adjust the cooking time to 7 minutes. 8. When cooked, let the unit naturally release pressure. 9. Remove the foil and serve the brownies in the ramekins while still warm. 10. Refrigerate the leftover in a sealed container for up to 5 days.
Per Serving: Calories 299; Fat 17.6g; Sodium 453mg; Carbs 34.65g; Fibre 3.2g; Sugar 12.68g; Protein 5.07g

Greek Yogurt Bundt Cake

Prep time: 10 minutes | Cook time: 35 minutes | Serves: 4-6

Nonstick cooking spray
360g plain flour
140g sugar
2 teaspoons baking powder
½ teaspoon baking soda

½ teaspoon sea salt
120g plain Greek yogurt, store-bought or homemade
80ml whole milk
4 tablespoons butter, at room temperature

1 large egg
1 tablespoon pure vanilla extract
Grated zest of 1 lemon
240ml water

1. Mist a suitable pan with cooking spray. 2. In a medium bowl, combine the flour, sugar, baking powder, baking soda, and salt. Add the yogurt, milk, butter, egg, vanilla, and lemon zest. 3. Add the water to the cooking pot, place the reversible rack in the pot in the lower position and drop the lower rack through the reversible rack handles. 4. Arrange the pan onto the rack. Pour the cake batter into the pan and cover it with foil. 5. Install the pressure lid and turn the pressure release valve to the SEAL position. 6. Select PRESSURE COOK, set the cooking temperature to HI and adjust the cooking time to 35 minutes. 7. When cooked, let the unit naturally release pressure. 8. Remove the foil and let the cake cool before unmolding. 9. Cut the cake into slices and serve. 10. Refrigerate the leftover in a sealed container for up to 5 days.
Per Serving: Calories 267; Fat 9.25g; Sodium 377mg; Carbs 39.12g; Fibre 0.9g; Sugar 13.84g; Protein 6.11g

Hazelnut Soufflé

Prep time: 15 minutes | Cook time: 10 minutes | Serves: 2

1 large egg plus 1 large egg yolk
2 tablespoons sugar
95g chocolate-hazelnut spread (such as

Nutella)
2 tablespoons plain flour
Nonstick cooking spray

Icing sugar, for serving

1. Place a trivet in the bottom of the cooking pot, then pour in 240ml water. In a medium bowl, combine the egg, egg yolk, and sugar, and whisk until smooth. Add the chocolate-hazelnut spread and whisk until smooth. Add the flour and whisk until smooth. 2. Spray two 150g ramekins with cooking spray. 3. Divide the Nutella mixture evenly between the ramekins. 4. Add 240ml of water to the cooking pot, place the reversible rack in the pot in the lower position and drop the lower rack through the reversible rack handles. 5. Arrange the ramekins onto the rack. 6. Install the pressure lid and turn the pressure release valve to the SEAL position. 7. Select PRESSURE COOK, set the cooking temperature to HI and adjust the cooking time to 9 minutes. 8. When cooked, let the unit naturally release pressure. 9. Remove the foil and invert the ramekins onto plates to release the cakes. 10. Dust with icing sugar and serve warm.
Per Serving: Calories 425; Fat 21g; Sodium 68mg; Carbs 50.23g; Fibre 3.2g; Sugar 41.5g; Protein 8g

Apple Rice Pudding

Prep time: 5 minutes | Cook time: 15 minutes | Serves: 6

480ml whole milk
200g long-grain white rice
240ml water

125g chopped peeled apples
100g sugar
1 tablespoon pure vanilla extract

1 cinnamon stick
1 large egg
240ml whole milk

1. In the cooking pot, combine the milk, rice, water, apples, sugar, vanilla, and cinnamon stick. 2. Install the pressure lid and turn the pressure release valve to the SEAL position. 3. Select PRESSURE COOK, set the cooking temperature to HI and adjust the cooking time to 12 minutes. 4. When cooked, let the unit naturally release pressure. 5. In a small bowl, whisk the egg with ½ cup of the cooked rice pudding and return it to the pudding along with the whole milk. 6. Stir the mixture at HI on SEAR/SAUTÉ mode for 2 to 3 minutes to thicken the pudding. 7. Discard the cinnamon stick and serve warm.
Per Serving: Calories 269; Fat 4.05g; Sodium 79mg; Carbs 50.88g; Fibre 1.5g; Sugar 22.77g; Protein 6.17g

Frozen Berry Crisp

Prep time: 5 minutes | Cook time: 15 minutes | Serves: 6

300g frozen berries (no need to thaw)
50g granulated sugar
Grated zest of 1 lemon
3 tablespoons freshly squeezed lemon

juice
30g plain flour
20g rolled oats
30g slivered almonds

1 tablespoon light brown sugar
½ teaspoon sea salt
3 tablespoons butter, cut into thin slices
240ml water

1. In an ovenproof pan that fits in the cooking pot, toss together the berries, granulated sugar, lemon zest, and lemon juice. 2. In a medium bowl, combine the flour, oats, almonds, brown sugar, and salt. Sprinkle the oatmeal topping over the frozen berries. 3. Place the butter slices on top of the oatmeal topping and cover the pan with foil. 4. Add the water to the cooking pot, place the reversible rack in the pot in the lower position and drop the lower rack through the reversible rack handles. 5. Arrange the pan onto the rack. 6. Install the pressure lid and turn the pressure release valve to the SEAL position. 7. Select PRESSURE COOK, set the cooking temperature to HI and adjust the cooking time to 12 minutes. 8. When cooked, let the unit naturally release pressure. 9. If desired, uncover the bowl or pan and grill for 2 to 3 minutes in the oven for a crispier topping. 10. Refrigerate the leftover in a sealed container for up to 5 days.
Per Serving: Calories 173; Fat 8.19g; Sodium 277mg; Carbs 24.56g; Fibre 0.8g; Sugar 16.33g; Protein 3.04g

Simple Chocolate Pudding

Prep time: 5 minutes | Cook time: 20 minutes | Serves: 6

1 large egg
70g sugar
3 tablespoons unsweetened cocoa powder

480ml whole milk
1 tablespoon butter
1 tablespoon pure vanilla extract

1 tablespoon cornflour
240ml water

1. In a suitable metal bowl, beat together the egg and sugar and whisk for about 30 seconds. Whisk in the cocoa until smooth, then whisk in the milk, butter, and vanilla. Whisk in the cornflour until smooth, between 30 and 60 seconds. 2. Cover the bowl with aluminum foil. 3. Add the water to the cooking pot, place the reversible rack in the pot in the lower position and drop the lower rack through the reversible rack handles. 4. Arrange the pan onto the rack. 8. Install the pressure lid and turn the pressure release valve to the SEAL position. 5. Select PRESSURE COOK, set the cooking temperature to HI and adjust the cooking time to 20 minutes. 6. When cooked, let the unit naturally release pressure. 7. Lift out the bowl using the trivet handles or sling. Once cooled, refrigerate the pudding to chill and set before serving.
Per Serving: Calories 138; Fat 5.53g; Sodium 54mg; Carbs 19.16g; Fibre 0.8g; Sugar 16.16g; Protein 3.38g

Vanilla Tapioca Pudding

Prep time: 5 minutes | Cook time: 6 minutes | Serves: 4

720ml water
180g medium tapioca pearls
480ml whole milk

100g sugar
1 large egg
1 tablespoon pure vanilla extract

½ teaspoon sea salt

1. In the cooking pot, combine the water and tapioca pearls. 2. Install the pressure lid and turn the pressure release valve to the SEAL position. 3. Select PRESSURE COOK, set the cooking temperature to HI and adjust the cooking time to 6 minutes. 4. When cooked, let the unit naturally release pressure. 5. Remove the lid and stir in the milk, sugar, egg, vanilla, and salt while the tapioca is still piping hot. 6. You can serve this pudding warm or let chill in the refrigerator.
Per Serving: Calories 318; Fat 4.89g; Sodium 351mg; Carbs 62.49g; Fibre 0.3g; Sugar 29.6g; Protein 4.37g

Filling Dump Cake

Prep time: 5 minutes | Cook time: 10 minutes | Serves: 6

200g plain flour
200g sugar
1 teaspoon baking powder

½ teaspoon sea salt
120ml water
1 can pie filling

4 tablespoons butter, cut into slices
Vanilla ice cream, for serving (optional)
Whipped cream, for serving (optional)

1. In a medium bowl, mix together the flour, sugar, baking powder, and salt. 2. Pour the water into the pot. Pour the pie filling on top of the water and do not mix. 3. Add the flour mixture on top of the pie filling and do not mix. 4. Dot the top with the butter. 5. Install the pressure lid and turn the pressure release valve to the SEAL position. 6. Select PRESSURE COOK, set the cooking temperature to HI and adjust the cooking time to 8 minutes. 7. When cooked, let the unit naturally release pressure. 8. Serve heaping spoonful of cake in dessert bowls. If desired, top with ice cream or whipped cream. 9. Refrigerate the leftover in a sealed container for up to 5 days.
Per Serving: Calories 299; Fat 8.01g; Sodium 290mg; Carbs 55.4g; Fibre 1.4g; Sugar 26.16g; Protein 2.84g

Conclusion

It's simple to throw ingredients into the Ninja and let it do its thing until it's time to eat. Use it to conjure up mouth-watering curries from Friday night fantasies or Sunday roasts that will solidify your position as the family cook to beat. You're pressed for time. This gadget is worth keeping on hand if you need dinner quickly because it can pressure cook 70% faster than conventional models and can also prepare food from frozen. In the end, the Ninja Foodi MAX 7.5L Multi-Cooker OP500UK offers a shortcut to preparing wholesome family meals without the need for any prior cooking experience.

Printed in Great Britain
by Amazon

24107090R00061